wARpeD RuleRS

M.J. Bennison

BANKHOUSE

To Judy
Fy ngeneth, fy nynes; yn gyntaf, yn olaf, am byth …

First published in the United Kingdom in 2013 by
Bank House Books
PO Box 3
NEW ROMNEY
TN29 9WJ UK

© Marcus Bennison 2013

British Library Cataloguing in Publication Data
A catalogue record for this book is available from the British Library

ISBN 9780957305816

Cover image:
A detail from a 1681 portrait of Carlos II of Spain, aged twenty, by
Juan Carreño de Miranda (1614–85). [courtesy Wikimedia]
Picture section images © Bridgeman and used with their
permission.

The 'Warped Rulers' logo is a registered design and may be used
only in connection with the promotion and reviewing of this book
and associated works without prior express consent of the author
and copyright holder.

Typesetting and origination by Bank House Books

visit these websites:
www.warpedrulers.com
www.bankhousemedia.com

Contents

GOD giues not Kings the stile of Gods in vaine,
For on his Throne his Scepter doe they swey:
And as their subjects ought them to obey,
So Kings should feare and serue their God againe
If then ye would enjoy a happie raigne,
Obserue the Statutes of your heauenly King,
And from his Law, make all your Lawes to spring:
Since his Lieutenant here ye should remain,
Reward the iust, be stedfast, true, and plaine,
Represse the proud, maintayning aye the right,
Walke alwayes so, as euer in his sight,
Who guardes the godly, plaguing the prophane:
And so ye shall in Princely vertues shine,
Resembling right your mightie King Diuine.

James I writing to his son, Prince Henry, 1599

Acknowledgements

Few creative processes are solitary. Invariably there are unforeseen influences; acts of sometimes unconscious generosity from many sources which aid the development of ideas. Therefore I must acknowledge people, places and an animal that have helped me in the creation of the following, inadvertently or not.

Firstly and perhaps most importantly, the influence of the celebrated playwright Peter Barnes, infamous for his play *The Ruling Class*, must be acknowledged. It was his sprawling, controversial play *The Bewitched* that first introduced me to the pathetic Carlos II of Spain and stimulated the debate within me as to how on earth such an incompetent could be allowed to remain on the throne of the seemingly most powerful nation on earth in the last years of the seventeenth century. Then I found more monarchs exhibiting bizarre behaviour. Their self-interested decisions, or those taken by the self-interested on their behalf, would change the course of world history. In discussions over searing curries, Peter – this kind-voiced, mild-mannered, but hugely passionate man – showed me the inherent corruption of preserving the status quo no matter what. Almost in spite of myself, I enjoyed his grim glee in the maxim that 'blind chance rules the world'. I am continuously astonished by the way he used words.

I have to thank my family in West Sussex for letting me start this journey. As I waded through the sometimes unfathomable oceans of information, I discovered just how many nations have suffered from utter incompetents and bizarre personalities as their heads – and survived. Several households helped me as I wrote – especially the Shaws, who generously put up with me as Justinian II lost his nose. My dear friends John Vincent Dryden, Nicky Carter and Simon Fletcher unstintingly supported me at times when I faltered. I am grateful to Mark Gillard for some invaluable assistance to solve a particular problem. Mark Brayne provided much-needed guidance and insight.

But the greatest gratitude is reserved for the Porter family, who welcomed me into their home and generously tolerated my monopolisation of their office as torrents of words poured out. I would not have completed these accounts but for them. The breathtaking Gower peninsula, over which I tramped while working out how to describe sometimes complicated situations, was a constant inspiration. Many thanks are due to Koda the Siberian husky, who was my enthusiastic companion as that astounding landscape was explored. I remember sitting on a cliff-top in a warm, wet gale on a darkening afternoon with the impatient dog tugging at my side and my flapping, damp-leaved notebook which would not take the ink, watching the waves and wrestling with how I could compare Sweden's Charles XII with his rival Peter the Great of Russia; it was one of the happiest times.

Gratitude must be extended to the considerate staff in the British Library on my occasional visits; but particularly I owe a huge debt to the pleasant, well-informed and apparently intrigued staff at the splendid Swansea public library. They fielded my obscure information requests and suggestions for extensions to their stock with patience, efficiency and good humour. Patrons who may be intrigued by the larger than expected store of Byzantine-related subjects there – no apologies, but it's partly my fault.

Thanks to Steve Lauder of Lauder Consulting for help with the cover design and for designing the Warped Rulers logo.

Thanks also to a nice chap whom I met in the crowded bar of the splendid King Arthur Hotel in Reynoldston. While we were waiting to be served, he listened with a broadening grin as I explained what I was attempting.

'Well, best of luck, mate; but I bet you don't do it!' he called cheerfully over his shoulder as he staggered out with a wobbly tray of drinks.

Well, mate, I needed it; and – you know what? I have ...

Introduction

Some are born great; some achieve greatness; some
have greatness thrust upon 'em
Twelfth Night – William Shakespeare

Take but degree away,
Untune that string and hark what discord follows!
Troilus and Cressida – William Shakespeare

This book is not a scholarly thesis. Nor is it designed to pioneer new ground in the history of these sometimes remarkable, often disastrous people. Nor is it academic history. It is a series of stories retold about inappropriate rulers who were incompatible with their roles and responsibilities through defects in mental health and personality, sometimes through genetic heritage and other times through outside circumstance. We will meet monarchs who should never have ruled; chiefs of countries who should have been actively prevented from wearing a crown.

James VI of Scotland wrote a treatise on kingship for his five-year-old eldest son in 1599. It was called *Basilikon Doron*. In this manual on how to behave as a king, he opined that because kings were divine representatives on earth, God had made a king 'a little God to sit on a throne and rule over other men'. The responsibility of royal celebrity turned some rulers' heads. There were some who were so far removed from reality that they never realised they and their actions were unreasonable. There were some who were tolerated by their advisors, despite their eccentricities, because of who they were and whence they came; and some hopelessly incompetent monarchs who were kept in their exalted position because they were exactly the figureheads that others needed to pursue their own agendas. Some found themselves where they were because of accidents of birth or mortality. You will meet monarchs who might have been regarded as geniuses in other, more enlightened ages. Others' inhumanity to their relatives and subjects is hardly believable. There were rulers who made themselves; some were made by others.

This is a series of bite-size biographies, perhaps to be read last thing at night or in the smallest room, which it is hoped will stimulate readers to mull over stories and the fates of their and other countries and the position of those nations in the world with these sometimes unfortunate people as their heads. Perhaps reading might make you want to find out more about those leaders and compare them with our contemporary leaders in politics or industry, who may have gained their positions of influence either by inheritance or their own efforts. Maybe it will cause you to wonder at what they have done (or not) both personally and throughout the world to change our little lives. Our ancestors were sometimes profoundly affected by the self-interested actions of these people often elevated to improper levels of power. Therefore you are perusing this perhaps not because of them but certainly in spite of them.

Read on and marvel that these people existed, and were allowed far too much power and influence and the means to put their actions into practice, despite their personal vicissitudes and their often inept and delusional behaviour.

And as you read, perhaps consider whether any of these remarkable folk remind you of anyone you know ...

Any factual mistakes are mine. There is always more to be discovered.

Chapter 1
Alexander the Great – So Much Too Soon

Our characters are the result of our conduct
Aristotle

Few individuals' deeds and character have reverberated through historical and legendary chronicles and individual and collective memories quite like Alexander III of Macedon, called 'The Great'. He was one of the first rulers to be so called; he is one of the few rulers in any civilisation throughout human history to deserve this appellation. He could lay claim to being the first legend in his own lifetime. No one so young has received such a title with so little qualification by future generations. No single conqueror can compare with him in terms of his imperatorial successes; not Genghis Khan, Kublai Khan, Julius Caesar, Charlemagne, Attila the Hun,

1

Alaric the Goth, nor Tamburlaine; not Henry V or VIII. Between the ages of twenty and thirty-one, practically single-handedly, he created an empire that spanned half the known world and would last in some areas for hundreds of years; and his Greek influence we can still observe in some of the most remote areas of the world. The vast scale of his legacy has influenced the traditional literature of India, Iran and Turkey and the oral storytelling conventions of the Middle East and Southern Asia. Indeed, he is the subject of ancient and medieval literature from India to Africa to Scandinavia to Iceland. In France, Racine wrote a play about him in the 1660s, and he has been portrayed innumerable times on film. A medieval epic based on a compilation of classical written sources and folk-tale, *The Alexander Romance* was told by medieval troubadours up and down highways, in inns and around campfires in half the known world. However iconic he is in Western Europe, his memory has been preserved even more strongly in Islamic countries than in the West. It was one of Sir Terence Rattigan's greatest professional disappointments that his 1949 play about Alexander's career, *Adventure Story* – a meditation on the nature of theosis (man becoming god) and the increasing isolation of the successful autocrat – was not a critical success. Dictators and their vicissitudes were still too much in the public conscience and memory at that time.

Alexander is the subject of Bangladeshi art in the sixteenth century and Persian poems in the twelfth; he is a component of one of the greatest of Islamic poetic romances – the *Shah-nameh* (the Book of Kings) written by the tenth-century genius Firdausi and an Iron Maiden song in the late twentieth. His story has been written by many people from Alexander's contemporaries to fiction writers from the twelfth century to the twenty-first. He is claimed as the legendary ancestor of the Malay royal family. Suleiman the Magnificent read a collection of Persian legends about Alexander throughout his life. Alexander's main biography by Arrian, written 400 years later and based on other lost accounts, has been pored over by scholars for its accuracy – and recent research has verified many incidents. Contemporaneous accounts are sparse; Callisthenes, the nephew of Aristotle and the official historian of the campaign, wrote reports until he was rendered unable, as we shall see. Alexander's military engineer Aristobulus wrote an account that he did not publish until many years after his emperor's death, perhaps because it was contentious and he knew what would befall him if he cast aspersions on powerful magnates or their descendants. Alexander's admiral Nearchus wrote a retrospective history that others have used in their stories. But much is lost or in fragments – the facts distorted in the retelling or recopied; there are too many instances in the story of Alexander where first-hand witnesses are silent; too many would-be biographers are writing too many hundreds of years after the events, and the mists of time force us to see only shadows. Much information needs to be authenticated and much never will be. Whatever new information we discover using modern research techniques, however much we cross-reference to try and create something that purports to be three-dimensional, it is likely that the personality of Alexander will remain an enigma and the subject for hot debate for evermore. He became the stimulation for adventurers like the American Josiah Harlan, who reinvented himself as an Afghan prince in the 1830s and was the inspiration for Rudyard Kipling's story *The*

Man who would be King (made into the splendid John Huston film); and the inspiration for historians, storytellers, travellers and romantics who want to stand where he stood; who need to see what he saw.

Some twenty cities are known to have been founded by Alexander; some fifty more claim him as initiator. There are dozens of cities in the areas that he conquered named after him, the most famous being Alexandria in Egypt; and later many towns in America named Alexandria or Alexander after a city, or the founder. Thousands all over the world have been named Alexander, but no one has achieved so much militarily and geographically so quickly. Pathan and Afghan tribesmen bear the Persian patronymic Sikander with pride; there are many Sikanders in Pakistan; Iskander is a traditional name in Islamic countries and also the name given to a Russian ballistic missile system. The national hero of Albania is George Kastrioti 'Skanderbeg'(1405–68) – so called from his Islamic name 'Iskander Bey' or 'Lord Alexander', given to him by the Turks because of his genius in the field. Skanderbeg changed sides and religion, defending the land of his birth and resisting his former masters for well over twenty years. Archbishops of the Middle East, eight popes and kings of Greece, Yugoslavia, Russia and Scotland have been named after this extraordinary legend in his own lifetime, Alexander, whose name means 'defender of men'.

There has been constant prurient speculation about his bisexuality (not that it mattered much in his society), his increasing paranoia through his sense of growing isolation, his all-consuming ambition and sometimes gratuitous cruelty; but these and other hypotheses about his conduct have only added to the mystique of the man. He created his own mythology and following generations have served him by raising his profile as the epitome of young, driven, brilliant, enigmatic conquerors. Was he the greatest achiever of all time?

His tomb in his most famous civic foundation, Alexandria in Egypt, was an object of veneration for 700 years, until it vanished in the Christian purge of paganism in the fourth century AD. He and his actions had become a cult with the focus on his last resting place. He imagined himself as a god; his mother certainly claimed that he was engendered by Zeus as his reputation for invincibility grew and Plutarch has him descended from Heracles. He could be the basis of the Indian god Skanda, the lance-bearer, whom Chandragupta worshipped. He saw Alexander himself in the flesh when he, the founder of the Maurya Empire, was young. In recent surveys, Alexander regularly emerges as one of the inspirations of presidents and peasants alike. Napoleon admired him; so did Stalin. At the turn of the fourteenth century, Edward I Plantagenet wanted to conquer like him if only he could slow down time; Roman Emperor Caracalla was obsessed with his achievements and drilled a by then old-fashioned Macedonian phalanx.

He is alluded to several times in the Biblical books of Daniel and appears as a historical figure as the First Book of the Maccabees commences; and as the 'Two Horned One', sacred to the Egyptian god Amun (the Ram), in the Koran. Greek coins found from Macedon to India have him wearing the ram's horns and an elephant's head to show his victories over Indian rajahs. But in some countries the horns have made Alexander into the Devil; an Iranian storyteller's backdrop of the story of Alexander portrays him wearing a horned helmet. He is lauded in Greece and loathed by the Zoroastrians, who blame him for the persecution of their fire worship. In Shiite folk plays he is portrayed as a British coloniser in a pith helmet, drinking and plotting with the last Pahlavi Shah of Iran, the Wicked Caliphs and Uncle Sam – the Great Satan. In rural areas of the Middle East, when children are not being good, the exasperated mother will sometimes threaten that Alexander, the dark spirit, the bogey man, will 'get' them.

Allah made Alexander, as Dhul-Qarnayn, 'mighty in the land and gave him means to achieve all things'. Contrastingly, he is called 'The Accursed' in the folk tales of the Middle East, and storytellers throughout the area encompassed by the Persian Empire have entranced audiences with folk tales about him for over 2,000 years. Many races claim descent from the Greeks, who were settled in the cities Alexander founded in what is now Tajikistan, Uzbekistan, Afghanistan and Pakistan. This is unlikely, as his forces were often in one place for only a matter of months. His battlefield tactics have been essential study for armed forces cadets to generals from that day to this and descriptions of his strategy are required reading in all military academies. Although he fought just five major pitched battles in his career, his ruthless ability to keep his increasingly disparate and disaffected forces loyal and cohesive against constant guerrilla warfare was an extraordinary achievement.

Whether he could have kept a unified empire is another question. Certainly the conquered tracts of land survived and in some areas even expanded under his military successors, the Diadochi, and it survived a series of civil wars between Alexander's generals in the thirty years after his death; so the internal administration that he partly inherited and partly refined seems to have been robust enough to have raised revenues and resources so that, had he survived, he would have been in a position to have conquered more of northern India, Arabia and threatened Carthage. If he had succeeded in subduing Carthage, the emerging Roman state (which was threatening Greek Sicily) would have been next on his list; there were many Greek settlements in southern Italy and Sicily and they would have been expected to support a Greek invasion. Carthaginian settlements in Spain would have surrendered to the unstoppable Hellenes. The Roman writer Livy speculates this far, but of course cannot have Alexander conquering his countrymen. However, had he lived into his seventies, Alexander might have welded all these diverse races into a colossal single world state under Greek cultural domination and produced enough heirs to ensure some sort of continuity. The history and culture of our world would have been very different. Plutarch speculates that Alexander would have thought that Western Europe was within his military grasp. The historian Arnold Toynbee wrote a mischievous alternate history of an idealised Hellene-dominated world state with railways and steamships invented in the second century BC, and ruled in the 1960s by an Alexander XXXV! In his poem 'The Clipped Stater' Robert Graves invents an Alexander who assumes he is divine because no other mortal can withstand him. Falsifying his own death, he vanishes into the interior. He fights as a common soldier further and further away from his empire until he reaches the borders of Mongolia. As part of his pay, years later, he receives a damaged and rubbed coin on which he recognises his own portrait as a god. Only then from his lowly state does he begin to understand what it is to be divine. The poem is dedicated to

Aircraftsman T.E. Shaw – who is more familiar to us as Lawrence of Arabia, in whose desert exploits the spirit of Alexander flowed.

But he is more than just one of the most able battle tacticians who have ever lived; more than one of the great conquerors of the known world; more than perhaps the greatest leader. Alexander was directly responsible for uniting great swathes of country under Hellenism; for making Greek the language of intellectuals and argument, wherever they came from. Through him, the idea of uniting all populations in a world society is formed. Through his tutor, Aristotle, some of the philosophical foundations of our Western so-called civilisation were based. The intellectuals in Rome tended to be Greek or had received Greek education; the fourth-century Roman Emperor Julian, called 'the Apostate' because of his re-introduction of the pagan Greek-based pantheon of gods, spent much of his twenties in Greek philosophy schools. Most, if not all the New Testament was originally written in Greek. Greek, not Latin, was the spoken *lingua franca* of the Eastern Roman Empire; Constantinople/ Byzantium kept Greek culture vigorous for close on another 1,800 years. Coins minted in northern India well over 300 years after Alexander's invasion still display Greek inscriptions and designs. Greek influence in art, sculpture and architecture is vividly evident in India and through the spread of Buddhism in eastern Asia, a thousand years later. The great statues of the Buddhas, cut into the cliff at Bamiyan in Afghanistan on the Silk Road to China showed by their style that they were almost certainly carved by the Greek Buddhist descendants of Alexander's empire in the sixth century AD, nearly 900 years after he had marched past. They were destroyed by the Taliban in

2001 because, in their opinion, they were un-Islamic, to international outrage. They would never even have been constructed had it not been for the overweening ambition, magnetism and charismatic genius of one young man, barely out of his adolescence, from well over 1,000 miles to the west, over 2,300 years before.

Alexander was born into a world of pan-national violence, internecine strife and constant dynastic plots in the Macedonian royal family in the capital, Pella, in July, 356BC. Macedonia's name is traditionally based on a pre-Greek word meaning 'tall', with the implication of royal impressiveness and sibling rivalry. Alexander's usurper father could have been described as a brigand in later times; his mother would have been accused of being a witch then and now. He grew up not so tall, but passionate, determined, wilful, indulged and, as an adolescent, over-aware of his vulnerability in an unprincipled, tempestuous royal family where amorality ruled; but as he grew older and more able to understand the way that royal politics worked, adapted his ruthlessness to achieve what he wanted. 'To the victor goes the spoils' goes the saying; if Alexander was to be a male Nike, then he had to ensure his succession – as we will see. He was the first legitimate son of the freebooting autocratic Philip II and his third wife (although some say his fourth, of the seven he is supposed to have had), Myrtale or Mistilis, who changed her name upon her marriage to Olympias, which was more acceptable to Macedonians. Philip had cut bloody swathes through opposition internally and externally, but he was an attractive, bombastic character, generous and cruel by turns, which to an extent made up for his lack of height (apparently only 5ft 2in). He organised internal security better than before, and so provided a stability of sorts, even though it was administered through a reign of terror. She was of the royal house of Epirus, which is situated to the north-east of Macedon, approximately where the Albanian coast is today.

To be a Macedonian heir to the throne was inheriting a perilous legacy – none of the previous four occupants had died of natural causes and only three of the last eight had expired naturally in their beds. Alexander was a true descendant of this restless, pugnacious, ambitious, unscrupulous family. Royal megalomania and accompanying paranoia must have been prerequisites in this area; his father Philip was only as strong as his last victory. One-eyed from 354BC onwards, he developed a single view to keep himself on the throne and his immediate relatives powerful but subservient and loyal. Demonstrated also was a sense of racial and national superiority among the Macedonians; other city-states and races not as warlike were considered inferior. Epirus and Illyria were neighbouring Balkan states with the same belligerent attitude; Illyria, situated to the north of Epirus, trained its women in arms as well as the men: today Albanians consider themselves descended from Illyrians. They were in constant conflict and yet sometimes were allied; there must have been grim mutual respect between these tribes as they developed into nations. Perhaps a comparison might be made between rival American Indian clans in the nineteenth century or competing families within the Mafia in the 1950s. Philip had beaten the Illyrians in battle earlier in his reign and extended the sphere of Macedonian influence as far as Lake Ohrid – not far from where the modern Macedonian/Albanian border is now.

Alexander's father was not the legitimate heir to the Macedonian throne; he was Amyntas IV's uncle.

When his brother Perdiccas III died in 359BC, Amyntas became the king; but he was only a baby and so Philip assumed the role of regent. Soon afterwards he appropriated the kingdom for himself. Amyntas was not considered a dynastic threat (he may have been feeble-minded) and was sidelined. Philip had several more wives. Many of his marriages were to seal political alliances – and there were many concubines to satisfy his lust, but Olympias was premier wife at the time she gave birth to Alexander. Before him there was only his half-brother, the illegitimate Philip Arrhidaeus, who was physically and mentally handicapped. From her marriage at the age of sixteen Olympias terrified courtiers with her vindictive, passionate, ruthless nature. She was as ruthless, violent and ambitious as any of the Macedonian royal line and a senior member of the feared Dionysian snake cult; it was rumoured that she slept with snakes. No-one was to come between her and her beloved son. She did not lack courage in her own family. Alexander's close relative on his mother's side was to be King Pyrrhus of Epirus, who loved war for its own sake, an ancient world forerunner of Charles XII of Sweden. He was to be the scourge of the Roman Empire for many years and the originator of the 'Pyrrhic victory', where the losses of the successful army were greater than those of the defeated.

Alexander's education was firstly from his nurse, the sister of Philip's trusted general Cleitus, who must have told him traditional stories, especially of heroes of the past in the Trojan War. We must remember that the great wars of the Greeks and the Persians, with the heroic battles of Marathon, Thermopylae and Salamis in which Alexander's ancestors must have participated, were almost within living memory, as we might regard the First World War. His namesake and ancestor, Alexander I, had broken his father's sensible diplomatic alliance with the Persians, advised the Greeks on defeating the Persian general Mardonius and slaughtered over 40,000 of King Xerxes' soldiers on their retreat from Greece after their defeat at the battle of Plataea. This was on the banks of the Strymon (now the river Struma in Bulgaria) in 479BC. By this time Alexander's father Philip was emerging as the strongest leader in the Greek peninsula. His long-term aim was a united Greek military expedition against the Persian Empire to settle old scores. This was a difficult task: the southern Greek cities had no wish to be led by a Macedonian, as not all the leaders would recognise Macedon as being truly Greek – a social and political problem that rumbles on today.

When Alexander was thirteen he was sent to be tutored in Mieza by Aristotle, whose father had been personal physician to Alexander's grandfather. Here he learnt to love the classics of Greek epic literature and art. Aristotle, perhaps the first polymath we know, instructed him in ways of thinking about the sciences, making sense of the natural world, philosophy and religion. Aristotle told him to treat all Greeks as equals, all other races as beasts or plants and although heir to a kingdom to remember his mortality. It is understandable, given the family's track record, that as Alexander grew in reputation, Aristotle was to despair of the divinity that he assumed.

After three years Alexander was considered of age to take responsibility for home affairs while his father departed on military adventures. So he bade farewell to Aristotle and became Macedonia's regent, crushing a rebellion by one of the insurgent tribes and founding his first city. He deported Macedonians to it to keep the local tribes quelled. He was his father's son; he learned how to be strong fast. The famous and probably apocryphal story goes that when Philip saw his son tame the wild black stallion Bucephalus, he said that Alexander should find a bigger kingdom to rule because Macedon would not be large enough for him. The irony in this story is that Philip's name means 'horse friend'. Whether this is apocryphal or not, Philip had good reason to respect his son; he returned to see that he had a competent war leader and administrator on his hands – a two-edged sword. The thought must have regularly passed through his mind that here was someone who might be impatient to rule and might want him out of the way; his assistant was always a potential rival; after all, Philip himself was a usurper and the prince's now bitter mother Olympias, divorced and sidelined in favour of other female charms, was always going to favour her son against himself, and so both were not to be trusted. Alexander was therefore sent off to quell possible rebellious disturbances in Thrace; if he came to grief in some obscure skirmish, Philip would have another reason to sleep more easily. He had to balance the power that his son's campaigns gave him against the threat that his continued success might constitute.

Other invasions, especially by the Illyrians, were repulsed; Alexander was demonstrably earning his spurs and he was nowhere near out of his teens. The southern Greek states were alarmed and formed an alliance against the warlike king and his son; despite Macedon making overtures to Thebes, they sided with Athens. Thebes and Athens were brought to battle with the Macedonians near Chaeronea, about 75 miles north-west of Athens, on 2 August 338BC. Thebes's professional, seemingly invincible, force of 150 homosexual couples, the Sacred Band, was annihilated, refusing to flee and dying where they stood. Alexander had made the first breach in the enemy defence with Thessalian heavy cavalry; the long spears of the Macedonian phalanx did the rest. Afterwards, father and son regarded the huge heap of slain – a testament of their heroic stand in a lost cause. At least three-quarters of them met their end that day; the Sacred Band never re-formed. Philip is traditionally supposed to have eulogised over them: 'Perish any man who suspects that these men either did or suffered anything unseemly.' The Roman biographer Quintus Curtius Rufus, writing nearly 300 years later, quotes the eighteen-year-old Alexander as he viewed the appalling aftermath of his first major battle: 'Holy shadows of the dead, I'm not to blame for your cruel and bitter fate, but the accursed rivalry which brought sister nations and brother people to fight one another. I do not feel happy for this victory of mine. On the contrary, I would be glad, brothers, if I had all of you standing here next to me, since we are united by the same language, the same blood and the same visions.'

The tall lion monument to these brave men which the Macedonians permitted the Thebans to erect in their honour, their deed equal to Leonidas's 300 Spartans at Thermopylae 140 years before, still stands on the site, although reconstructed. Philip's victory meant that half of Greece was now his, and he sent Alexander to negotiate generous terms with Athens; he needed all his rivals on his side. The Greek city-states, bar Sparta, elected Philip as head of the Corinthian league. But Alexander trusted no-one. His attitude was reinforced when a daughter of one of his Macedonian-born generals took Philip's fancy. A male heir to the throne from this union would be racially pure, whereas

Alexander was only half Macedonian and perhaps would favour Epirus to legitimise the affront to his mother. He would not have precedence to the throne and therefore was much more vulnerable. And so it proved. The story goes that there was a family row at the wedding, where Alexander confronted his father about the succession (the dynastically legitimate Amyntas IV was still alive), and a drunken, mistrustful Philip drew his sword on Alexander. However important he was to his father militarily, he was too much of a rival to be allowed to speak out publicly against his king. Mother's and son's positions were soon untenable, and they feared for their lives. With Olympias, Alexander fled the court, to Epirus and Illyria, both of which were viewing the potentially destructive strife in their rival nation's royalty with interest. He left his mother with her kinfolk and spent some months in Illyria, where he was welcomed even though he had been in conflict with them recently. He was close to the country of his birth, but far enough away to be safe. Philip looked as if he was searching for a wife for his physically and mentally disabled son Philip Arrhidaeus, and Alexander sent an actor to Caria in Asia Minor to tell the Persian satrap (provincial governor) there, who had offered his daughter as a suitable wife, about the shortcomings of his half-brother. Alexander was in danger of losing his inheritance to an incompetent illegitimate of whom he seemingly was very fond. Philip Arrhidaeus accompanied him on his travels, and on the death of Alexander became Macedon's king in name only under the regency of Antipater.

In 336BC Philip was assassinated at the wedding of one of his daughters by someone whom he trusted but who secretly bore a grudge against him. The

Macedonian army immediately acclaimed Alexander as king; but nearly all the other Greek states rose in revolt, thinking that for all his promise a teenager had neither the experience nor the charisma to inspire loyalty, nor the stamina to take them on all at once. He acted with amazing decisiveness and ruthlessness, both in internal politics and abroad. He had Amyntas IV, who had never been regarded as a threat to his father's throne, and other royal princes less close to the accession murdered, absolutely ensuring his succession in his own country. Using his heavy cavalry as a kind of flying column he swiftly outmanoeuvred the Thessalonians in the north-east. They immediately capitulated, and Alexander added their cavalry to his. He was back south at the gates of Corinth in a few days. Athens realised that she was in no position to resist and sued for peace. The other members of the Corinthian league unanimously elected Alexander as head, at the age of twenty. Alexander added their forces to his army and then swept north again to deal with a serious revolt in Thrace. Once this was dealt with, he had to take care of revolts in Illyria, towards the west on the Adriatic coast, at whose court he had been a guest but a short time before, and then deal with a rebellion by other tribes all the way back past the north-east extremity of Macedon on the banks of the Danube.

He was right to trust no-one. While Alexander was hundreds of miles away on his northern border, Thebes and Athens perfidiously rose again in rebellion. In their arrogance, the southern cities had again misjudged the firebrand Macedonian. As Alexander swept down from the north, Athens thought better of it and backed down, but inexplicably Thebes decided to fight. There were not enough Theban resources: their citizen army had not recovered from Chaeronea; there was no new

Sacred Band. The result was inevitable and brutal. Alexander razed the city to the ground, leaving only the temples and the house of the poet Pindar, possibly because he had written an ode in praise of his ancestor Alexander I. The inhabitants were either massacred or sold into slavery. Thebes's territory was divided up among the stronger members of the Corinthian League. Alexander had shown that even at this young age he was not to be trifled with and there would be no mercy. There were no more domestic revolts in the next few years. The cavalry force that had sped to all parts of the emerging Macedonian empire putting down insurgencies he welded into his famous Companions.

Barely out of his teens, Alexander had made it clear he was the uniting leader that the Greeks had been looking for; young, educated, determined, ruthless and ambitious to the point of mania, tactically amazingly astute, brave to the point of foolhardiness, an example to his peers and an inspiration to the rank and file. Although he was under average height and in some busts hardly idealised in looks, no-one had ever seen his like. He threw himself into preparations for the great family project – the revenge invasion of the Persian Empire. This was to be another Trojan war, some thousand years later; heroes would be created and reputations forged, so that in later times Alexander and his generals would be regarded as almost superhuman.

Alexander started to believe his own publicity; in the face of enormous odds he was invariably victorious. Perhaps his mother was right: he was the son of a god, maybe the son of the king of the gods as Robert Graves makes him claim. It is unclear whether at the outset in 334BC he had any idea how long this expedition would take, or if his ambition stretched to conquering the entire known world; but within his forces there were geographers, artists, scientists and natural historians. There was also an official chronicler, the historian Callisthenes of Olynthus, whose reports were sent back to Macedon every year. This was no mere raid to liberate the Greek cities of the coast of Asia Minor from their thrall to the Persian Empire. This was a deadly serious long-term expedition, and the Persians were to underestimate him at their peril. But misjudge him they did. They must have known that Alexander was going to attempt an invasion, as the preparations must have taken some time. They took their time to collect an army, which gave Alexander time to conduct a pilgrimage to Troy to view the site of *The Iliad*, his favourite tale, an annotated copy of which was given to him by Aristotle and which he took with him on all his campaigns.

The famous Gordian knot legend, where Alexander cuts a knot that cannot be untied with his sword to prove that he will conquer the world, may only be a tall tale, but it illustrates this young man's ability to try innovative and dramatically decisive methods of solving problems. Already Alexander's reputation was secure. At the first major military encounter on the Granicus river, the Persian satrap's army was smaller than the Macedonian. Despite their superiority in numbers, the only time when he would have that advantage, the young and impetuous Alexander nearly came to grief in what would become a trademark headlong cavalry charge across the river. He was knocked temporarily unconscious by a blow from a mace in the thick of the fighting, but his life was saved by his friend and mentor Cleitus, called 'The Black', who killed the Persian perpetrator before he had time to finish him off. The gods were with Alexander; his life looked charmed. The more successful he was, the more he craved success. His cry to his father that there would be no more lands to conquer was to prove prophetic some nine years later.

At the subsequent huge battles of Issus and Gaugamela, which destroyed Darius as a king and commander, Alexander's tactics still involved enormous personal risk; modern wargamers have rarely re-enacted Gaugamela, especially without the young king being critically compromised. In the 2003 re-enactment as part of the BBC TV series *Time Commanders* both Darius and Alexander are killed. But at both Issus and Gaugamela, at the moment Darius was personally threatened, he seemed to have a crisis of confidence and fled.

The character of Darius has gone through some revision recently. He is not the coward the Greek propagandists would have us believe. At Issus and Gaugamela the main point in those defeats should be that he remains alive to be the focus of the resources of the Persian Empire, so his retreat is an understandable strategy. He seems to have been a mild-mannered and just ruler and willing to learn from military mistakes. But he was regarded as semi-divine by his subjects; there is a story of a successful Greek mercenary leader having the effrontery to criticise Darius for not paying for more of his troops as the basis of Darius's heavy infantry. This was too much an insult to Persian honour, and the Greek paid with his life. If there had been a battle of personalities at this time, Darius would have lost. If he had remained, the history of the world would have been very different.

The myth is enhanced by the famous mosaic made perhaps 200 years after Alexander's death from a contemporaneous painting, discovered in Pompeii in

1831, of the critical confrontation of Alexander and the Great King in the battle of Issus. Alexander, at the head of his Companions, is making straight for the Darius with his huge eyes wide open in excitement and fanatical resolve – *'pothos'* – because he is almost within striking range. He has a long lance in his hand with which he has transfixed a member of Darius's personal bodyguard – perhaps a valued general or a family member. He is helmetless; the artist needs to identify Alexander, so has used some licence in portraying him thus; but also he is depicting that Alexander is heedless of all dangers, utterly confident that he will be personally victorious. His gods are in the ascendant. It all looks too much for the half-veiled Darius, whose chariot is on the turn (his charioteer is whipping up the horses desperately) and whose eyes show the apprehension of the realisation that here is his nemesis. His hand goes out to Alexander, palm outwards; is this a gesture of accordance of status or an admittance of defeat? This could not possibly have been the only artwork illustrating this subject. All over the ancient world there must have been others in Greek and Roman villas depicting this and other scenes in Alexander's life.

To Alexander, and much more to the army, the risks he took only added to the talismanic charisma surrounding him. He was devout; he sacrificed to the gods at the beginning of each day to keep them on his side. Here was a man on whom the gods smiled. Here, the army thought, was a man who achieved godlike acts. Here was a man who was proving to be superhuman; the rumour mill ground out the stories that made him a god or the son of a god, as his mother claimed. Here was another Achilles, a demigod – a personification of the memory of the heroic times he loved hearing about when gods and men were closer and the world was a place where heroes were created. In between the battles of Issus and Gaugamela, he conquered Egypt and listened to the lectures on living gods. He visited an oasis dedicated to Amun in the desert and was hailed as a reincarnation of the god by the priests. Well, they would, wouldn't they? He was venerated as a living god while staying in Memphis. He could not lose. When he had established his rule in Baghdad Alexander adopted Persian costumes and rituals that implied his deified status; this was not popular with the Greeks and intensified the alienation of his officers.

After Issus, Darius's harem, his family and enormous treasure fell into Alexander's hands; after Gaugamela, riches and land beyond even his wildest dreams were solely his. He treated the Persian erstwhile royal family with respect; as the years went by he became extremely fond of Darius's mother. Perhaps he saw in her some aspects of his own mother, whom he must have adored but maybe found a trial. Perhaps here was a quasi-Oedipal substitution process. The warmth of the relationship seems to have been mutual; Curtius, writing nearly 400 years later, says that when she heard of Alexander's death the old queen refused food and pined away. He needed intimate company even more now he was lord of lands to the end of the earth. He took Darius's title of *shahanshah* – King of Kings. He could command anything; he owned everything he could; he could do anything. All this at just twenty-five – the rock star of his age with the lifestyle to match; he must have known that his name would be bruited further than he could imagine or even the most fanciful geographers could draw. No wonder his head was turned. Gaugamela was a victory borne out of

21

battlefield tactics which, had they failed, would have been regarded as folly. The fate of the known world turned in a few hours; the gods had spoken.

During the next few years Alexander travelled further than he could probably have imagined, possibly to places where no Westerner had ever been. He was determined to capture Darius alive and nothing would stand in his way. After Gaugamela, Darius had become increasingly fugitive with fewer and fewer followers, but Alexander wouldn't give up; he kept hounding him, getting closer and closer. They were now in the eastern part of the Elburz mountain range, east of what is now Tehran, just south of the Caspian Sea. The story goes that the dust from the Macedonian cavalry could be seen on the horizon when Bessus, Darius's second-in-command, stabbed his king to give the Persian forces time to get away. He knew that Alexander only wanted Darius. But the Great King was dead before Alexander galloped up. For once he had been thwarted.

Later stories have them meeting as Darius breathes his last. Firdausi seizes this moment and transforms it into one of the great scenes in all fiction, retold by traditional storytellers for close on a thousand years, sometimes using a backcloth of a scene in a dramatic style that can still be experienced from Turkey to India. Darius gives Alexander his kingdom and his soul to God. He dies holding the Macedonian's hand, and Alexander mourns for him in the traditional Middle Eastern way, as David mourned for Saul and Jonathan, tearing his clothes and throwing dust on his head. Alexander becomes an Iranian hero because of his respect for the Great King. Of course this is exactly what Alexander wanted: to be the great ruler of this enormous empire he had to forget much of his cultural heritage; he had to become Persian. As he now relentlessly pursued Bessus as an act of revenge for his frustration in not meeting the Great King when he was alive (and perhaps the sop to his ego of receiving his personal surrender), he explored areas of Darius's empire that the Great King would not have known. He encountered opposition from his army, both rank and file and commanders. They thought that with Darius dead the adventure was over and they could go home. Not a bit of it: Alexander was determined to rid himself of all focuses of national resistance; he knew that in an empire this vast central control with him as pivot was everything. And it had to be through military means; he had to destroy to build again. It is what he did in Macedon, which was a geographical and political pinprick compared with this vast empire with its different races – he eliminated everyone there who might have opposed him. This included leaders and followers; massacre of males, especially those of military age, became the norm; sometimes, as in the dreadful legend of the Branchidae, whole populations were put to the sword. Hunting down Bessus took a year, but even with him publicly tortured before the army and then slowly put to death before the Persians, there were still revolts to deal with in this impossible terrain, notably from a Sogdian chief Spitamenes, a kinsman of Bessus, who has become locally immortal through his trenchant guerrilla tactics against the much more powerful and high-handed invader. Spitamenes betrayed Bessus to Alexander and was himself killed by his soldiers after a disastrous defeat against Coenus in 328BC. The story is still recalled that his head was sent to Alexander as proof of his death, but his garlanded, mummified body is venerated in a hidden cave above the remote Tajik resort of Iskander Kul (Alexander's Lake).

During his drive to quell revolts and uprisings and

indelibly stamp his authority to the furthest edges of his influence, Alexander and his army saw many remarkable things. He thought he had seen the great world-encompassing Ocean at the southern tip of the Caspian Sea; he climbed the foothills of the Pamir Mountains – still extraordinarily remote to Western eyes today; when he reached the Indus, there still was more to see and explore and conquer. Here we see him once again as the pupil of Aristotle: one of his teacher's more famous maxims is that 'all men by nature desire knowledge'. He was nearly always militarily successful (news of the rare reverses were always suppressed) and always an inspiration to his followers. He was wounded in the legs, throat and head at various different times, but recovered remarkably quickly. On the Indus he very nearly died, but his iron constitution won through and he remained the talisman to his army, now composed of huge numbers of polyglot mercenaries taken away from their homelands where they might foment mischief, organised around an increasingly grizzled, battered and discontented core of Macedonian veterans.

The great Indian king Porus was well aware of Alexander years before he saw him; his neighbour in Taxila had already submitted, but when he appeared, defeated, before Alexander after the king's hardest struggle at the battle of the Hydaspes in 326BC, he had the distinction and confidence in himself to ask to be treated like a king. Porus was apparently very tall – another potential Macedonian; perhaps Alexander saw in his dignified mien a confidence that he began to lack. 'Be careful of what you wish for,' runs the old proverb in Aesop's Fables; 'you may get it'. By the time of his victory against Porus, he had still never lost a battle and perhaps the spectre of failure began to be more potent than failure itself. Before the battle of the Granicus – only the second major pitched battle he had commanded – he is said to have given away all his property to companions and soldiers. One of his closest generals, Perdiccas, asked: 'What do you leave for yourself?' He answered: 'Hope.' This demonstrates that Alexander knew there were many outcomes to a battle – including his own demise as a leader, through capture or death. Five years later the thought of failure was an abomination.

With great power comes huge suspicion of others' envy and motives. Alexander had success beyond his wildest dreams so soon. He knew in his heart of hearts that the flatterers were wrong; he was capable of seemingly superhuman feats and therefore could prove there was no one like him; but he was mortal. His experiences in Greece after his father's death and his ancestry meant that treachery was almost to be expected. He risked injury and death in action with increasing recklessness, and there were times when he was incapacitated through wounds or disease and therefore vulnerable to *coups d'état*. He nearly died of the effects of an arrow wound in the course of a siege on the Indian border; he was often ill through the effects of self-indulgence, including infamous bouts of heavy drinking, and it is possible he became an alcoholic; he punished his body through forced marches almost as much as the common soldier. He was the king and emperor; he felt that everything devolved upon him; his authority was not to be questioned: these are all elements of developing paranoia. As in all great magnates before and since, whatever their background, anything that he did, thought or speculated upon that might even hint at weakness and fallibility could not be tolerated. So he began to be suspicious of colleagues who had given no evidence through thick and thin that they were disloyal. Many of his generals were also his father's. But he came from a violent, suspicious family where colleagues were always potential rivals, greedy for power.

Alexander's empire, power and influence were many times greater than his father's, almost beyond imagination; therefore so was his sense of suspicion. Lord Acton's famous expression about all power corrupting and absolute power corrupting absolutely was never truer than here. He killed his friend Cleitus, the brother of his childhood nurse, who had saved his life at the battle of the Granicus, in a drunken brawl. A possible plot to assassinate him had come to the knowledge of Philotas, his commander of the Companions and the son of his father's best general, Parmenion. There may or may not have been a serious plot on Alexander's life; Philotas may or may not have been implicated if there was, but was slowly tortured to find suspects and then brutally executed by the army – some say with stones, others that he died from many spear wounds. His father, Alexander's trusted general who had been such a military bastion for him and his father, had been posted far away across the desert at Hamadan. He was a general like Cleitus, one of the old school of Macedon, deeply aware of his racial and cultural roots and profoundly suspicious of Alexander's enthusiastic absorption of Persian values. He was implicated just because he was who he was, as well as what he represented, and was swiftly murdered on Alexander's orders before the news of his son's death reached him. The loyalty Parmenion had showed both Alexander and his father counted for nothing. 'Not for Parmenion to consider what he should receive but what Alexander should give' ran the old saying, demonstrating the king's distorting and disturbing sense of rectitude. This was an incident that echoed down the years, particularly in the turbulent seventeenth century where the role of a king as God's earthly representative and the relationship between a monarch and the people was deeply questioned. Plays based on the Philotas story by the English Poet Laureate Samuel Daniel in 1604 and the Prussian Enlightenment philosopher Gotthold Ephraim Lessing in 1759 were unpopular because of the contemporary constitutional situations they satirised.

Alexander could not understand why his army refused to move from the Persian Empire's established farthest eastern border. The rank and file, such as were left from the original army, depleted through casualty and far-away settlement, at last had had enough; they had followed their demi-god to what they thought were the ends of the earth to find that the world was far bigger than they had imagined. They had been away from Macedon for a long time, some for over eight years, and had been forced to become more oriental as their great Greek leader had become a Middle Eastern-style potentate. The tyrannous demi-god had been so used to getting his own way for so long that he never emotionally matured, so he indulged in a series of spectacular adolescent tantrums. He had his mother's devil in him. He raved, he argued, he sulked and threatened – but eventually even he had to give in. His petulant will was not as strong as his followers' resolve. The monsoon was at its height; everything was rotting and wounds were gangrenous. The army slouched south downstream along the Hydaspes/Indus for months, almost as if Alexander hoped that even then there would be a change of heart before the great river became too much of an obstacle to ford. Constantly they were challenged by the native population. Alexander was badly wounded when besieging a city. At last they turned their backs on the river.

Arrian thought that Alexander's army's appalling march west across the Gedrosian (now the Makran) desert in southern Iran in 325BC seemed to be so that he could demonstrate that it could be done. The trek was completed, but at an enormous cost in men and supplies. The army could have been transported by ship along the coast far more easily and safely; Admiral Nearchus of Alexander's newly built fleet in the Hydaspes followed the coast from the mouth of the river and arrived in Susa in Persia without much mishap. Plutarch reckoned that less than a quarter of the men who started the journey from the Indus to Baghdad arrived. Arrian thought that the toll was worse – that most of the army with all its camp followers perished. Such a waste of life and potential mattered little to Alexander by this time. He had become another pitiless potentate like Darius, Pol Pot or Stalin, able to command multitudes in the field and utterly indifferent to individual suffering. Back in Babylon, he could raise new armies of Persians trained in Macedonian warfare which would not prove so intransigent, obeying him like the god he must be. Then he could campaign back east to the furthest reaches of India; perhaps even fight China. He could journey west to Arabia and Carthage, then threaten Rome, and then maybe explore and conquer as far as the remote, misty Britannic islands by sailing the great world-encompassing Ocean. The gods would still be with him.

Why should an autocrat seemingly deliberately rid himself of his countrymen – the cornerstones of his military success? Was this dreadful trek revenge for disloyalty? Did he need his Macedonians any more? He had already started to retire his fellow-countrymen, either homewards or sometimes in forcible settlement in the furthest reaches of the empire, much as his Persian predecessors had done years before. There is the dreadful story that may or may not have a basis in truth, which was retold by Curtius, of the Branchidae, a priestly clan who incredibly hailed from the Ionian Greek city of Didyma (modern Didim on the west coast of Turkey). Alexander found them in Bactria and massacred them because they had cooperated with the Persians in a revolt of the Ionian Greek cities against Xerxes over 150 years before and then been exiled to this remote location. In the 1990s Michael Wood encountered the Kalash, a remote community in the North West Frontier province of Pakistan who claim direct descent from Macedonians. Indeed, some possess blue eyes and blond hair. Genetic research has not yet proved the link.

Alexander seemed to want to mingle Macedonian blood and values with Persian. He ordered marriages between them on his return to Susa in a vast Moonie-like ceremony; he married Persian princesses himself. This may be because the Persians always revered their leaders as semi-divine and Alexander could pursue his plans without opposition. On his return to Persia in 324BC he immediately planned an invasion of Arabia (was the Gedrosian desert march a rehearsal for the Arabian?), and purged his army of all opposition. In a mutiny at Opis over forcible repatriation he personally killed potential ringleaders in the midst of the army. This must have been a calculated risk, like many of his cavalry charges in pitched battle. Was he personally courageous or had his mind been turned by his self-image? If he had been killed this would have been interpreted as classic hubris.

Alexander was becoming more and more divorced from reality. He believed more in omens and trusted his friends less and less; he saw alternate agendas and believed his own publicity. His great boyhood companion (some say his lover and alter ego) Hephaistion had died suddenly in the autumn of 324BC. Hephaistion had long taken advantage of his privileged position with the king; he aspired to godhead himself and was loathed by the majority of the other older generals. Alexander hysterically mourned his lifelong companion; he would not be consoled. He was feeling more isolated and was increasingly aware of his generals jockeying for position. Too many of his tight band of supporters had their own reasons for flattering him.

He was entranced by the beautiful eunuch Bagoas, who was Darius's slave before him; privileged and egocentric, he indulged the king in orgies and huge drinking bouts. Alexander was losing control. More appalling acts of butchery followed. In an expedition against the Cossaeans of the Zagros Mountains, Plutarch claims that Alexander 'massacred the entire male population from the youths upwards'. Wood recalls the *Iliad* parallel with Achilles sacrificing Trojan youths over the grave of his lover Patroclus; perhaps this was Alexander's thinking.

Other important characters in this story met unexpected and precipitate ends. Callisthenes, Alexander's historian, was implicated in a plot involving some of Alexander's noble Macedonian attendants and was hanged; the pages were stoned to death. Alexander's treasurer and boyhood friend Harpalus, who was excused military service because of his lameness, fled with some of the treasury twice and was eventually tracked down and disposed of in Crete; the rest of Parmenion's immediate family died suddenly from illness or unfortunate accident. General Coenus, the victor over Spitamenes, possibly the spokesman for the rest of the commanders in their refusal to go farther east or maybe just the scapegoat, succumbed to fatal illness quite soon afterwards. His brother Cleander, who was one of the officers who had killed Parmenion, was accused of embezzlement, cruelty and extortion and was eliminated, as were some of Parmenion's other generals, Sitalces, Heracon and Agathon, on similar charges. Others in power, who were not Macedonian, considered themselves unsafe. The satrap Astaspes was accused of high treason for not providing enough help to Alexander in his invasion of India, and was executed. So were other Persian satraps, Abulites and his son Oxarthes, the latter run through by an incandescent Alexander, perhaps because they had tried to bribe him for their lives. Another satrap neglected to send presents to Bagoas as well as Alexander; he was murdered soon afterwards, as was the Macedonian Polymachus, who had counselled against Alexander taking Bagoas's advice. Bagoas took his revenge in accusing Polymachus of desecrating the tomb of Cyrus, the greatest of the Persian kings, the founder of the Persian Empire and a god in his own right to the Persians. His surprisingly modest tomb can still be seen at Pasargadae, where it is due to be restored. Anyone who opposed Alexander was in peril of their lives, and it is surprising that so many did. The number of internal conflicts must imply that Alexander's sometimes drink-inspired paranoia ruled in the last few years of his life. His mistrust of everyone's motives in Babylon resulted in dithering; waiting for omens and the debates of soothsayers, rather than making judgements based on fact. His overwhelming ambition seemed to have deserted him, despite the grandiose plans for expansion the next year. This is from a man who had just completed a campaign of nearly 20,000 miles; much of the last thousand on foot and suffering the after effects of wounds and illness. Alexander turned in on himself. He received letters from his mother doubting Antipater, the regent, of Macedon's and Greece's loyalty; dying, he was well aware that after he had gone the surviving generals would fight over what they considered their legacy.

Alexander died fast. It is well known that he imbibed to excess, and in this year (324–3BC) of relative inactivity in Susa and Babylon he would have had more opportunities to do so. Macedonians were infamous for their binges. The traditional view is that he died of a fever brought on by excess of alcohol and consequent liver failure, complicated by the punishment that he had given his body in over ten years of constant campaigning. Perhaps it was malaria, which if severe enough could induce organ failure. Even today many retirees (miners, for instance) after a vigorous working life do not react well physically or mentally to enforced leisure, and many die or become permanently incapacitated a short time after retirement. However, Paul Doherty has put forward a compelling case for Alexander's death by arsenical poison and suggests that Hephaistion may well have gone the same way. As we have seen, Macedonians rarely died of natural causes, and Alexander seems to have been ill for less than three weeks. He was a month short of his thirty-third birthday.

Alexander's Persianisation programme cannot have endeared him to his Macedonian leaders. Both Persians and Macedonians regarded each other as barbarians. He had married Roxana, a daughter of Oxyartes, a minor and half-wild satrap of a province seemingly at the end of the earth and almost on the roof of the world, to the consternation of his generals. To make Roxana a concubine would be all very well; but his first wife? His legitimate successors to this enormous and ever-growing empire would be half-castes. But that is what he wanted.

Alexander had inaugurated a military training in Greek style and tactics for Persians and the families of rank and file retirees who had opted to go home; their children were enforcedly left so that an integrated Macedonian-Persian hierarchy and military could develop. It seemed that Alexander was becoming more Persian than the Persians. No wonder the generals felt that they would become marginalised and therefore personally more vulnerable.

Doherty makes much of the fact that the searing June heat did not corrupt Alexander's dead body; arsenic has preservative qualities. This could have been interpreted to a credulous public that Alexander was indeed a god. He suggests that General Ptolemy was the instigator – because the body was spirited away to what became his territory in Egypt, where Alexander was considered to be Amun on earth. Ptolemy was one of Alexander's most trusted officers – a member of the seven-strong special bodyguard of the king, only three of whom survived the full years of campaigns. After some time residing in state in Memphis – sacred to Amun – Alexander's body was finally laid to rest in Alexandria, to develop into his greatest civic foundation, on the Nile delta. There his tomb was venerated for the next seven centuries.

Ptolemy largely kept out of the internecine strife that followed as the fourteen other generals tore at each other's throats, and he died of old age, unlike most of his compatriots. His dynasty lasted longest; it ended some 350 years later in the suicide of Cleopatra VII, her lover Marcus Antonius and the murder of her son by Julius Caesar, Ptolemy XV, better known as Caesarion, on the orders of the first Roman emperor, Octavian (later called Augustus), in 30BC. Augustus is supposed to have said that two Caesars was one too many. He was the stronger.

Alexander is supposed to have bequeathed his empire 'to the strongest'. 'The strongest' in Greek is *Kratistos*, but his voice was very weak; it could conceivably have been misheard by his surrounding generals and hangers-on as Craterus. Craterus, in his late forties, perhaps the last of the old school of Philip's commanders, was absent from the great king's deathbed, because he had been sent home with a column of demobbed veterans. If he had been there, there might have been more Macedonian blood spilt on Alexander's still warm corpse. He lasted less than two years before he was trampled to death by his own horse in battle with one of his erstwhile colleagues. In the next fifty years the diminishing numbers of *Diadochi*, the successors of Alexander, the generals and their descendants, fought each other, plotted with and against and assassinated each other. Hundreds of thousands of lives were ended on the sword-points of their individual ambitions.

Roxana was pregnant when Alexander died, and towards the end of 323BC bore the half-Persian half-Macedonian son and heir that the Macedonians dreaded – Alexander IV Aegus, 'The Shield'. The young dowager could be just as callous as the men: she murdered the Persian widows to make sure of her son's succession, and then mother and son were sent for their own protection to be with her mother-in-law, Olympias, in Epirus – a long way from Persia. Olympias was still spitting fire and seeking revenge against anyone whom she thought was her son's murderer. She had the harmless Philip executed in 317BC. Rivalry, vengeance and political machinations were never far from the snake-queen's mind. More of her political meddling caused her to invade Macedon, now governed by Antipater's son, Cassander. The incursion did not go well and she found herself holed up in the city of Pydna – later the site of two calamitous defeats at the hands of the Romans, which would cause the end of Macedon as an independent country. She surrendered to the governor in 316BC, on the promise that her life would be saved. At the age of fifty-nine she should have trusted her instincts, experience and violent heritage. Cassander did not stick to his part of the agreement. She was condemned for the atrocities she had committed for more than forty years by the families of those she had had killed, and was summarily executed without trial. Her exalted son could not have organised it better. It is said that Cassander denied her burial rites, so that her ghost would never find rest. Already in his mid-thirties, Cassander was Alexander IV Aegus's regent; as was usual the regent's ambition was to be King of Macedon, and Alexander was recognised by most of the empire as the legitimate dynastic successor. Now that the young prince's unspeakable grandmother was dead, he didn't have her political intriguing to worry about; but Cassander waited, perhaps to ascertain if natural causes would carry him off. As the years passed he realised that the half-Macedonian half-Sogdian prince was attracting far too much attention from potential rivals and backers, even though he was safely immured far away in the north-west, in the fortress of Amphipolis under the supervision of Glaucias, a Companion veteran of Gaugamela. Cassander needed to prove that he was *Kratistos*; that might was right. He might not have many more years to rule. He grew impatient, and mother and son were poisoned by 309BC. Cassander assumed the throne, ruled for another twelve years and, unusually for this dynasty, died in his bed.

Cassander had married Thessalonike, a half-sister of Alexander the Great; his third son was called Alexander. He reigned as Alexander V, the last King of Macedon to be called so, with his brother Antipater, who murdered their mother in 295BC, and ousted him because he had his mother's favour. Alexander V ingloriously re-invaded Macedon, having sold great areas of his birthright for a mercenary army. It was all to no avail; he was assassinated a year later after three years of vicious, unprincipled, shameful, fraternal scrabbling for the crown of a much less significant country. The violent, amoral, merciless, hubristic chronicle of the House of Macedon would continue for 150 more years. Even this struggle would be a sideshow to the ugly dynastic turmoil of the inheritors of Alexander's Middle Eastern empire.

Chapter 2
Roman Rulers –
Man as Emperor as God

Nothing happens to any man that he is not formed by nature to bear
Meditations – Marcus Aurelius

For all its seemingly inexorable expansion and influence up to the end of the second century AD, the Roman Empire was rarely secure internally. However, by the time of Marcus Aurelius's death in March of AD180, possibly of plague, maybe at Bononia on the Danube, it had enjoyed an unprecedented century of political stability, economic and social development, because there had been few threats to its domestic security. The Renaissance philosopher Niccolo Machiavelli and the great eighteenth-century historian Edward Gibbon called the autocratic predecessors of Marcus Aurelius (Nerva,

Trajan, Hadrian and Antoninus Pius) and himself the 'Five Good Emperors', because there was a largely undisputed succession after they had died in their beds, leaving the empire in the hands of their adopted sons. 'If a man were called to fix the period in the history of the world, during which the condition of the human race was most happy and prosperous, he would, without hesitation, name that which elapsed from the death of Domitian to the accession of Commodus,' opined Gibbon. Some scholars have included the Five's predecessor Domitian, because his ruthless control steadied the empire after the débâcle of the so-called Year of the Four Emperors (AD68–9) following the end of the Julio-Claudian line with Nero's suicide. Domitian's inclusion would make the number six.

It ought to have been seven. There was every reason to believe that Marcus's son, Lucius Aurelius Commodus Antoninus, would continue the line; he was admired in battle and well schooled in the philosophy of government by his remarkable father, who had died during a campaign to further subdue the Germanic tribes on the northern frontier. He was raised to Caesar status at the tender age of five with his younger brother Marcus Annius Verus, who did not survive long, and for the next fourteen years he was groomed for succession, being raised to Augustus in AD177, with the same status as his father – but only in name. He lived in the shadow of his father for the rest of his life.

It started so well, as many of these stories do. Immediately Commodus made his way to Rome, accompanying his father's ashes, to enjoy the peace his father had won for him and the empire, to great acclaim from the citizenry in a spectacular Triumph. This abrupt retreat from the frontier was against his late father's wishes, but it probably turned out to be a sensible decision; it was already doubted whether the empire possessed the resources to keep expanding forever. However, by this action Commodus relinquished the strategic advantage the Romans had wrested from the German tribes; the empire never reasserted itself to the same level. The money saved by curtailing military activity he spent on personal aggrandisement. The army suffered through this lack of investment with a consequent loss of morale and discipline, especially in the Praetorian Guard. No wonder that the contemporary historian Dio Cassius described Commodus's reign as 'a golden age turned to iron and rust'.

It could be conceived that the rapturous reception he received on his return to the capital that October started to turn his head. There may have been some instability inherited. Commodus was the eleventh child of thirteen born to Marcus Aurelius and his first cousin Faustina. Only five of Commodus's siblings had been spared to mourn their father. Perhaps the genetic bottleneck was demonstrated by his neurotic tendencies. Although unbiased sources are sparse, it seems that Commodus was generous to the people and remained popular with the general public for the majority of his reign. Regarded as a hero, he was determined to live up to that reputation. However, unlike his father he did not see the need to be involved in the minutiae of administration, and after a purge of his father's experienced advisors he left state affairs in the hands of his chamberlain, Saoterus, a freed slave who had shared his chariot during his triumphal entry into Rome – when he would traditionally have warned his master that he was mortal. There were rumours that he was the emperor's lover. Popular he may have been with the Roman mob, but Commodus had made many enemies among the great of the capital. Promotions of favourites, most of whom were of low birth, led him to barely surviving a royal family coup within the first two years of his reign, largely because the two aristocratic relatives sent to kill him were impeded by the emperor's bodyguard.

Saoterus was implicated in the plot that guaranteed Commodus's fall in AD182; Marcus Aurelius Cleander, a freed slave and the emperor's most powerful favourite, was ruthless enough to have him eliminated, probably by the prefect of the Praetorian Guard, who was by now only loyal to those who paid him. For Cleander money talked: everything had its price, and he sold privileges to the highest bidder. In AD190 there were twenty-five *suffect* consuls – 'replacement' consuls when there was no need for replacements – a record in Roman history. Every one of these positions was sold by Cleander to wealthy senators who were desirous of influence. One of them was a young aristocrat named Septimius Severus, who had already been raised to senatorial rank by Marcus Aurelius, and had the head of the Praetorian Guard murdered so that he could take over. He used the Praetorians to keep the mob down, but unrest at his policies, coupled with food shortages, made the ordinary soldiers side with the population. The Praetorians were cowed. The corruption of Cleander was evident to ordinary Romans and he did not last much longer: he was sacrificed to quell an ever more restive mob by an emperor who only wanted to save himself, and turned his back on his servant. Cleander's head was tossed to the baying mob.

The autocratic nature of his predecessors meant

that Commodus's cult quickly became one of flawed personality. He believed his own publicity. Too indolent to earn acclaim by his own industry and exploits, he created it for himself. He could not be seen to fail, and had to be bigger, stronger and more godlike than any of his predecessors. The way he changed his name during his reign is a case in point. On his accession he changed his first name from Lucius to Marcus, presumably in honour of his father. Fair enough. In AD182 he named himself Pius and in AD185 added Felix. Well, he was emperor. In AD191 he gave up the name Marcus, restored his original Lucius and added Aelius, connecting himself with his illustrious predecessor Hadrian; which, given his self-imposed charisma, is understandable. But then he went too far. By the end of AD191 he had dropped the title Antoninus and demanded to be glorified as Lucius Aelius Aurelius Commodus Augustus Herculeus Romanus Exsuperatorius Amazonius Invictus Felix Pius, adding two titles – Dominus Noster (Our Lord) and Orbis Pacator (Pacifier of the World) – for good measure. These titles have been found on contemporary inscriptions all over the Roman world. Herculeus comes from his increasing delusion that he was the modern manifestation of the god Hercules, and the club and the lion skin associated with Hercules became Commodus's insignia. To reinforce this delusion he demanded that he be called Hercules, son of Zeus rather than Commodus, son of Marcus. Exsuperatorius demonstrated his arrogant pre-eminence over all; Amazonius linked him again with Hercules and the warrior Amazons; and Invictus emphasised what he thought was his all-conquering destiny. Commodus's megalomania touched everyone in the empire: he decreed that Rome was to be named after him; so were all the legions; and many of the months of the year were renamed after himself or given Herculean connotations.

Commodus confirmed his self-imposed dominance in the gladiatorial arena on innumerable occasions; he fought and was never allowed to be beaten. His naturally left-handed exploits became ever more ridiculous, and it was increasingly obvious he did not have sufficient skill to compete, mirroring his predecessor Nero's incompetent exploits on the stage. But more than anything Commodus loved the sight of blood. He killed innumerable lions, panthers and other wild beasts for public entertainment, particularly delighting in severing ostriches' necks with special arrows with half-moon-shaped tips, which decapitated them so cleanly that they still ran headless afterwards. He is reported to have approached the dais on which the senators sat, threateningly waving a severed ostrich head, with the implication that he would do the same to them if they did not acquiesce to his wishes. Commodus moved his headquarters to the gladiator school, where he enjoyed fighting the gladiators with his iron-bound club; bouts he always won, of course. He adopted yet another name, that of a renowned gladiator of past times: Scaeva. When his bloodlust was up, no-one was safe.

The senate was cowed; fear stalked the palace corridors and the debating floor of the senate. The palace household finally acted. Fearing murder herself, Commodus's mistress, Marcia, prepared a bowl of poisoned drink. The emperor greedily consumed it, but it didn't work: he started to vomit it up. Marcia knew she had gone too far and was sure to pay the ultimate price. Perhaps in panic, she called for Commodus's personal trainer, the wrestler Narcissus, and he strangled the half-poisoned egotistical emperor. All Rome breathed again.

Commodus has been portrayed in two films, as a raving schizoid by Christopher Plummer in *The Fall of the Roman Empire* in 1964 and as a blood-soaked tyrant by Joaquin Phoenix in *Gladiator* in 2005. Both films showed how far the role of emperor was debased in the twelve years of Commodus's rule. The final scenes are similar: Commodus dead in the gladiatorial ring and the emperorship being sold off to the highest bidder. Edward Gibbon was of the opinion that the reign of Commodus marked the beginning of the end of one of the great empires of global civilisation. It looked impregnable in AD180 – but how fragile it all was.

Commodus was murdered on New Year's Eve AD192. The freefall into moral bankruptcy of the Roman Empire continued. The fabulously wealthy Publius Helvius Pertinax won the auction to become emperor and was proclaimed by the Praetorian Guard on New Year's Day, AD193. His tenure lasted precisely eighty-six days before his acclaimers became so disaffected that they murdered him in his turn. He was the first of five candidates who claimed the throne that year – hence the Year of the Five Emperors. Didius Julianus won the next auction for emperor by offering 25,000 sesterces to every praetorian, and was reviled throughout the empire for devaluing the currency. With rival Septimius Severus at the gates of Rome, and the by then moribund Praetorian Guard offering little protection or resistance, Julianus was murdered by a soldier on 1 June. Other generals in further-flung parts of the empire were claiming the throne. Thanks to many battles between different Roman forces in the succeeding four years, the army was severely weakened, both in manpower and in generalship. At last, in a titanic two-day struggle that involved more Roman troops fighting each other than had ever been recorded before (the contemporary historian Cassius Dio claims up to 300,000), Severus triumphed over the governor of Britain, Clodius Albinus, in February AD197, at Lugdunum (Lyons). The consequence was that for the next fourteen years Rome lived under the sometimes tough rule of Severus, and some stability was restored within the empire.

Perhaps solidity had been achieved in the empire, but not within Severus's family. Septimius fathered two sons in quick succession by his Syrian Arab wife Julia Domna – Publius Septimius Geta and his elder brother Lucius Septimius Bassianus, later named Marcus Aurelius Severus, called derisively Caracalla, after the Gallic hooded tunic he made popular. In future generations disgust at his actions meant that the emperor became more known by his nickname than by his real title. The brothers loathed each other. As Severus aged and became more infirm, he became increasingly concerned about this sibling rivalry, which had become mutual hate. Cassius Dio relates the advice the old man gave to his warring sons: 'Get along; pay the soldiers and ignore all the others.' How he and the rest of the empire must have wished that the brothers had heeded this. Severus promoted both to joint Augusti with him and tried to use their energies and capabilities in Britain, where he was consolidating the empire's position after the stripping of regular legions from the island by Clodius Albinus. Caracalla would be in charge of military matters and his younger brother would deal with civil administration – in which he proved adept. Caracalla's jealousy and indignation at his brother's growing influence and heightened regard by his subordinates grew as his father's health slowly deteriorated.

Septimius Severus died in York in AD211, with his sons' rivalry at its height. In his will the dying emperor instructed that they should rule jointly. Neither was likely to obey this; both were out for sole power. The brothers continued their manoeuvres against each other and their supporters. In December of that year Geta was stabbed to death; some stories say Caracalla killed him with his own hand while Geta was in the protective arms of their mother, who had been a significant influence on Severus's policies and had tried to mediate between her sons for years. His father's ruthlessness and occasional vindictiveness in defence of his emperorship and dynasty was well known, expected and respected; but Caracalla didn't know when to stop, and he summarily executed several of his own relatives whom he thought might have supported Geta. Included in the massacre was Geta's wife, all her family and innocent multitudes that might have been associated with them, however marginally. Cassius Dio estimates that when the bloodbath was over as many as 20,000 Romans and high associates had been eliminated. Caracalla damned his brother's memory, expunged all the public inscriptions to him and destroyed all his statues. Usually the punishment of *damnatio memoriae* was meted out by the Senate only to considered traitors of the state, and rarely to emperors.

Caracalla's name has resonated throughout history as the epitome of evil, as much as anything because of his ungovernable temper, his malice and his extreme cruelty. One of his busts shows an aggressive-looking, perhaps paranoid young man with an infuriated, puckered brow, in the act of turning his head to the left as if to verbally lambast someone behind him or possibly to confront somebody who might be attempting to do him harm. Constantly restless, mistrustful and suspicious, deferential to nothing but the army, on which he increasingly depended, craving the guidance of soothsayers and fortune tellers above his own civil and military advisors (those who dared), he would brook no opposition; everyone whom he saw as representing any kind of criticism he violently eliminated. Edward Gibbon called him 'the common enemy of all mankind'.

Caracalla remembered insults. Everything was taken personally. Publicly derided by the Alexandrians when the murder of Geta was officially described there as self-defence, he took revenge for the slur by butchering a deputation of the leading citizens who gathered to welcome him to the city in AD215 – almost four years later. His ghastly, corrosive temper may have been caused in part by some unspecified long-term illness that may have given him pain, because we know that he attended the shrine of a Celtic god at Aurelia Aquensis, now Baden-Baden in Germany, and visited that of Aesculapius, the god of medicine, at Pergamum, on the Turkish Aegean coast.

Although he gained some kudos with the army on a campaign against the Germanic tribes in 213 by raising their wages, sharing their route marches with them on foot, partaking in their rations and even grinding his flour with them, Caracalla was never popular. He attempted to model himself on Alexander the Great, demonstrating his underlying desire for personal military glory – especially on his campaigns in the east. He adopted Macedonian costume and even recruited a body of Macedonian infantry whom he trained into a proper phalanx, even though this had proved inferior to Roman fighting formations hundreds of years earlier.

Following in the steps of Alexander on a campaign into Parthia in the spring of AD217, Caracalla was assassinated near Harran while urinating at the roadside: a fittingly ironic and ignoble end to a violent career. The conspiracy against him was almost certainly organised by a general and administrator called Macrinus. He had no aristocratic heritage and took the role of emperor in the face of the surviving Severans and the legitimate line; it was a terrible risk to take, as he had been implicated in the murder. He spent his brief reign campaigning in the east. It was impossible for him not to have made enemies of the Severan women, notably Julia Domna, who had lost both her sons brutally; but soon after Caracalla's murder she followed him to the grave. Some reports say she died of the cancer from which she was already known to be suffering; others suggest she starved herself to death. The focus moved to her sister, Julia Maesa, her niece, Julia Soemias, and her good-looking great-nephew by Julia Soemias, Varius Avitus Bassianus.

Septimius Severus had always appreciated his Syrian wife Julia Domna's advice and always defended her views on how he should govern; there were many malicious rumours about her personal agendas, possible affairs and her ambitions for her own family. Theirs was the leading family in Emesa (modern Homs in western Syria, not far from the Lebanese border), where the men were hereditary priests of the Syrian sun god Elagabal. Julia Maesa's grandson Bassianus had been appointed the high priest at the tender age of fourteen, at the time of Caracalla's death. Julia used her wealth and influences to persuade the local legion to revolt. His father, grandfather and uncle had all died in AD217 and, as the next Severan, Bassianus was pitched into the limelight. Severan family power was being wielded by his mother and especially his grandmother. Macrinus could see his authority ebbing away as more soldiers flocked to the rebels, and he wrote to the senate in Rome denouncing the rival, calling him the 'False Augustus' and claiming he was insane. Whether he knew if this was true or not is difficult to say. Defeated outside Nisibis by the Parthians and again near Antioch by the dissident forces, Macrinus realised that he had almost no chance of sustaining his claim to be emperor and publicly removed the Imperial insignia to save himself. It didn't; he was hunted down and executed.

We now come to one of the most bizarre episodes in the history of the Roman Empire, made infamous by the gossip of contemporaries, the descriptions by Cassius Dio and his colleagues and the fascination of later civilisations, notably the controversial Victorian Dutch painter Sir Lawrence Alma-Tadema, whose sensuous depictions of indulgent luxury and decadence were enormously popular in the later years of the nineteenth century. Bassianus took as his Imperial designation the name of the sun god whom he served. He, his mother and grandmother made their way to Rome. Marcus Aurelius Antoninous Elagabalus, as he was now officially known, took his Syrian culture and religion with him.

The opulent extravagance of the east amused the Romans, used as they were to the excesses of their emperors. But this adolescent's indulgent behaviour outpaced much of the hyperbole. As high priest of his cult, he was already so close to being a god that he thought he was divine. Married as soon as he arrived in Rome, aged no more than fifteen, he quickly gained a reputation for luxurious excess. Then he embarked on a series of homosexual adventures, notably with the charioteer Hierocles. His first marriage was a disaster and a divorce was quickly arranged; another followed without issue; and while that was still extant there was a third to an image of a Carthaginian goddess, with whom what fruit could emerge can only be imagined. By now Elagabalus must have imagined that he and his namesake god were one. He then went through a form of marriage with his handsome fair-haired athlete and tried to make him a Caesar.

Yet another marriage insulted the Romans. This was to Aquila Severa, a Vestal Virgin (a priestess of Vesta – whose well-being was seen as fundamental to Rome's security). Even though the symbolism might have been understood, for many Romans this was a sacrilege too far. Like the others, this marriage did not last long, nor did another to Anna Faustina – after which he added insult to injury by remarrying Aquila Severa. Elagabalus was married five times in four years.

Narcissistic and exhibitionistic past reason, Elagabalus behaved more and more like a woman. He rouged his face and painted his eyes; grew his hair long and wore a hairnet; had all his facial hair pulled out so that he could look more feminine. It was whispered that the emperor dressed himself as a female prostitute and touted for business like a common whore, first on the streets and then in the palace itself, charging high prices. The gossip was that he wanted a vagina implanted in his body; the first transsexual Roman emperor. He wondered whether he should be castrated. He liked being found *in flagrante delicto* by Hierocles, so that he could enjoy being punished by his partner; he was often seen sporting black eyes and other physical evidence of masochism.

Elagabalus rewarded his favourites from low backgrounds with high office. He incensed the contemporary commentator Herodian who fulminated, 'The emperor was driven to such extremes of lunacy that he took men from the stage and the public theatres and put them in charge of the most important Imperial business.' His conduct completely demeaned the office of emperor. The great and ancient Roman Empire's leader had no dignity, no gravitas; he was a laughing-stock. As a ruler, the Syrian sun god was a black hole.

Increasingly alienated from his grandmother, who realised that her attempts to promote him were headed for disaster, Elagabalus still had the support of his mother; but the senate had little idea who was really pulling the strings of power. Government stagnated; councils were supine; public dissatisfaction increased. Several names are mentioned in the historical record as potential rivals to this effeminate teenager for ultimate power, but although one of the legions that initially supported him was disbanded when it transferred its allegiance to a rival, there does not seem to have been a full-scale revolt. His exasperated grandmother transferred her attention to Elagabalus's cousin Alexianus, now renamed Alexander, only a teenager himself and not yet competent to take the reins of government, but not prone to the excesses of his cousin. Alexander was hauled out of the emperor's presence and given lessons in government and martial strategy. Although Elagabalus had reluctantly adopted Alexander and allowed him to be promoted to the rank of Caesar, he wanted an heir himself. How this was to happen is anyone's guess, as he seemed incapable of furthering a heterosexual relationship.

There was no way in which an indulged, inexperienced, immature, self-obsessed youth like Elagabalus could cope with the responsibility of being the figurehead of the most powerful institution in the world. He used the emperorship as his plaything. Being made emperor when he was already the high priest of a god that he thought was greater than Jupiter, he assumed he was capable of anything. Throughout the last year of his occupation of the throne – for it could scarcely be called a reign – he began to find that there was a consequential limit to his actions. His was the petulance, cruelty and spite of the most spoilt of children – always pampered, always expecting the best and never having to struggle for any of it.

Even Elagabalus was aware that there was another candidate for his throne: someone who might have been more competent; someone who was more popular. He foolishly attempted to eliminate Alexander as a rival by having him murdered, which signalled the end. Towards dusk on 11 March AD222 the eighteen-year-old Elagabalus and his mother were themselves murdered, and their mangled bodies were cast into the sewers that led into the river Tiber; from the highest to the lowest in a few swift moments. Mother and son subsequently suffered *damnatio memoriae*; his favourites, including Hierocles, were similarly brutally eliminated. The emperor who thought he was god of the sun had plummeted humiliatingly in a bloody evening. His grandmother followed him not long afterwards; we don't know how.

There must have been older folk who had lived throughout the whole of the reigns between Marcus Aurelius, who had died in AD180, and Alexander Severus, who restored some order but was assassinated along with his mother in AD235. Any of them with knowledge of Roman politics must have thought that the empire was doomed, because of such intrigues at the corrupted black heart of government and with such capricious occupiers of the throne.

But, as we know, the empire was to endure for many more generations; the emperorship for more dynasties.

Chapter 3
The Byzantine Heraclian Dynasty – Rise, Fall and Fall Again

All that is human must retrograde if it does not advance
Decline and Fall of the Roman Empire
Edward Gibbon

By any standards, Flavius Augustus Heraclius (*c.*575–641) was as extraordinary a ruler who has ever lived. The namesake son of the powerful Armenian-born Exarch of Carthage, he practically single-handedly rescued the failing Eastern Roman Empire from a gruesome legacy of increasingly incompetent and harsh rulers, internal anarchy and potential mortal threats from abroad. His career ensured the preservation of the Eastern Roman Empire and the Greek culture it developed for the next 800 years. If he had not existed, the Eastern Empire would almost certainly have been so riven by internal dissension that it would not have been able to withstand the invasions and sieges by other races and cultures during the next decades. His reign heralded a different kind of empire: more forward-looking and increasingly more eastward-regarding and Greek in nature. However, in just over a century his dynasty had ended in insane revenge, corporeal mutilation and butchery, with appalling scenes recurring throughout the century.

Heraclius's renown has echoed through history. His exploits were the focus of two frescoes by the renowned Italian painter Piero della Francesca in the fifteenth century. His relationship with his physically unprepossessing and brutal predecessor Phocas was the subject for a play by the French dramatist Corneille in the seventeenth century; and he was the subject of a great Swahili Islamic poem, one of the first to be written down in that language, composed in what is now Kenya in 1728, which shows the regard in which, even at that late date, he was held by the Muslims. His reputation and legacy was still potent, over a thousand years after his time and thousands of miles from his empire. A tradition from Arabia tells that the prophet Mohammed sent couriers to Heraclius with a letter inviting him to convert to Islam. Muslim tradition reports that Heraclius interviewed an envoy of Mohammed. The envoy's summary of the interview showed that Heraclius could rationalise conclusions; so much so that there is a belief among the Faithful that the emperor converted and was a closet follower of the Prophet. Whether this story is apocryphal or not is open to debate – but it shows that often an enemy's respect for a leader is more telling than allies' support; much like the relationship five centuries later between Saladin and Richard the Lionheart.

Handsome, strong, dynamic and charismatic, Heraclius was revered as the saviour of the Eastern Roman Empire and one of the greatest of Byzantine emperors, but in later life it was clear that he experienced delusions and irrational fears. This may have been because of a form of post-traumatic stress syndrome; Heraclius experienced many personal mental and physical crises in his reign, during which he travelled more widely than even the celebrated founder of the Eastern Roman Empire, Constantine – and his empire was larger. Only a few years after he had seemingly secured the south-east flank of the Byzantine Empire by neutralising the Sassanids in four campaigns, he had to contend with the seemingly indestructible tide of Muslim conquest, culminating with the catastrophic defeat of a mighty Byzantine army on the Yarmuk, a tributary of the Jordan, in AD636. John Julius Norwich calls him 'the first Crusader', but Walter Kaegi dismisses this title, suggesting that the upholding of the Christian religion was only one of several reasons for fighting the Arabs. However, the seventh-century Byzantine court poet George of Pisidia goes out of his way to mirror God's actions in the emperor's against the Persians, but also used the analogy of the Labours of Hercules as illustration of the great obstacles with which his emperor had to contend. Because Hercules was not a god (although he looked godlike), the Church could identify with Heraclius as the instrument of God rather than God himself.

The reign of Heraclius can be summed up in his two entries into Constantinople and his great triumph in Jerusalem; the first triumphal, but in different ways. In 610 he was the blond re-creation of Hercules, filling the citizens with hope for the future; then in 629 he entered Jerusalem, 'The City of Peace', carrying the True Cross at the end of his campaigns to neutralise the Persians. The grateful citizens regarded their emperor as victorious, but they must have been shocked to see how greatly changed he was; worn out in the service of the empire. Likewise his pathetic creeping into Constantinople in 638, when it was obvious that he was completely broken physically and especially mentally, having seen all his hard-won gains at the expense of the Persians swept away in a few short years by the seemingly inexorable advance of the forces of Islam, of which, at the beginning of his reign, he would have been utterly unaware.

It had all started so well. The existing occupier of the throne, Phocas, a short, stocky, ferociously ugly, bearded ex-foot soldier from Thrace, had violently overthrown the legitimate Emperor Maurice in 602 – the first time that this had happened in the history of Constantine's capital. The army had revolted against twenty years of Maurice's obsessive meanness towards them and unremittingly high taxes on the suffering population. As the legions marched on Constantinople, so the empire's government dissolved. The emperor and his family fled to a monastery on the other side of the Bosphorus, but he was quickly found and dragged out. Revenge for his frugality was swift and typically merciless. His six sons and his brother were executed before his eyes before he suffered the same fate. The bodies were thrown into the sea where they were objects of fascination for the locals – a scene that was replicated just over a hundred years later. The male heads were publicly exhibited, and the traumatised empress Constantia and her three daughters were incarcerated in nunneries.

Phocas's rebellion was initially against Maurice's parsimony, so one of the first acts in his reign was to lower taxes, which made him popular with the army (on which he depended) and citizenry for the first few months; then his increasing paranoia engulfed him. The reputation he had for gratuitous cruelty while a soldier was proved innumerable times during his increasingly cruel and chaotic reign. John Julius Norwich grimly comments that his character was not as prepossessing as his appearance. The Persians to the south-east and the Avar tribes in the north-west began to reorganise themselves and threaten the borders. Agricultural production fell; the capital starved. Phocas paid ever more in tribute to stop invasion by the Avars and the Persians, but it didn't stop them: the Persians appeared on the other side of the Bosphorus during his reign, and the citizens fearfully watched the glow from the enemy campfires. The empire was in danger of imploding through pressures from outside and increasing internal anarchy.

The rebellion had to come. It began in Carthage, North Africa, in late 608. The Heraclians, father and son, began to mint coinage in their names, once they could count on the Exarchate army's support. Carthage was a long way from the capital; Phocas's expeditions to combat the upstarts ended in hard-fought failure in Egypt. Slowly but inexorably, much like his own rebellion but on a far vaster scale, the number of rebels grew as they approached the capital. Cities and Greek islands needed little persuasion to go over to the Heraclians. Egypt was kept quiet by Heraclius's uncle, Nicetas. Phocas had sown the wind; he was now reaping the whirlwind. He reacted in a typically vicious, malicious manner – Maurice's wife and daughters were torn from their cloisters and put to the sword, a useless, self-destructive gesture. But nothing could stop the Heraclians. Their triumph was inevitable; the surviving generals went over to them, as did the emperor's bodyguard, headed by Phocas's own son-in-law, Priscus. On 4 or 5 October 610 Heraclius sailed up the Golden Horn and entered the city without opposition. Unlike the emperor he had usurped, Phocas did not flee; there was nowhere friendly he could go. He was shorn of the purple regalia and brought to his young, tall and heroic rival on board his flagship. The physical contrast between the emperor and his rival could hardly be more different. J.B. Bury tells that Heraclius demanded, 'Is this how you have ruled, wretch?' Phocas, who had ruled by the sword, must have known that his days were numbered. Showing some spirit, he retorted, 'And will you rule better?'

It is not reported whether Heraclius replied. What is told is that Phocas was instantly killed on the deck; his head was hacked off, his body was torn apart and his genitalia ripped off. Some stories record that the ex-emperor's body was mutilated by Heraclius himself. Phocas's pathetic gory remnants were paraded throughout the city. Later that day the god-like rebel was crowned and married. There are no contemporaneous accounts of Phocas's reign; all were written later and all aggrandising Heraclius and his achievements. But there must be no doubt that the reign of the previous usurper was an unmitigated disaster and Heraclius saved the Byzantine Empire. The story goes that the father of Heraclius saw his son crowned and died soon afterwards, his life's work completed – almost as if father and son were God-given to preserve the state in its direst hour. Perhaps this was propaganda, but it was compelling nevertheless.

From then on fate overtook Heraclius. Although the Byzantines were defeated by the Persians in 613, in 626, inspired by Heraclius's example, the Byzantines survived a siege by a combined host of Avars, Slavs and Persians estimated at over 80,000. Within a few years Heraclius, as a true descendant of the spirit of Heracles, had rendered the apparently all-powerful Sassanian Persian Empire impotent; his bravery was the stuff of legend. His example inspired; his armour was as golden as his hair; in him flowed the spirits not only of Heracles but of Alexander. By 629 he had neutralised the Avars on the western border. In 614 the Persians under Chosroes had taken possession of Jerusalem. In the process of winning the cataclysmic battle of Nineveh in 627, Heraclius killed the opposing commander in single combat. The Sassanian defeat prompted a Ctesiphon palace coup the next year, which resulted in the overthrow of Chosroes and a peace offered by his son Khavad II, who agreed to withdraw from all conquered territories. His father, by now an old man, was imprisoned in a tower and, like Maurice, was forced to watch his children killed, one by one; then he was slowly shot to death with arrows. It was no more than he expected; he himself had tortured and killed his own father to seize the throne. As what he considered the pinnacle of his achievement in 629, Heraclius personally restored the True Cross to Jerusalem. According to tradition, this most precious of Christian relics had been discovered by Constantine the Great's mother Helena 300 years earlier and taken to Constantinople; now it was back where it belonged.

Although he seemed to be initially Western Roman in sympathy with a Roman first wife, Heraclius seems to have set up a resurgent, vigorous, Greek-speaking Byzantine Empire with a separate identity from

Justinian I's Rome-based remnants in the West, and with territorial ambitions over all the Middle East. He was addressed as the Greek *Basileus* rather than the Latin *Imperator*. He instigated much internal governmental and religious reform, especially his reorganisation of the empire into administrative areas called Themes, carrying on the work of his predecessor Maurice. After ruling for twenty years, an achievement in itself given the upheavals of the world at that time, surely he could afford to rest on his well-earned laurels?

However, only three years later Heraclius was the first head of a Christian state to contend with the titanic military onrush under Islam out of the Arabian Peninsula in all directions, which swamped the Sassanid Persians like a never-ending swarm. In the last twelve years of his reign even he was not able to prevent enormous tracts being torn out of the southern flank of the empire for the new faith; Egypt, Mesopotamia and Syria, which had been gained in previous years, were lost, some areas permanently. Heraclius managed to consolidate what remained, but at enormous cost to himself physically and mentally. His descendants were not as strong in either areas – so most of his personal foreign policy achievements were short-term. John Julius Norwich speculates that if Heraclius had died in about 630 he would perhaps have been regarded as one of the greatest rulers of all time. As it is, he and his exploits are known far more in the Muslim world than in the Christian.

Heraclius's last eleven years are a personal tragedy. At some point it became obvious that dropsy, the constant curse of the Byzantine emperors, was affecting him; the Church grimly regarded and self-righteously observed the effects of divine revenge. There is a story that the poor previously godlike emperor could not urinate properly, and had to place a board in front of him so he did not soak himself. How were the mighty fallen.

Heraclius was capable of controversial actions that seriously undermined his reputation at home, notably his second marriage with his niece, Martina. His first wife, Fabia, renamed Eudocia on her coronation, had died probably in 613 after the birth of their second child, from an epileptic seizure. She had been adored by the Byzantines. Later (Norwich says it was 'shortly afterwards'; others contend that it might have been as much as ten years on) Heraclius entered into a marriage with this much younger woman, which the patriarch Sergius and most of the Byzantines found repugnant because of the degree of blood relationship. There were public disturbances against the marriage, and even George of Pisidia, always there to praise the emperor, seems to criticise him. Nevertheless, it took place, no doubt presided over with the utmost unwillingness by Sergius. The new Empress Martina was almost universally detested because of the marriage, and the patriarch expressed this in no uncertain terms to Heraclius, but the emperor seemed to appreciate the risk he was taking and assumed responsibility for the consequences. This marriage and the many children from it seriously complicated his domestic and religious policy; it also made the question of the succession far more difficult, because many half-brothers would compete for the throne. However, the emperor and his young wife seemed soulmates; they were rarely out of each other's company. She cannot be faulted in her loyalty. Like Eleanor of Aquitaine in the Second Crusade, she journeyed with her husband on his campaigns against the Persians; perhaps she gave birth along the way, for she appears in Antioch, hundreds of miles from Constantinople, with an infant. There were ten children from the marriage; at least two were handicapped and some died young, thus proving to the Church that God frowned upon this seemingly happy family. We must speculate on whether the close blood tie was a factor in their familial tragedies.

John Julius Norwich tells a story, already retold by the Byzantine historian Nikephorus a hundred years after Heraclius's death, that in his later years the emperor developed a phobia of the sea and almost fatally delayed an important expedition against Islamic forces because of his illness: he could not bear to cross the Hellespont from his beloved palace of the Hiereia to enter Constantinople. Lord Norwich quotes Nikephorus's source that a bridge of boats was made with green foliage on either side so that the paranoid man could not see the water as he travelled across. Another relates that a boat was similarly fitted out and he was transported with his eyes firmly closed. Heraclius's most recent biographer, Walter Keagi, dismisses these stories of mental instability, feeling that they were largely a response to the reactions of a physically spent, increasingly ill and disappointed man, well-aged in an era of mostly short lives. However, all of his successors who lived to any sort of age displayed emotional instability. The Byzantines were used to their emperors becoming unbalanced. In the 570s one of Heraclius's predecessors, Justin II, became increasingly unreasonable and physically violent, only being quelled by the utterance of the name of an obscure Arab chieftain whom he had never met, but of whom he seemed irrationally terrified. In his more lucid moments he realised (perhaps he was persuaded by his wife Sophia and his closest advisors) that his competence to rule was collapsing, and abdicated four years before his death.

Heraclius and Martina's surviving son, Heraclonas, was made joint emperor with Constantine, his son by his first marriage to Fabia/Eudocia. Constantine was already in declining health and died after a reign of three months, probably from tuberculosis. Of course it was easy for a hostile public to suspect that the stepmother had poisoned the stepson in favour of her own natural son. Martina's ambitions for her sons meant that she would rule through Heraclonas, who was still a minor. Eventually she was not only regent but ruler in all but name. The military, the civil administration and the people were all against her. No woman had ever ruled before; the empire under female domination must be doomed. The massive incursions made into Byzantine territory by the Arabs in the late 630s, so soon after the Byzantines' triumph over the Persians, were blamed upon her. Soon after Constantine's death there was a rival claim centred on his son, Constans (also the product of an ecclesiastically disapproved marriage – Constantine and his wife Gregoria were second cousins – but their marriage did not seem to excite anything like the public opprobrium that Heraclius and Martina's did). Martina's tongue was cut out and Heraclonas's nose was slit, so that they could never again be claimants to the throne – for it was tradition that only individuals without physical blemish should rule in Constantinople. They were exiled to Rhodes. An Armenian source says that she was killed; but whatever happened to mother and son, they vanish from the story.

The Heraclian dynasty lasted just 101 years. The last occupant of the throne, Justinian II, displayed instability bordering on insanity; perhaps understandably, when his story is heard. Inheriting the Byzantine throne in 685 on the sudden death of his intelligent and able father, Constantine IV, in his early thirties from dysentery, Justinian tried to model himself on his illustrious namesake predecessor from 150 years previously. Arrogant and quarrelsome, he was barely sixteen when he ascended the throne; and despite those traits he looked as if he might well prove as successful as Justinian I. He presented all the energy of the founder of the Heraclian house and much of the shrewdness and perspicacity. But he also displayed some of the mental imbalance displayed by both his great-great-grandfather Heraclius and his grandfather Constans II in their declining years. In his case the madness manifested was a concentration of his infamous temper into acts of unbridled and unjustifiable cruelty.

Again, Justinian's reign started so promisingly. He led a successful expedition against the Slavs in the west in 688–9, and as a consequence transported thousands of them to parts of Anatolia (southern Turkey) which had been depopulated for over 200 years. He then proceeded to tax them unmercifully, with the consequence that when the Arabs invaded again in 691 many of these new citizens, with no loyalty to their recent master in what they saw as a foreign land, and with some justification for their actions deserted to the enemy. As punishment, it seems that several thousand men, women and children of Slav origin living in Bithynia in the north of what is now Turkey, many miles from where the original incident occurred, were methodically butchered and hurled into the Sea of Marmara.

Being an obsessive individual, Justinian would go to any lengths to get what he wanted. The most brutal methods of raising taxes from the suffering population were used. Whipping, roasting over slow fires and smoking victims into unconsciousness were only a few of the means Justinian sanctioned to satisfy his demands for money to fund his manias, which included building. Status didn't matter; rich and poor alike were pitilessly squeezed. By this and other policies Justinian rapidly acquired an unpopularity only achieved by Phocas, of whom his great-great-grandfather Heraclius had ferociously disposed in 610; one of the few blots on his early career.

In 691 Justinian sent to Pope Sergius I in Rome the results of the debate of a huge synod of eastern bishops, the Quinisext, giving the high-handed order that the pope approve the listed 102 religious principles without exception. Some of these were utterly insignificant – even irrelevant – in Roman ecclesiastical eyes. However, the banning by the Eastern Church of the popular metaphor of Christ as the sacrificial Lamb was refused outright, and Sergius, in an act of defiance and disapproval, deliberately added the *Agnus Dei* to the Latin Mass, where it has remained to this day. On receiving this news Justinian ascended into one of his now familiar apoplectic rages, decreeing arrests, mutilations and banishments of Roman officials, and anyone else who might be construed to be in any way connected to what he considered the heretical Church in Rome.

Eventually, enough became enough. In 695 the aristocracy revolted under the leadership of a recently disgraced general, Leontius. The twenty-six-year-old Justinian was arrested and deposed. He was ignominiously paraded for public vilification, and his predatory tax-gatherer enforcers were dragged by their heels through the streets before being burnt alive. As a gesture of remembrance of his friendly association with

Justinian's father, the new Emperor Leontius spared the son the same fate; but like those of his ancestors his nose and tongue were mutilated to prevent him from regaining the throne. He was exiled north to Cherson in the inhospitable, uncivilised and far-away Crimea. From that day to this he has been known as *Rhinotmetus* – Slit-nose.

Not much later, how the Byzantines must have regretted Leontius's comparative mercy. The new emperor was an unmitigated disaster, supervising the loss of Byzantine Carthage, where Heraclius's father had been Exarch, to the now Muslim Arabs. Three years later in 698 he was deposed and mutilated in his turn by Apsimar, a German vice-admiral of the Carthage-bound relief fleet that turned traitor. His name was quickly changed to the more appropriate Tiberius. He fared better, inflicting defeats on the Arabs with the aid of his brother, Heraclius. The reputation of the name lingered.

In the far-away Crimea no-one dared resist a vengeful Justinian, allied to the Bulgar King Tervel and now married to a sister of a Khazar khan. We do not know her real name but we must render her much sympathy. She was just a political pawn, and she even lost her own identity; Justinian renamed her after his first wife, Theodora. He had been fulminating against his successors and plotting his return for years with other local magnates, so much so that the authorities in Cherson were increasingly eager to be rid of him. In the spring of 705 he and an army suddenly appeared before the walls of Constantinople; to the refined citizens he must have seemed a vengeful ghoul at the head of a horde of Slav and Bulgar sub-human barbarians. Tiberius fled to the now Turkish mainland. The city fathers decided on the lesser of two evils, and reluctantly re-received their ruthless ex-emperor rather than be ravaged by his crude creatures.

The next years were awash in merciless blood; no-one was safe from the mutilated emperor's ire. His two predecessors were soon found, publicly humiliated and executed. Tiberius, Apsimar's brother, the best general Constantinople had at the time, was hanged from the walls together with all his staff; the patriarch who had crowned Leontius and Tiberius was blinded and exiled to Rome. Paul the Deacon, in his *Historia Langobardorum*, which was written some eighty years later, related the dark tale that the paranoid, pitiless emperor ordered the execution of anyone he surmised was opposing him almost as many times as he wiped phlegm from his non-existent nose. He was losing his grip on reality. When a naval expedition to punish rebellious Cherson was swamped by a storm on its way home, with the deaths of over 70,000 men, he is said to have burst into peals of hysterical laughter.

It could not last. Justinian's insane purges of the highest echelons of command, like Stalin's purges of the Russian officer class in the 1930s, resulted in too many military setbacks. The whole of the Crimea rebelled again, and a second army, sent to raise the siege of Cherson in 711, joined the besiegers under a hard-nosed, callous Armenian mercenary commander called Vardan. As soon as Vardan had realised that he could aspire to emperor, he had taken the much more acceptable patrician name of Bardanes Philippicus. He marched south. What was left of the fleet followed, hugging the coast and cutting off any escape over the Black Sea. Justinian was not in Constantinople because he was on his way east to quell a minor uprising in Armenia, but as soon as he heard he turned back towards the city to confront the northern rebels, 'roaring like a lion'.

He was just too late. Intercepted at the twelfth milestone from Constantinople, Justinian was arrested again; but this time there was no Leontius to offer mercy. He deserved none. There was not even a public humiliation this time; his head was summarily sliced from his body at the milestone. It was displayed for all to view in Constantinople; some stories say that it was exhibited in Rome and Ravenna as well. His corpse was hastily heaved into the nearby Marmara, no doubt to be watched by many as it pathetically floated past. The Slav holocaust of twenty years previously had been avenged. Justinian was forty-two years old. His wife had already vanished.

The butchery didn't end with the emperor's murder; there was still the heir to the throne to be disposed of. Tiberius, Justinian's six-year-old son by his Khazar wife, had been swept off by the late emperor's mother, Theodora, into sacred sanctuary in the Church of Mary, the Mother of God next door to the huge royal palace of Blachernae in the northern extremity of the city, next to the Theodosian Walls. Bardanes Philippicus must have thought that the tiny Tiberius was an important rallying point for all those still loyal to the Heraclian line, as he was the only legitimate successor to Justinian – and therefore he constituted a personal threat to his ambition. He sent a deputation of soldiers to search for the child, who was discovered in the church, crouching on the high altar; the most sacred location in a long-sacred building. He was desperately hanging onto his grandmother and clutching sacred relics, including a fragment of the True Cross, one of the most venerated relics of the whole Church. The sacred rights of sanctuary were ignored by the new emperor's gang, and regardless of his frail grandmother's imploring and curses, he was wrenched from her failing grasp by one of Philippicus's agents, no doubt wailing with fright. He was dragged outside the sacred walls, and in the porch of another church nearby his clothes were ripped from him and he was 'slaughtered ... like a sheep'.

Thus ended the Heraclian dynasty of the Eastern Roman Empire. It had started in such hope for reconstruction and revival, with such a contrast in physique and personality. It had been successful beyond its founder's dreams; now it was deliberately demolished in infanticide and tainted ignominy.

In the same year – 711 – the Muslim Arabs invaded what had recently been Byzantine territory in southern Spain; they would remain there until 1492. Twenty years later they were threatening northern France. The Byzantines never held land in Western Europe again.

Bardanes Philippicus lasted only two years before an internal rebellion deposed and blinded him. In the next decade three more emperors sat uneasily on the throne of Constantine; and the great empire was plunged again into the internal strife that had been mirrored a hundred years before. It seemed almost as if Heraclius had never been; never ruled.

Chapter 4
Charles VI and Henry VI –
Inherited Insanity

Madness in great ones must not unwatch'd go
Hamlet – William Shakespeare

Throughout Europe's long and varied history, crowned heads understood that their marriages were initially for political purposes rather than love and mutual attraction. Very few of them thought that they were in control of their choice of marriage partner; even less did they think that their opinion on the subject of dynastic progress was worth much. Many were engaged almost as soon as they were born, for dynastic, political or financial gain by the older generation. Royal futures were speculated upon, planned and mapped before royal children were even aware that they had futures. As in previous centuries it was accepted that lives rarely reached the accepted span of threescore years and ten; they were abbreviated through inherent vulnerability to disease and violence in men, the added complications of childbirth in women, and famine in both. Adulthood was agreed to have begun by the age of thirteen and many young men and women – we would see them as still boys and girls – were often married by this time. Young princesses were often pregnant at twelve. The phrase 'till death us do part' was often the short-term rule rather than the exception. Nearly half the population of Europe had succumbed to the ravages of the bubonic plague known as the 'black death' in the middle of the fourteenth century, and the average life-expectancy throughout that century was a little over thirty. Class was no protection, and the need for repopulation was great. Princes and princesses were pawns, procreative slaves and puppets for their elders and masters – sometimes not even their royal relatives, but powerful commoners, who saw an advantageous marriage as a means to cement power and influence over the crowned head, especially if he was a minor.

As time went by and royal families became more intertwined, there were fewer candidates of appropriate status or political and dynastic power who were not related in some way. As the 'great and good' aspired to become greater and better in their own eyes, they became infinitely worse in terms of their gene pool. The French from the twelfth to the nineteenth century were ruled by two families; the Spanish from the fifteenth to the twentieth by two; the Russians from the tenth to the twentieth by two; the Austrians from the eleventh to the twentieth and the Bavarians from the eleventh to the nineteenth by one. All were plagued by mental and physical disability, and inherited weaknesses – for instance susceptibility to haemophilia and to physical fragility and illness, often caused by manifested or inherited venereal disease. If there was a genetic weakness in the main branch, it often appeared among progeny of cousins, uncles, nephews and nieces. The British have been ruled by at least six families and cadet branches in the 950 years since the Norman Conquest – and even they have not been immune from inherited physical and mental difficulties. Even in the populist 1960s and '70s, when there were no national alliances that needed to be sealed by royal marriages, there was constant press speculation as to whether there was an appropriate Protestant princess with whom the Prince of Wales could sire the next generation of royal Protestants. In medieval Europe the Catholic Church tried to curtail interrelated marriages because it was against canon law. However, religious leaders, even the pope in Rome or Avignon, could be bribed, persuaded or forced into providing dispensations by the magnates on whom they were dependent for survival. After all, they would probably not be alive to view the fruits of their enforced liberalism.

Charles VI ascended the French throne in 1380 on the death of his father, Charles V. The father was cultured, shrewd and highly intelligent; but a fatalist – strange-looking, long-nosed and odd-bodied, with a weeping abscess on his left arm, possibly the effect of an assassination attempt – for these were violent times and noble loyalty could not always be assumed. He was assured that when the carbuncle dried he would not live long, so it seemed that he was always in a hurry to secure France by proving to be an astute and resourceful head from the start of his reign. Charles V not only alleviated the threat of more English territorial gains in France but restored much of the national terrain, through diplomacy, for sixteen years. He was perhaps fortunate that Richard II's English foreign policy was just as conciliatory. At the same time he quelled inevitable internal unrest by nobles and peasants; often caused by voracious levels of taxation, including a hearth tax that would affect anyone, whatever their status. His son was extraordinarily popular at first and deserved the title of *Bien-Amie* – the Well-Beloved. This sobriquet would change.

Charles VI's mother, Joanna of Bourbon, had died giving birth to his youngest sister Catherine in 1378, to the great grief of her husband (unusually this was a marriage where there was genuine affection between husband and wife). Of the seven children of Charles and Joanna only two – the future Charles VI and Louis, Duke of Orleans – survived to maturity. The Bourbon family were already displaying mental instability, for Joanna's father, Peter, the first duke (killed at the battle of Poitiers in 1358, at which King John II had been captured), and her brothers demonstrated intermittent volatile behaviour. She seems to have had a nervous breakdown after a birth in 1372. Her son Charles was married at seventeen to Isabeau of Bavaria, who was from the ancient Wittelsbach family (which displayed both spectacularly talented and insane members in later centuries). Isabeau was thrust into a position of strength; how she dealt with it was a significant factor in the story of France during her husband's decline into incompetence. Women of all classes were not expected to survive confinements, which were usually many. They were second-class citizens, and Christine de Pisan, the first woman to earn her living by writing, often complained that women were denigrated in a man's world despite their intelligence.

Charles VI's France had borders that would be unrecognisable to modern eyes. The English held land in Brittany in the north-west, in the Pas de Calais in the north-east and around Bordeaux and Bayonne in the south-west. There had been war in France between England and France for years. Although the royal families of Valois in France and Plantagenet in England were related through marriage and descent from the Normans, the French objected to the claims of the English to be kings of France through the female line, adhering to Salic law. This prohibition, which prevented women from inheriting land, was supposedly founded on a law of the Salian Franks, who first organised the kingdom that became France, and it meant that no descent through a female could be accepted as legitimate in French eyes.

Despite his father's political and military labours, Charles was born into a country that was still racked by war and rumours of war. France and England were involved in what was to become known as the Hundred Years War – a sporadic conflict that lasted for more than a century, concerning the disputed royal succession to the French throne and possession of the land of France itself. Within this war there were internal civil conflicts between the great families, each vying to influence a throne occupied by weak monarchs who acted unpredictably.

Twenty years before Charles was born, the treaty of Bretigny had made much of the land of France tributary to English influence, if not to its direct rule. Charles's grandfather, John II, called the Good, had been a prisoner of the English. He was released once a third of his ransom had been paid. Unbelievably, even for that time, he voluntarily returned to imprisonment in England as a matter of honour to his bond when a prince of the blood, also a prisoner of the English, escaped. He left his country without a ruler or a purpose by sacrificing his nation to his chivalric conscience, and died in voluntary captivity in 1364. During the next sixteen years Charles V wrested back much disputed French territory by diplomacy, bribery and neutralisation of military threats by avoiding set-piece battles. Despite the unpopularity of swingeing taxation, national morale was rising within France when in early September 1380 the king's arm abscess suddenly dried. True to the prophecy, Charles V quickly gave up his hold on life, revoked the hearth-tax and 'slept with his fathers' at the age of forty-two. The *Bien-Amie* began his reign when he was no more than twelve years old. With the king still a minor, a regency council to protect the young king's interests with a senior noble at its head was needed, but as nobles were potential rivals for power this was a difficult role to sustain. The dukes of Berry, Bourbon and Burgundy were all out for their own ends, under the pressured chairmanship of Louis, Duke of Anjou as senior aristocrat. Within a month Louis had bowed to demands from the others that the young king be declared of age.

Like many princes, Charles's general health was not of the best and he was frequently indisposed. This was not unusual in an era when life was often short, most doctors were unskilled and treatment was brutal. In early 1392 Charles was seriously ill, going down with a fever and losing the hair from his head and the nails from his hands and feet. Dr Vivian Green suggests that this could have been encephalitis or typhoid (either disease could have been a factor in hastening the king's mental decline), or some form of inherited syphilis. However, the king would have had what was thought to be the best of care, and was especially fortunate in that the great doctor Guillaume de Harcigny, although fabulously ancient for the times (probably in his early eighties), was still alert, shrewd and respected. By early summer his patient was not yet completely recovered, and still displayed intermittent low fever and verbal incoherence.

The old Breton warhorse Olivier Clisson, Constable of France, who had lost an eye in battle, advised the king that he should rule without the influence of the great lords. Charles managed to do this in 1388 at the end of his teens, replacing the lords with other advisors, including, of course, Clisson. These were five courtiers – not great lords or vastly wealthy magnates, just a group of five men who swore allegiance to the king and interdependence on each other. They were derogatorily described by the affronted aristocrats as the Marmousets. John V, Duke of Brittany, was an old enemy of the constable and attempted to have Clisson murdered in 1392 by Pierre de Craon. Although Clisson was wounded, his iron constitution helped him recover. De Craon fled to his master in Brittany; the king viewed this as a personal affront. To punish the duke and his conspirators, the king (still not in the best of health) and the constable raised an army and marched in the high summer of the year.

Progress towards the duke's lands in the north-west of France was slow. The weather was oppressively hot and sultry, but Charles was impatient to get on. As the army entered a forest near Le Mans, a beggar (some say a leper) suddenly emerged from the undergrowth. 'Turn back, noble king,' he yelled, grabbing the king's bridle. 'Go no further! You are betrayed!' Although the man was beaten back by the royal attendants, he was not arrested, and the chronicler says that he followed them for about half an hour, repeating his warnings.

The army kept on at a snail's pace through the gloomy trees in the stifling heat. We can only imagine what was going through the minds of the royal army on that oppressively hot morning of 1 August 1392. Whatever their education, training and knowledge, they were still uninformed about so many things and suspicious of everything that could not be explained positively. Forests were places of dread to them, full of threats, of magic, of malevolent spirits and shadows. Eyes were everywhere; ears pricked for any sound that might be hostile. Everyone was aware that this would be a good place for an ambush, if the Duke of Brittany was prepared; he must have been forewarned of an expedition of this size. With the great lords all jockeying for position around the young king, the potential for plots and betrayal was rife. No aristocrat who had something to gain from influencing the impressionable monarch trusted the others. There would have been some individuals who knew that they would benefit from the king's death; everyone was aware. Some armour must have been worn, which further intensified the heat and feelings of oppression. The tension was almost visible.

The army stumbled on through the forest's shades, finally emerging in a cloud of dust at about midday. The heat dropped onto them like a thick blanket and one of the pages slumped forward drowsily, dropping the king's lance and clanging it against a helmet. The king was riding a little apart from his companions to get out of the way of the dust. Wide-eyed, he shuddered, drew his sword and swung it about his head. 'Forward against the traitors!' he cried. 'They wish to deliver me to the enemy!' In his overwrought state, he thought everyone was attacking him, and defended himself valiantly against his imagined foes, cutting and slashing with his heavy broadsword at anyone who came close. The horses bucked and shrilled, the silence shattered by panicked shouts and yells. Once Charles's sword had been broken it still took many knights to subdue him and lie him on the ground. With the king were several who would not move again. Among them was a popular knight from Gascony, the Chevalier de Polignac, who was much mourned.

The king lay as if transfixed, with his eyes flicking wildly from side to side, finally slipping into a comatose state, in which he remained for two days. When he recovered consciousness he seemed to recognise no-one. His advisors sent again for the renowned Guillaume de Harcigny. The chronicler Jean Froissart described the illness as *une chaude maladie* – either delusions brought on by the summer heat or, more seriously, the heat of humours to the brain. Doctor de Harcigny recognised symptoms that had been evident in the king's mother's breakdown twenty years before, and sensibly prescribed a period of rest and good food. Charles slowly recovered during the following months, and in the autumn gave thanks for his recovery in the cathedral of Laon, de Harcigny's home city.

A political as well as a medical reason for the king's illness had to be found, and the scapegoat became Clisson; his influence was blamed for Charles's indisposition. He was stripped of the constableship and, as the king failed to recover quickly enough, he fled to the lands of the same Duke of Brittany who had attempted to have him killed only months before. He became reconciled to his erstwhile murderer and acted as his advisor until the duke's death in 1399. He then became protector of the duchy in the years before his own death in 1407, well into his eighties. In such ways were loyalties transferred at this time. Being king and therefore God's temporal representative, as well as the personification of the country, did not necessarily mean that Charles was the most powerful man in France.

Meanwhile, the king's illness meant that his uncles could regain power without his objection. Guillaume de Harcigny had suggested that Charles's fragile mental state meant that he should not be worried about matters of state, or anything else that would cause him trial, so while he was recovering and in no position to defend his advisors the Marmousets were deprived of office and imprisoned. The lords were supreme again and the king's role reverted to an emasculated cipher. Not that it seemed to worry Charles. He could enjoy himself as much as the next person, and continued his slow recovery to a state where he might assume some responsibilities again. The court entertainments helped; they were extravagant and often dissolute, and he enjoyed them, provided that the queen did not get involved.

The year 1393 began with every hope that the king would make a complete recovery. He was still known as the Well-Beloved; not many were of the opinion that his eccentricities of behaviour were anything but a passing phase: royalty was often subject to these episodes. The long life of Guillaume de Harcigny was ending at last, so he could not be called upon for diagnosis or advice about treatment. On the evening of 28 January a grossly bad taste masque was organised by the queen to celebrate the third marriage of a lady-in-waiting. The centrepiece was a troupe of six young men who wore outlandish, uncivilised costumes and played randy savages. They wore masks to conceal their identities, because of the nature of their performance, and their costumes were made of linen or hemp impregnated with wax and resin, so as to render them 'shaggy and hairy from head to foot'. The organiser of this entertainment, Huguet de Guisay, well known for his indulgent sadism and debauchery, but a favourite of the king, knew that this was a fire risk, so fire was prohibited. As the performers pranced about, making obscene sexual gestures, the king's brother, Louis, Duke of Orleans, arrived in the room with his entourage. They were bearing lighted torches. A spark fell from one of the torches onto one of the dancers' costumes.

When material coated with resin ignites, it not so much burns as explodes. The heat is intense and instantaneous. When wax is added to the resin the heat is just as concentrated but the burning lasts much longer. It must have constituted the medieval equivalent of napalm, engulfing the performers in almost liquid fire. With terrifying rapidity the flames passed between the dancers. Courtiers tried to rip the costumes off the victims, which resulted in their clothing catching fire. The queen had hysterics; only she knew that the king was one of the dancers. Chaos ensued, with panicking courtiers dashing to get out of the room colliding with other courtiers, servants and attendants who were rushing in to help. The screams of the horrified audience combined hideously with the agonised cries of the sufferers. The ghastly odours of burning material and roasting living flesh were overpowering. The young Duchess of Berry displayed both bravery and presence of mind by flinging her skirt over a dancer who was not completely immolated – and the flames were smothered. Under the smouldering remains of his costume was the king. Four of the other dancers died after immense suffering, including Huguet de Guisay. This tragic episode became known as the *Bal des Ardents*, with the ironic pun on 'ardents' – 'men in extreme love' and 'men burning'.

Although there is no direct connection between this horrific incident and the king's decline into madness, there is no doubt that it must have had a profound effect on a man who had already demonstrated mental frailty. Six months later, in the summer of 1393, he could not recognise his wife or children; he didn't believe that he was married and refused to answer to his name. He developed a hate for the royal coat of arms and tried to scrub it from his gold plate. Doctor de Harcigny's replacements, Renaud Freron and then William de Haresley, did not last long. De Haresley thought that the incident in the forest was the source of the king's madness, coupled with the inheritance of his mother's nature. Freron was possibly the victim of the king's delusions. In November 1395 the poor king was observed rushing from room to room in the Hotel de St Pol, yelling that he was escaping from his enemies, until he collapsed. Freron might have been in the group that tried to help the distracted man. It is said that internal doors were walled up afterwards to prevent the scandal leaking out. France was a large and proud country with ancient traditions: the idea of nationhood was emerging, and to have the personification of that nationhood displaying such mental incompetence was an insult to the country and could be seen as a metaphor of its internal corruption. Any royal family that viewed France with acquisitive eyes would use that ineptitude as political proof of the degeneration of its temporal power, and the ruling family's right to continue. There could not be a worse prospect for French monarchical (and therefore national) prestige.

It became worse. The king was mad more often than he was sane. In early 1396 Charles began to forget who he was, and schizoid behaviour ensued. He called himself Georges and again did not recognise his royal coat of arms, thinking it was a lion with a sword thrust through it. Sometimes he was lethargic; at other times he was charged with manic and unfocused energy. He damaged himself and his possessions; many items were broken. At other times he announced that he was made of glass, and had iron rods inserted in his clothes to prevent himself being shattered. The royal accounts show that a gown was cleaned after the king urinated on it. He seems to have recovered from this episode, but not for long. By 1405 he had been unshaven, unwashed and verminous for months.

Queen Isabeau simply couldn't cope. This maniac, the king and her husband, with whom she had had twelve children in a little over twenty years, couldn't bear her being close to him, and she was banished from his presence. With her blessing a mistress was installed, a beautiful and kind young woman called Odette de Champdivers, a former mistress of his brother Louis. She cared for her distracted charge for many years and provided him with a daughter, Margaret. Instead of grasping the opportunity to steer her adopted country towards the stability that her husband could not provide, Isabeau feathered her nest and those of members of her Bavarian entourage. Louis also tried to get what he could from his influence of the regency over the increasingly inert king. He was rumoured to have had an affair with the queen to reinforce his ascendant position, and disputed the legitimacy of the influence of John, Duke of Burgundy, who had emerged as the strongest candidate. Louis also did his best to frustrate all John's policies, which would have benefited Burgundy as well as France. Internecine strife developed, which threatened to break into civil war – the last thing that the country needed. On 20 November 1407

Louis and John made a solemn pact of reconciliation in the presence of the whole court, for the good of the country. But their hatred and rivalry ran too deep. Three days later Louis was surrounded as he mounted his horse in Paris; his arms were chopped off to render him helpless before he succumbed to the fatal thrust.

This murder pitched France under its helpless king into a civil war between the Burgundians and the adherents of the family of Louis, the Armagnacs, which would last for several generations. The English, now free of internal rebellions, watched and waited for their opportunity, which would have come earlier if Henry IV had been in better health himself. He died in 1413, and, once home affairs had been stabilised and rebellions neutralised, his son, Henry V, sailed for France on a punitive raid in August 1415. This ended with France's defeat at Agincourt. The battle has been well documented and its course need not concern us here; what should be emphasised is that the French nobility managed to forget their differences in the short term and fight against the common enemy, at enormous cost. John the Fearless, Duke of Burgundy, was significantly absent, however. Two of his brothers were killed, together with Jean de Croy, John's chamberlain, and two of his sons.

Not only was the country headless because of the king's madness, but many prominent members of the nobility were now dead or captured by the English, who wanted enormous ransoms from their families. National morale plummeted. The disaster at Agincourt was only the start. The country was headless.

Henry V could see that the crown of France, so long coveted by the English, was within his grasp: the enemy was too disunited to provide a co-ordinated opposition. In 1417 Henry invaded again, and most of

Normandy succumbed to his methodical siege tactics; the French would not meet him in pitched battle. By the summer of 1419 Paris was under siege, having been captured the year before by the Burgundians. The Dauphin Charles and John, Duke of Burgundy met on the bridge at Montereau-Fault-Yonne, to the east of Paris, ostensibly, John thought, to discuss how to continue to appear united in the face of a seemingly all-conquering enemy. But this was not what the Armagnacs had in mind; John was murdered on the bridge. The effect of this was that his son Philip, called 'The Good' and King Charles's son-in-law since 1409, would openly favour the English; his father never had. Even so, events did not stop him from swapping allegiance between the French and the English whenever it suited his purpose for the next twenty-six years.

With the English all-powerful in the north and south-west, Paris in enemy hands and the Burgundians ready to invade from the east, Queen Isabeau and her advisors had little choice but to negotiate. The crushing terms of the treaty of Troyes in 1420 were enough to make any French nationalist weep. The main conditions were that the French princess Catherine would marry Henry V and he would be regent of France until her pathetic father's death. Thereafter, any heir (presumably the son or daughter – in English law, contrary to the French Salic law) would be acclaimed King or Queen of England and France. The crowns would be united; but France would be the vassal of England. The new dauphin, the heir to a non-existent throne, would be ostracised – a prince without a country. Even if he claimed what was left of France, in territory terms it was little more than half its size on the accession of Charles VI the Well-Beloved, now called the Mad. One wonders whether any details of the disaster were communicated to the king, so deep in lunacy was he; and if it was, what sort of reaction there could have been.

Although he had secured what many of his royal predecessors had yearned to do, the energetic Henry V still wanted to reinforce his rights to the mainland by more conquest. In 1421, while raising levies for the army in England, he had lost his deputy, the Duke of Clarence, killed in battle against a Franco-Scots army, but he was back in Normandy in 1422, taking Meaux Castle by storm in the late spring. He must have known when the treaty was signed that Charles had been suffering intermittent bouts of fever and, now in his fifties, couldn't be expected to live much longer. But it was the much younger and more vigorous king who departed first. By 31 August Henry was dead, probably of dysentery, at Vincennes Castle, east of Paris. He and Catherine had performed their prime function as members of a royal dynasty, as the French Queen of England had given birth to a son, the putative king of both countries, on 6 December 1421. He was just eight months old when his father died. Charles's tortured life ended in a stupor caused by a form of malaria on 21 October 1422 in Paris. Odette's name was on his lips as he descended into coma. He had outlasted Henry by less than two months. God had moved in a mysterious way His wonders to perform. Those seven weeks probably sealed the fate of both countries for the next 400 years.

Charles's maternal genes sealed the fate of his grandson. Henry VI grew up seemingly intelligent, alert and eager to follow his father's example. However, he was very much of his maternal grandfather's frame of mind when he was young – well intentioned but prone to tantrums. As soon as it was considered that he was physically able to endure it, the child was crowned king in England on 6 November 1429. Charles the Dauphin had already been crowned King of France in Reims on 17 July, just short of his twenty-sixth birthday. Henry of England was crowned King of France at the end of 1431; he was only nine. The French had an adult and intelligent king, not a man of physical action (the Valois never were) but inspired by Joan of Arc, a girl who seemed to be a gift from God, leading them to success against the hated English. They entertained the prospect that their king would be an influenced minor for several more years.

By the time Henry achieved his majority, the political and economic situation at home and in France was deteriorating, and the council of ministers that had ruled in his name was proving not to be up to the task. Neither did the king have the right character to assert his authority, although he made an effort. He was more interested in learning and religion, and his grief at his inability to cope with political and temporal problems was expiated in confessionals. The problems that he inherited were too difficult for him to deal with intellectually and practically; he relied far too much on poor advice from a faction led by the Beaufort family. His assessment of personality was at fault; he trusted flatterers and favourites. This led to the young king's increasing unpopularity in court, where the Yorkist faction, descended from the murdered Richard II, arguably had a better claim to the throne than he. There was not enough of France secured under his father to generate the revenue to pay for the upkeep of garrisons against a hostile native population. English possessions inexorably ebbed away after Joan of Arc's example reasserted French nationalism, encapsulated by the relief of Reims – which allowed Charles VII to be crowned in 1429 where all French kings had been for time immemorial. Joan of Arc's death at the stake in Rouen in 1431 united France as a nation in its hatred of the English; the lands so hard won by Henry V vanished; eventually even the citizens of Bordeaux, who regarded themselves as English, having been ruled by them since the days of Henry II, succumbed to French rule after the disastrous English defeat at Castillon in 1453.

It is difficult not to have some sympathy for the young king. His father was an impossible act to follow – a legend in his own lifetime; lionised in death; a universally respected man of action; a national superstar, free from the skulduggery that surrounded his father's seizure of the throne, coupled with the murder of Richard II in 1400. Henry V died knowing that he was secure at home, militarily the strong man of Europe, universally respected and feared, at the height of his powers. He never seemed to personally fail or make mistakes, and could afford to be his own man, supported by efficient and loyal magnates and churchmen, idolised by the military and commoners, both in the field and at home. Henry VI possessed none of his father's earned charisma; he took after his mother's side, being less active and more bookish. He was unfortunate that the great leaders were becoming older and the advisors, largely the Beauforts, were not as shrewd. The country was declining in agrarian and military terms. However much Henry wanted to succeed the problems were too complicated for him to solve. But he was the king; he knew the buck stopped with him, and as he grew older he could see the country made great by his father going to rack and ruin. He was blamed for bad harvests, rising prices and a seemingly unending stream of bad news and military reverses from a resurgent nation across the Channel. National morale was collapsing even in the first twenty years of his life; law and order was breaking down; the Beauforts were feathering their nests at the expense of royal land and revenue, as they had done since they had assumed the guardianship. Henry had put his trust in them when he was not able to make decisions for himself, and his emasculated will was never sufficient to oppose them. By the time he was old enough to take on the reins of government, corruption and weak government were endemic; it was too late for lasting reform. He was not strong enough to slow the charge downhill.

It seems unusual that the great magnates were so tardy in arranging a royal marriage for their young charge; this could have been because the king was suspected of not being capable of making appropriate decisions when he achieved the age of responsibility. It was the Beauforts who suggested the beautiful and proud Margaret of Anjou, the niece of the French king, as a way of promoting peace in France while still retaining land won by Henry V. Margaret had been brought up in a cultured female-dominated household in the Duchy of Lorraine. Her mother spent her married life supporting her gentle father's claim to the kingdom of Naples. Her father's mother, it is said, ruled Anjou 'with a man's hand'. Marriage negotiations were protracted, but finally a deal with Charles VII, as the French king, was brokered. The terms were extraordinary: there would be no dowry and the provinces of Anjou and Maine would revert to French rule. This was no negotiation from an English position of strength; it was kept secret because it would have been very unpopular in the country at large. On 23 April 1445 the marriage was celebrated in Titchfield

Abbey in Hampshire, a monastic house famous for its learning, possibly because the Beauforts wanted it to happen as soon as the bride had landed. She was just fifteen; Henry was twenty-four. Margaret had passion and strength for both of them, and ruled increasingly on her own as the king was overwhelmed by problems that he knew he did not have the authority to resolve: he might have already been deeply depressed by the time of the marriage. It was the queen's duty to support the interests of the English Crown, and this she did – heedless of her personal unpopularity. She was viewed as an adult in those days, and in the middle of her teens her word was law; but even she could not hold her adopted nation's headlong decline.

Government became more and more sporadic as factions bickered among themselves, and king and parliament were openly ridiculed. Even three years before his marriage there had been unrest and personal insults concerning Henry's mental competence. The crisis deepened in 1450 as the Duke of Suffolk, the leader of one faction, was banished and assassinated; then the bishops of Chichester and Salisbury were murdered. Jack Cade, an ex-soldier, led a crowd of peasants from Kent and Sussex in rebellion against the king, protesting against heavy taxation. A royal force sent against them was surprisingly defeated near Sevenoaks, and Cade's unruly mob surged into London, confronting and killing John Stafford, the Archbishop of Canterbury, and Henry's treasurer, Sir James Fiennes. Their heads were jammed onto spikes and, in a graphic demonstration of peasant opinion, were exhibited in the act of kissing each other. The army didn't defeat Cade; it was the Londoners themselves who, tired of the peasants' excesses, ejected them from the city. Cade was hunted down and killed in Sussex.

It took a long time before Margaret became pregnant; rumours were rife that the king could not father a child, unlike his grandfather and uncles who, despite their mental frailties, had had many children. Eventually Margaret was delivered of a son, christened Edward on 13 October 1453, and the rumour mill ground out many potential fathers. The king was absent from the baptism; he was sinking into a quietening, darkening, mentally somnolent world of his own. By then he had received the news of the defeat and death of the Earl of Shrewsbury at the battle of Castillon. This pitched him into a state of physical and mental paralysis, incapable of response. He was not to know it, but Castillon was the last battle of the Hundred Years War. In the thirty-one years of Henry's reign, the third of France won by his illustrious father's acts of arms had been almost completely lost; all that was left of the vast English possessions of a few years previously was a small area around Calais.

In January 1454 the queen and the Prince of Wales travelled to Windsor to meet the king and his court. There, the physical manifestation of Henry's mental illness was graphically exhibited. John Stodely described how the Duke of Buckingham took the infant Edward in his arms, 'beseeching the king to bless him; and the king gave no manner answer. Nevertheless, the duke still abode still with the prince by the king; and when he could no manner answer have, the queen came in, and took the prince in her arms and presented him in like form ... but all their labour was in vain, for they departed thence without any answer or countenance, saving only that once he looked on the prince and cast his eyes down again without any move.'

There were no more royal children. The Lancastrians depended on Edward, for their confidence in his father had long evaporated. The king was gripped by an ecstasy of inaction. Without his input, government could not function. For nearly eight months the king remained silent and almost immobile; he had no memory of who he was or what he was supposed to do. No major appointments were made in these months. The doctors were at a loss, and subjected the royal personage to purges and ointments, diets and suppositories to no avail. There may have been a trepanning operation, where a hole was drilled in his skull, supposedly to release pressure on the brain. By the autumn Henry was recovering, but slowly. On 30 December 1454 he could not recall who his son's godparents were. One of them, the successor to the murdered John Stafford, was Archbishop Kemp of Canterbury, who had himself died earlier in the year – but Henry could not recollect this. He was lucid enough to be present when parliament met in July 1455, by which time the royal faction, supported by the Lancastrians, had been defeated at the first battle of St Albans. As the autumn progressed Henry sank into a depressive trance again. No legislation received the royal signature between 12 December 1455 and the following 2 March. Government stopped. The country teetered on bankruptcy; the currency was devalued; no-one knew who was in authority; civil war and anarchy loomed. It was four years before the nobles' self-control broke.

On 23 September 1459 the Lancastrians' forces were beaten in an extended skirmish at Blore Heath in Staffordshire, starting the most brutal of the phases of the civil war. After reverses on both sides the king was captured in another Lancastrian defeat at Northampton the following July, and taken back to London. Presumably he was either uncooperative or, more likely, so ineffective that they lost patience with him, and on 7 October 1460 parliament recognised the legitimacy of Richard of York's claim to the throne. Henry was perhaps forced to agree that Richard would succeed him, and not his own son. Possibly he did not know what he was agreeing to – but his wife did.

Margaret became *de facto* the military leader, organiser and recruiter of the Lancastrians and chief champion of their cause; she supported the foundation of Henry's kingship. This stance the Yorkists found abhorrent: their leader, Richard, Duke of York, had the better dynastic claim and an ancestral murder to avenge. For the next eleven years England's nobility and their retinues tore into each other for royal, personal and local causes, in what the Victorians would romantically call the Wars of the Roses. After the successful conflict at Wakefield in December 1460, the Lancastrians were nearly always defeated in battle, but Yorkist nobles were also casualties: for example, Richard, Duke of York was killed at Wakefield at the end of 1460. With Margaret guiding Henry in a recruitment campaign in the north, Richard's son, Edward, had himself hurriedly crowned king in London on 6 March 1461.

On the 29th, Edward's claim to the throne was immeasurably strengthened on a windy, snowy Palm Sunday. Perhaps as many as 28,000 men were killed at the battle of Towton in Yorkshire, when the huge and confident Lancastrian army suffered another shattering defeat. This bleak sixteen hours remains the bloodiest day in domestic military history: 1 per cent of the whole population of England was wiped out in less than a day. A.A. Gill reckons it to be the equivalent of 600,000 killed today; almost nuclear in its calamitous losses. It completely eclipses the casualty estimate of the first day of the battle of the Somme. Margaret and Henry fled to Scotland, where the 'auld alliance' with France was still strong. Because he was ambitiously writing for hopeful recognition by Elizabeth I, a descendant of the Lancastrians through Catherine, Henry V's widow, Shakespeare gives a speech to the weak but saintly king mourning the appalling loss of life. Was he really aware of what had happened, or the consequences for his cause? Shakespeare is fascinated by Henry VI: he appears in four plays, more than any other character. It shows that his mythic reputation as a devout, naïve monarch was still potent over a hundred years later.

In contrast, Edward was physically impressive, another Henry V forty years on. Extraordinarily tall for the time, he was vigorous and outgoing, charismatic, strong and handsome, shrewd and resourceful; a natural focus and leader, compared with the small, fragile, depressive Henry VI. In 1470 the Lancastrian cause was briefly ascendant through the work of the 'kingmaker', the Earl of Warwick, at the second battle of St Albans; the king apparently laughing and singing as the carnage raged about him. He was restored to the throne, and Edward fled to his sister Margaret, the Duchess of Burgundy. As Henry was paraded through London as the restored head of the country, the people could see for themselves that he was even more unfit to rule, especially compared with the young king-in-exile. He was described by a contemporary observer as 'not so worshipfully arrayed, nor so cleanly kept as befitted … a prince'. Of course, Warwick ruled in Henry's name; the ageing and vague king became a cipher again, just as he had been when he was a babe in arms. The wheel of fortune had come full circle.

Warwick immediately over-extended his power by declaring war on Burgundy. The duke, Charles the Bold, and his duchess were only too pleased to support her brother's cause. As soon as Edward landed in the north with renewed forces at the duchy's expense, Henry offered himself back to him, naïvely thinking that Edward's protection meant he would be safe from being a constant, helpless pawn. At the foggy, chaotic battle of Barnet, in April 1471, Warwick was killed and the Lancastrians fled. Less than a month later, on 4 May, Margaret's last force was annihilated at Tewkesbury, where Edward, the seventeen-year-old Prince of Wales and the last hope for the Lancastrian cause, although exhibiting his mother's courage and will, was captured and killed. This was the end for Henry; he was no use to anyone any more; he vanished soon afterwards, probably murdered on about 21 May. He was not yet fifty years old. Edward had another kingly quality: he was ruthless.

Henry's body was taken outside the city to the obscure Chertsey Abbey where it was hurriedly interred, and Edward hoped it would be forgotten. But when someone famous dies memory plays tricks and the myths appear. The Lancastrian Tudors were keen to rehabilitate the late king to the detriment of the Yorkists. In 1485 his body was taken to a more appropriate site, St George's Chapel, Windsor, on the orders of Henry VII – the lucky Lancastrian victor of the battle of Bosworth, where the impetuous Richard III was killed. Rivalry was still strong: the civil war was not yet over, and for the first years of his reign Henry VII was concerned that he was not dynastically secure. Miracles were reported at Henry's tomb, perhaps encouraged by Tudor propagandists; hymns and prayers to him as a putative saint still exist. But he never officially became one, much as the early Tudors tried.

Captured at Tewkesbury, Margaret was immured first in Wallingford Castle, where her husband had been educated as a child and, ironically, dowager Queen Catherine and Owen Tudor had consummated their relationship, which would end in an undisputed Lancastrian ruling dynasty; and then she lingered in the Tower of London, watched, alone, bereft of husband and only child within a month and broken in spirit at last. Her life had been full of disappointments. She had selflessly tried to keep her incapable husband as an effective prince and his family's cause as a military force. Margaret was ransomed back to France in 1475 and lived a further seven years in increasing poverty. The Lancastrian Henry VII would ascend the throne of England by right of conquest less than three years later.

Henry VI's predicament was that he could never rule on his own. He lacked the will, intellect and confidence to make himself independent from his advisors; he did not possess the judgement to realise that his advisors were not furthering the causes of the country, and his self-confidence was further emasculated by his dogmatic queen. The rapid loss of the French possessions and increasing social unrest at home heightened his unpopularity, especially when he was compared with his illustrious father. Henry's increasing understanding that he was incapable of changing the course of events brought on a destructive depression from which he was never afterwards free; and this became so deep and stupefying that he was considered insane. Because of his inability to conduct himself as he would have liked, and his strong wife's inability to realise that his cause was lost before it started, his depression was intensified. Henry did nothing when doing anything would have been applauded. While he did not demonstrate schizophrenic behaviour like his grandfather, he is likely to have inherited mental and moral weaknesses that are attributable to his genetic heritage, through the Valois connection.

A positive reminder of Henry VI, however, is some extraordinary architecture, notably Eton College, which he founded, and the chapel of King's College, Cambridge. He apparently wanted to be a monk, perhaps to run away from his responsibilities. If his father had lived, the cup of royal obligation might have been taken away from him by younger brothers. And there certainly would have been more children; Catherine and Owen Tudor had a large family. But if Henry V had lived longer, his son would still have had governing responsibilities, because there would have been a continental empire in France to oversee. There is no guarantee that he would have been equal to this, but he would have learnt more from his father than from the Beauforts, who cynically used him for their own ends. They were not the first to exercise their power through an incompetent superior, and they certainly wouldn't be the last.

The next King of England, who, it could be argued, demonstrated such obsessional behaviour that he could be called insane, was Henry VIII, born twenty years after Henry VI's death and descended from his father's Valois widow. Insanity can be inherited.

Chapter 5
Juana *La Loca* –
The Spanish Tragedy

... no fury like a woman scorned
The Mourning Bride – William Congreve

Many monarchs have acquired nicknames, epithets or sobriquets describing their apparent central aspect in popular terms – some in their own lifetimes. Alfred of Wessex is called the Great, the only English king to be named so, but was not so-called in his lifetime; his far-distant descendant, George III, was dubbed the Farmer, almost to his face; Prince Henry of Portugal was designated the Navigator, because of the number of exploratory voyages he sponsored. In France this imagery became common. Louis IX was canonised as St Louis; his father was known as the Lion; his sons, kings in their turn, were called the Headstrong, the Tall and the Fair. Descriptions were also defamatory: Charles III, king of western France and Holy Roman Emperor in the ninth century, was named the Fat – not the only French king to be so styled; his nephew was Charles the Simple; Charles's brother was Louis II, the Stammerer. Many of the later Merovingian kings who ruled much of what became France between the fifth and eighth centuries were so short-lived and ineffectual that in later times they were called *les rois fainants* – the feeble, cipher or puppet kings, as was Louis V, the last of Charlemagne's dynasty. On the Iberian peninsula Henry IV, Juana of Castile's half-uncle, was nicknamed the Impotent. The whisper went that his connective tissue was too thin at the base and too big at the head. However, few have been called as was Juana – *la Loca* – the Mad. Juana was the third child and second daughter of Isabella I of Castile and Ferdinand II of Aragon of the royal house of Trastámara. They were second cousins, and the last nationally born Spanish monarchs. Misunderstood in her day and still misunderstood now, she was a victim of cruel fate and the attitudes of the times. Ignored while she lived, she has fascinated historians and creative artists alike for over 200 years. Plays were written about her in the nineteenth century; she was one of the most celebrated subjects of the Spanish artist Francesco Pradilla Ortiz in the late nineteenth century; films were written with her as a major focus in the twentieth century; Gian Carlo Menotti composed an opera *La Loca* in 1979; and a commercially successful novel about her was written in 2006. The historian Sir John Elliott comments in his book *Imperial Spain* that in Juana's time Spanish society drove itself in a ruthless, ultimately self-defeating quest for an unattainable purity; and not just racially or culturally. During her lifetime this society was forcibly mutated into one with an ultra-orthodox rigid Catholic outlook. All Jews and Moriscos (the descendants of the Arab Muslim invaders of Iberia in the eighth century) who did not convert were expelled by 1502. Recusants (non-converts to Catholicism) who stayed were tortured and burnt. The rest of the nominally Catholic population's religious views were refined by the relentless reinforcement of the infamous Spanish Inquisition, inaugurated by Isabella and Ferdinand, and mercilessly organised by Isabella's confessor and the first inquisitor, Cardinal Torquemada. This coercion seems to have been reflected in the newly unified country's attitude to dynastic purity through the Habsburgs. Although Juana of Castile was not a Habsburg, she married one. Thus she mingled her neurotic tendencies, inherited in part from her Portuguese grandmother, with the burgeoning moroseness of the Spanish branch of the great European dynasty. Her mother had been fervently zealous about ridding the far south of the country of the last vestiges of other religions, almost to the point of fanaticism. God had spoken to her; this was her personal crusade to save more souls for the cross. As much as anything, this was why she decided to sponsor an itinerant Genoese obsessive by the name of Cristoforo Colombo, whom we know as Christopher Columbus, in his ostensibly hare-brained scheme to find a new route to the East Indies. Priests went with the explorers as converters of any indigenous populations as a prerequisite of her sponsorship of the expedition. The obsessive nature she bequeathed to her daughters was one of the first signs of Juana's perceived mental instability. Born in November 1479, younger sister to Henry VIII's wife Catherine, Juana demonstrated the intensity of feeling so eloquently shown later by her elder sister far away in England. She arrived in a world where, whatever their status, women expected that they would be controlled by men. The enormously influential Italian Catholic theologian Thomas Aquinas (1224–74) had taught that women were weaker in body and mind and that men should protect them (this was reinforced by the teaching in the first letter of Peter, chapter 3, verse vii). As far back as 1402 the first woman to earn her living by writing, Christine de Pisan, was complaining about inherent misogyny as men followed Aquinas's views. The Semitic teaching of the Old Testament, which Christians had inherited, had always reinforced male superiority – and men grabbed this religious underpinning of their views with enthusiasm. Juana's remarkable mother was queen of a more progressive society, a rare exception.

Juana was described as an intelligent and beautiful girl with the typical Trastámara red-auburn hair, unusually well educated even for a princess, interested in music and religion and speaking several languages; yet still subject to others' machinations. She soon understood that life was fleeting and transitory, experiencing family death many times in her childhood. As the third child she was never expected to inherit anything, and could therefore be used as a marriage pawn to ally the newly united Spanish royal family to other powerful European dynasties. She was well aware that she was a family chattel – very valuable politically but nevertheless a chattel – and consequently would not be in control of her marital destiny. She would marry someone who was not of her own choosing (she would probably never have met him), but would enhance the political and material legacy of the Trastámaras. Suitable families were few and far between, so although she might not have known the individual she would have known about the dynasty.

As it turned out, Juana gained an exceptional match. She was married at sixteen to Archduke Philip I, often called the Handsome, of Austria. He was the son of the Holy Roman Emperor Maximilian I, and ruler of an area now approximately covered by Flanders and the Netherlands in his own right. He was two years older than she; she was very fortunate in that many noble young ladies were married to men who were widowers and much older. The story goes that when they first saw each other she fell in love with him, and he in lust with her.

The Trastámara dynasty was not supposed to end with Juana's generation, nor was it realised that the Habsburgs would become so wrapped up with the fate of Spain. It was an inspired political match for the Habsburgs, however, as Juana's elder brother and sister died without issue, leaving her as the sole heir to vast possessions in the New World and Europe. Suddenly the opportunity to rule the greatest empire in the world fell into the Habsburg lap. But this was in the future. At the time of their marriage, Philip's immediate priority was running the Netherlands. He hated the formality of the Spanish court, and so initially Juana was left to fret in Spain. Her mother would not let her travel to Flanders because of winter storms at sea; so Juana demonstrated her disfavour by sulking for thirty-six hours, sitting outside the portcullis of the castle near Medina del Campo, from which previously she had tried to escape.

When Juana eventually joined Philip in Brussels in late 1496 it was much to his displeasure. Her hysterical, jealous and overbearing nature was demonstrated in her mistrust and possessiveness; in her insistence to be constantly in his company. She seemed to be barely under control, and his treatment of her hardly helped her equilibrium. As Philip was serially and publicly unfaithful to her, she became understandably more humiliated and overwrought. This melancholy state was exacerbated by her isolation; she was shorn of her Spanish entourage one by one. The last was her treasurer, who had been secretly spying on her for her husband. Even accountants have their price.

In the next ten years she bore him four daughters, who all became queens, and two sons, the Holy Roman Emperors Charles V and Ferdinand I. But, cast between an egotistical and hedonistic husband whom she idolised and a politically manipulative and unrelenting father of whom she was afraid, great strain was put on her perspective. And fate intervened as mentioned above: her brother John died aged eighteen in 1497, possibly from tuberculosis; her elder sister Isabella succumbed in giving birth to her son Miguel, who breathed his last in his turn on 19 July 1500 – he was not yet two. The death of this infant ensured that from that date Philip found himself married to the heiress to the throne of Spain with a seemingly limitless empire and resources. Aragon had suzerainty over Sardinia and most of southern Italy. Castile had incorporated the kingdom of Leon and after 1492 the whole of Granada. By the time Juana became heiress the whole of what is now the West Indies and Central America lay before the Spanish, ripe for conquest. Therefore Philip was to be king on the death of Isabella or Ferdinand, whichever was the later. His match was fortuitously greater than he could ever have imagined; because a married woman, whatever her status, was not allowed to own property, all of Spain would eventually become his. God had smiled on the Habsburgs by ensuring the extinction of the Trastámaras. One can imagine the cries for justice to the Almighty by the fanatical, distracted, increasingly morose queen.

Juana's behaviour as a wife was becoming intolerable to the Flanders aristocracy. Her moods became more intense and extreme, and first her husband (who always had his own agenda) and then the rest of the Brussels court began to suspect the balance of her mind. She noticed the change in Philip's public attitude to her. Suspecting that it was the influence of a current mistress, she stabbed him in the face and attempted to cut off her hair. This was hardly conduct to endear her to him, so as marital relations became more distant – the opposite of what she desired – this melancholy isolate took to her bed and, as it is chronicled, 'almost went out of her mind'. When Isabella died in 1504, the hapless Juana was pitched into a vicious wrestling game between her father's and her husband's ambitions, and the machinations of dynastic politics. Her Castilian mother's influence had evaporated, so she inherited that crown with all its power – but it was not hers. There were too many important, cold-blooded, ruthless men around her.

After Isabella's death Philip returned to Spain to pursue his claims to the throne of Castile through his wife's birthright, so he came up against his father-in-law – who needed his depressed daughter for his own purpose: to keep the thrones of Aragon and Castile under his dominance. Although his and Isabella's marriage had joined the two most powerful kingdoms in Spain it had by no means secured the alliance. In Juana's mother's Castilian law, women could succeed to the throne; a privilege her father's Aragonese law did not permit. His thirst for power and ambition for immediate personal aggrandisement were at their height when fate intervened: the young Archduke, one of the prevailing political figures of his age, probably went down with typhus, commonly known as jail, camp or ship fever, caught through ingestion of louse excrement, and died fast at Burgos in November (some say September) 1506. He was just twenty-eight years old. Corrupting lice infested all ranks.

Juana's reaction to her husband's death was predictably morbidly melodramatic. Pregnant with her sixth child, she constantly speculated on whether Philip had been poisoned; she all but accused her own father of being instrumental in a murder plot, for father and son-in-law had long been at loggerheads. When she travelled on the long pilgrimage to the south to visit her mother's tomb in Granada cathedral, she took Philip's coffin with him. Evidently she could never be parted from Philip's embalmed body; often she had his coffin opened to prove that no-one from Flanders had stolen his corpse. She would gaze on it and touch it 'without any emotion ... she shed no tears'. Yet she had to be torn away so that the painful journey could resume. Nevertheless, even Juana had to limit her mourning when a greater ordeal arrived, and she gave birth to her daughter, Catherine, at Torquemada in January 1507. Even when she became queen Juana would never reach Granada alive, although her dead body would eventually be carried to the newly constructed royal mortuary chapel in the cathedral as a lasting symbol of Catholic control.

After her mother's death Juana's pitiless father ruled with her, or rather for her. She was sidelined from her inheritance because her father used her depressed mental state as a precedent for persuading the *cortes,* the representative assembly, to give him power as regent of Castile. He tried to force Juana's abdication through mental incompetence in 1506; she refused to sign the documents. Eventually he secured regency over her in 1508, and she fought her father for the next seven years for recognition of her inheritance.

On Ferdinand's death in early 1516, Juana was perhaps the biggest female landowner in the world. Ironically, by this time she was publicly regarded to have become so mentally unstable that she was deemed a liability and incapable of ruling, and for the next thirty-nine years she was to remain increasingly incarcerated in the fortified convent of Santa Clara in Tordesillas. She had performed her prime function: there was a male heir and a spare, and four daughters with whom to seal advantageous alliances. As soon as she was deemed to have a weakness in terms of ruling (after all, her mother was a hard act to follow) she was manipulated into political impotence by her father and later by her son, who had inherited all the ambitious ruthlessness of his father.

Philip was initially laid to rest in a nearby monastery. From a window Juana helplessly regarded his resting place. She inexorably sank into melancholy as she gazed. Meanwhile, in a desperate attempt to revive the Trastámara dynasty through the Aragonese male line, and to further deny Juana her Castilian inheritance, Ferdinand married again a year after Isabella died. His bride was a southern French noblewoman who was a closer relative than would be considered proper today, and perhaps because of this the product of the marriage, Juan the Infante, did not survive, dying soon after his birth in 1509. Spain was destined to become a *de facto* Habsburg province under the powerless and increasingly myopic watch of the last Trastámara.

When Ferdinand died in early 1516, Juana's son, Charles, visited her in her prison. Having not seen his mother since he was a child, he was shocked at her deteriorating appearance and demeanour, but even at sixteen he had no intention of sharing power with her. Her youngest daughter, Catherine, had been her constant companion, and when Charles decided that the time had come for her to go to court to enter the marriage stakes, Juana exploded in hysterical passion – but no-one took any notice. For the next decades, under constant watch and increasingly bereft of liberty, she inexorably declined. Incongruously, at her death Juana was still the titular ruler of Spain; but throughout her life she had been manipulated and forcibly ruled in turn by husband, father and son. She was a focus of a local rebellion against the Habsburgs by the *Comuneros* between 1519 and 1521, when Tordesillas was captured briefly, but only a focus. The rebellion met its end in a disastrous defeat for the local rebels and the leaders were immediately executed; one wonders whether she knew it was going on, let alone the outcome. She was so much sunk into herself and so much a victim of misinformation by her jailors that effectively she was insulated from the world. Eventually she was confined in a windowless room – an apt metaphor for the degrading condition of her existence. The bird was singing, but the cage walls were so thick that no-one heard. She imagined monsters torturing her: a spectral cat was tearing her into pieces and devouring her soul. Juana survived into her seventy-sixth year, deprived of freedom and more and more physically crippled, dispossessed because of her perceived mental incapacity. She was primarily a victim of the vigorous ambition of her family and the sad misogyny of the society in which she lived.

Juana is buried with her parents and her husband in the Chapel Royal in Granada. Her coffin is huddled in a corner of the vault: you would not recognise it if it was not pointed out.

Was Juana mad? Would she have been viewed so today? Was this nature or nurture? She was certainly born of parents who were too closely related and had to rely on a papal dispensation from one of the Borgia popes to marry in the first place. There was a streak of melancholia and derangement emanating from her maternal grandmother, Isabel de Braganza, who was incarcerated in the last years of her life, tortured by ghosts. The first instance of her grandmother's insanity seems to have been some form of post-natal depression after the birth of Juana's mother, and certainly there seem to have been elements of this in Juana, especially after the birth of her youngest daughter.

However, her depressive nature was taken advantage of by her husband and her father; by the time Ferdinand had finally failed in perpetuating the Trastámara dynasty, Charles was of the age of majority and had not seen his mother for many years. Any filial love was superseded by his ambition. He secured his grip on power by locking his queen mother away. As Machiavelli wrote, 'Ambition is so powerful a passion in the human breast, that however high we reach we are never satisfied.'

Juana was a victim of her mental instability and the high politics and low intrigue surrounding and asphyxiating her. No-one cared about her as a human being; they only cared about her position and how they could exploit it. And these people were her immediate family. Such was the way with European royalty in those days.

Chapter 6
Ivan the Terrible –
Protector Turned Predator

*... whether it be better to be loved than feared or feared
than loved? It may be answered that one should wish
to be both, but, because it is difficult to unite them in
one person, is much safer to be feared than loved ...*
The Prince – Niccolò Machiavelli

When you are given the privilege of visiting one of the great cities of the world, perhaps for the only time, the urge to visit everything is overwhelming. There are only so many days and so much to see. So it was when the family found itself in Moscow. We walked around Red Square, and were denied a visit to St Basil's Cathedral because of a security alert. We regarded Lenin lying in state, looking a little green around the gills, and some vast and forbiddingly magnificent rooms in the Kremlin. We took a bus tour round the great circles of the city and were astonished at the identical monumental skyscrapers nicknamed Stalin's Seven Sisters. We wandered around the new cathedral of Christ the Saviour and goggled at the monumental and barbaric statue of Peter the Great. We drifted around the shops of iconic department store GUM, failed in our attempts to decipher Cyrillic and joined the millions who have been amazed at the Metro's architecture and design. We strolled down Old Arbat Street, where we parents tried not to discover McDonald's. We cruised on the Moskva river.

One of the places on my list was the great Tretyakov Gallery – one of the most significant art collections of the world. Nicki was quite enthusiastic about this, but we were both a little concerned about Suzie. We had talked to her about art gallery tours as an essential part of the holiday, but there's many a slip between an initial agreement in the UK and the real thing several thousand miles east. How much of this kind of culture could we expect an eleven-year-old to take? We were going to the Winter Palace in St Petersburg a couple of days later; I couldn't have her bailing out of that unique art encounter because of a bad experience in Moscow. So we approached the building with some trepidation, paid our dues to a fierce-looking red-haired lady at the kiosk and embarked on our journey, expecting any time after the initial ten minutes an explosion as Suzie reached the end of her art appreciation tether.

Ten rooms negotiated, we regarded some landscapes and some satiric socialist-leaning rural scenes. We explained as best we could what the paintings were and why they had been exhibited the way they were. We asked whether she was enjoying it and learning anything, and she nodded in that noncommittal way which regularly sets parents on edge. Was she enjoying or enduring? She knew it was what we thought she should see.

Twenty rooms. She was lagging; was she flagging? The personal tension was rising and Nicki and I exchanged glances. Any moment now she'd blow. Then we entered a series of chambers exhibiting the work of the Ukrainian-born Ilya Yefimovich Repin, the great nineteenth-century socialist painter. There was so much to see; some paintings we recognised but most were new and all were fascinating. I lost all track of time and space as each painting, each story clamoured for my attention and admiration.

Suddenly I realised that I'd wandered off, so I quickly retraced my steps. I found Nicki. No Suzie.

'Where is she?'

'Don't know. I think she could have gone back to the entrance.'

I groaned inwardly; then reflected that this wasn't too bad; well over twenty rooms of a serious gallery endured by an eleven-year-old. The portraits would have to wait for another year – if there was one. Hot chocolate in the café as a reward for her staying power, maybe?

We slipped through one room and then into another. Then ...

Suzie was standing stock-still in front of a large painting, transfixed. The scene was called *Ivan the Terrible and his son Ivan on Friday, November 16, 1581*. We gazed at the scene as a family; she seemed not to realise we were there at first. The picture seemed to suck us in; it wrapped itself around us. No-one else seemed to be in the room. Then, very quietly, still staring ...

'It's the eyes, Dad.'

Ivan's eyes seared out as he gazed into the middle distance; himself half-mad, but fully aware; traumatised at what he had done to his son. As Tsar of all the Russias, he could do anything within reason, but here was something he could not undo; here was the consequence of one passionate, paranoid act of a dictator who had lost control in one mad moment. This state of mind was extraordinarily intensely portrayed by Repin. I sighed with relief, because up to a point the culture marathon had been justified. I was so grateful to her. I didn't tell her why the date was so important in the title of the painting; I thought I might be pushing my luck. So, Suzie, I'm telling you now.

With the benefit of hindsight, we can make cases for certain dates and sometimes specific times as being watersheds in the story of our world; we can argue that the world was never the same after that time. All incidents must be personal choices, but perhaps we should consider about 4pm on 14 October 1066, on Senlac Hill near Hastings, when traditionally it is told that Harold II was struck in the eye by an arrow, within a few minutes of Saxon victory in some opinions. Or maybe the early afternoon of 18 June 1815 at Waterloo, when a sick Napoleon was in agony through an attack of piles and had to relinquish overall command of the French army for several hours when Wellington's 'infamous army' seemed to be at his mercy and the relieving Prussians were still too far away. Or perhaps approximately 7.55am on 7 December 1941, when the first Japanese bombs and torpedoes crashed through American battleships at anchor at Pearl Harbor, and Admiral Yamamoto's reported fears that they were awakening a sleeping giant were realised.

Certainly what happened in that room in the Kremlin on that fateful date changed the story of Russia, and it could be argued that the energy from this single, insanely angry blow still reverberates in Russia today – and therefore wherever Russian history and culture have an influence. Repin must have been aware of this to include it in the title of his painting, almost as if it should be nationally remembered, like Christmas. As American President Truman furiously commented of 7 December 1941, so 16 November 1581 lived 'in infamy' in Russian history, and therefore reverberates throughout the history of the world, joining the ripples of all the other tiny events that sooner or later make revolutions. The vast country was never the same after those tragic events.

Ivan was the fourth of his name of the original Scandinavian Rurik dynasty of the Swedish tribe of the Rus; he could trace his line back to the mid-ninth century, when the semi-legendary Rurik explored south-east from Sweden through the endless marshes, lakes, rivers and forests, searching for trade routes. He established himself in a settlement which became Novgorod, on the banks of the river Dvina. After his death the commercial capital moved from Novgorod to Kiev and then, hundreds of years later, to Moscow – all the time increasing tributary land and extending its political and economic influence in all directions. An isolated and marginal trading post in bleak, marginal land had become a mighty empire. Ivan's father, Vasili III, was the last Grand Prince of Moscow, although called tsar (Caesar). Through his ruthless and expansionist policies Ivan was crowned the first of the tsars of Russia; another step up the self-aggrandisement ladder, above the law of man and towards God. Ivan was expected to be an autocrat like his father and his father's father, and so on down the mists of time; he had to be. He reinvented the role of despot. Like Alexander the Great, he became a victim of his own charisma; there could be no opposition to his will. He was God's minister on earth. Therefore he was God.

All Ivan's time was spent in reinforcing his position by whatever means were at his disposal. There could be no half-measures here; no compromise in how he ruled. He executed absolute power – and, as William Pitt the Elder declared in a speech to the House of Commons in 1770, 'unlimited power is apt to corrupt the minds of those that possess it'. The assembly of the nobles, the Duma, was never a representative parliament, merely an advisory council of the great, who often owed their nobility to the ultimate sponsor and protector: the tsar. The idea of kingship in what had become Russia had hardly progressed in the 800 years since it had been founded. A constitutional monarch was an alien thought throughout Europe in Ivan's time, but Russia didn't elect a representative parliament until 1906 – the last European country to do so. There would never be a Russian Magna Carta. Ivan was expected to be ruthless, unpredictable and amoral. The divine right of kings was never stronger than in Russia, but he was the dark, brazen god of Exodus, who could not be disobeyed: 'for I the Lord thy God am a jealous God, visiting the iniquity of the fathers upon the children unto the third and fourth generation of them that hate me ...' Repin's portrayal graphically shows this.

Ivan was the first ruler of Russia to be widely known in England, largely because of the activities of the Muscovy Company. This was created in 1551 to promote trade between England and the vast, vague expanse that was Russia to the English. The country was portrayed to an ignorant, credulous population as a cruel land of snow and vast forests, inhabited by strange, brutal people who seemed hardly human. Maps of the area were few and imprecise: towns were few, rivers long and meandering, the animals illustrated strange and probably from the cartographer's imagination, and enormous tracts of land labelled 'Terra Incognita'. It was not until England's first governmental representative Anthony Jenkinson's travels in the 1560s and '70s that the fog of ignorance slowly began to clear. The first Russian monarch to be described in any detail contemporaneously was Ivan IV, Vasilovich, popularly called the Terrible but more accurately *Grozny* – the Awesome; a name and cliché that have echoed down the corridors of time whenever gratuitous depravity, ultra-indulgent behavioural extremes and the practice of individual cruelty are discussed.

Ivan was the first-born of his father's second marriage. The prime function of all hereditary rulers is to make certain the succession, to ensure continuity and guarantee as far as possible that the family keeps its position. It was what Rurik's descendants had done for hundreds of years. In the whole history of Russian monarchy only two families have occupied the throne for extended periods of time, the Rurikids and the Romanovs; and they were related through the female side.

Twenty years of barrenness with his Tatar first wife, Solomonia Saburova, eventually caused Vasili III, Grand Prince of Moscow, to annul his marriage, and in 1525 at the advanced age for those times of forty-seven he married Elena Vasilyevna Glinskaya, of mixed Lithuanian and Serbian descent and the niece of the influential boyar Michael Glinski. She must have been no more than fifteen years old. The Orthodox Church objected to Solomonia being put away and confined in a nunnery, but a dictator must have his way. After a worrying few years where it looked as if God's censure had spread to her fertility, Elena bore him two sons – Ivan in 1530 and his deaf-mute brother Yuri two years later. Vasili was grateful and relieved. So the great white tower of the Ascension church in their estate at Kolomenskoe rose in 1532 to celebrate the continuance of the line. It was 'highly remarkable for its height, beauty, and lightness and was like no church like this one in Russia before', gasped an astonished contemporary chronicler. Despite Vasili's gift, the Church still disapproved of the marriage, and the spurned first wife was canonised after her death in 1542. Yuri's condition was further evidence of God's continuing disapproval. The line was perhaps at long last beginning to fail; it had ruled its expanding empire for nearly 700 years.

Not that this seemed to concern Vasili. As he was expected to be, he was an autocrat who was only as strong as his last demonstration of power. Throughout history the Russians have respected strength – physical, mental and temporal. Brutality in maintaining power has always been appreciated: even today Vladimir Putin is often portrayed as a hard man, bare-chested and enjoying the simple outdoor life, riding horses and climbing trees, displaying that particular strain of outdoor *machismo* so dear to his nationalist supporters. In this he is a direct descendant of the practice of demonstrating personal and implied mental strength so embraced by predecessors like Stalin, Catherine the Great and Peter the Great, all authors of their own personality cults and admirers of Ivan. There is a Russian nationalist movement that advocates sainthood for this terrible tsar. Many despotic leaders have demonstrated the paranoia and habitual suspicion that accompanied those who have so much power, and rule by fear. To rule Russia one had to be a giant, physically or by reputation and unconcerned about any consequence of action. And because the idea of Mother Russia was so powerfully, contradictorily amorphous, a leader needed to rule by intelligence, intellect and instinct, with the private self-doubt inherent in that near-paranoiac state; the suspicion of disloyalty of everybody – even trusted family members – and the viciousness born of the basic desire and impulse of self-preservation. This was and has always been the law of the jungle – to the victor the spoils.

But it is the fate of the families of ruthless rulers to constantly bear tragedies; to bear the brunt of rebellions against unjust displays of power. Ivan's was no exception. Death came unexpectedly to even the most vigorous in those days in that cruel country, whether from violence or sudden corporeal weakness. When Ivan was three years old his strong, energetic father died fast; a boil on his leg swiftly led to irresistible septicaemia. His deathbed wish to Prince Ivan Belsky was that his wife was to act as regent for his first-born son, now proclaimed the new Grand Prince of Muscovy. This would be a daunting task for anyone, but for an inexperienced widow in her early twenties, who had just lost her much older but still energetic husband very fast and had another son (who was not yet a year old) with profound difficulties, the task seemed almost impossible. Continuity was vital to internal peace, and central control was essential. Any weakness would be seized upon by internal rivals and by opportunists from bordering states. Reporting to the dowager princess was regarded by the Russian nobles as insulting; what was Vasili thinking? Sources are sketchy, but the dying grand prince must have thought that she was equal to the task; despite her youth she must have been a formidable woman, but she also needed to be supported by equally hard men.

Elena set about her task with determination. Rivals to the throne were thrown into prison or exiled to their estates, principal among them being Vasili's younger brothers, Yuri of Dmitrov and Andrei of Staritsa. We will hear more of Andrei later. Elena also instituted financial and other internal reforms at home. The transition from princedom to regency was not exactly smooth, but within a few months she had established herself as the central power. The Lithuanians tried to take advantage of the minority of Ivan to restore land conquered by his father in 1534; Russian forces under Prince Obolensky-Telepnov (rumoured to be Elena's lover) and Prince Ivan Shuisky intercepted them. This was the fifth war between Lithuania and their Polish allies and Muscovite Russia in less than forty years; it would be the last for some time.

Elena attempted to assert royal authority over this vast area, but she could not have eyes everywhere; there were conservative anti-reformists, jealous and frustrated rival families and native and foreign opportunists willing to risk all for ultimate dominance. It is not surprising perhaps that when she died suddenly at the age of about twenty-eight in 1538 that poison and plots were whispered. Her contemporary supporters called the five years from 1533 to 1538 the 'reign' of Elena; it was more of a juggling act. Ivan was eight, and still far from an age where he could assume power. This was a critical time for the Rurikid dynasty. It didn't matter how long the family had been on the throne, or how many extraordinary ancestors glowed in their heritage; it was the present moment that was important. Everything ends: Alexander's vast empire had flown to pieces as soon as his eyes closed for the last time through lack of central control and too many powerful rivals; so had Tamerlane's.

In 700 years the tiny ninth-century Swedish trading state of Novgorod had acquired vast tracts of land, and become an enormous empire with no real eastern borders, rickety and riddled with corruption. The means of raising imperial funds for external war and internal stability were unreliable at best.

This was the time when the princely boyar families should have gathered round the institution of the princedom and its young occupant. If Rurik's line was to continue, the only hope seemed to be Ivan. Yuri's deafness and inability to speak rendered him inadequate for anything except a figurehead. But Ivan was growing up strong, already drinking heavily and displaying that streak of indulgent cruelty so prevalent in Russian rulers. Although great nobles gathered around the princes, they were rivals for the power of protection and the fabulous wealth and privilege that came with it. They were aristocratic gangs who thought they were above the law. A well-aimed bullet or a blade from an ambitious rival might secure a new dynasty or ensure an *eminence grise* behind the incompetent Yuri, thus feeding on the ruined body of the dying dynasty – but the boyars and the princes concentrated on short-term aggrandisement, manipulating the young princes for their own ends. The heirs of the Rurik line were bullied and humiliated, coerced and used as levers for whichever nobles happened to be in the ascendancy. These were members of the Belsky, Glinski, Kurbsky and Shuisky families, among others; the Shuiskys with their military prowess eventually triumphed, but not for long. All these aristocratic but often barbaric families were ruthless and distrustful, giving no mercy and expecting none. Many of them were relative newcomers, only powerful for 200 years or so, but some could trace their supposed ancestry back to the misty Rurik. The Shuiskys were descended from a cadet branch of the Rurikids; the Belskys from the Grand Duke of Lithuania, one of the last pagan rulers in Europe in the thirteenth century. In Ivan's time Lithuania stretched in a vast swathe between the Baltic and Black seas, taking in most of what are now Belorussia and Ukraine and providing a barrier between Poland and the emerging state of Russia. Many of the leading families had adopted the title of prince – literally from the Latin *princeps*, designating a leader or chief. They were rarely princes of the blood through direct descendance from the family of the monarch, as we in Western Europe would understand; they acquired their titles through ownership of estates or by gift of the grand prince, together with lands held on behalf of the monarch. Feudalism was alive and well all over Europe and no more so than in the under-developed Russian hinterland. The great princely and boyar families enjoyed a degree of autonomy in their often far-flung lands, which sometimes made them *de facto* monarchs – and a constant danger to the grand prince. Vasili controlled them much as his ancestors did, by being one step ahead of them in cunning; by bribing them, flattering them when they did his bidding, never trusting them and violently revenging himself on them should they prove disloyal.

To influence a young child it is vital that you have constant access to him, so you can foster his intellectual and political dependence on you. If the child is potentially in a position of power, you can secure enormous privileges from someone who has little idea of the consequences of his generosity. The tutorship of the two princes was therefore the ultimate short-term privilege and a long-term investment, and Princes Ivan Belsky and Michael Glinski grabbed it. Belsky had been at Vasili's deathbed almost until the last. Not only were they responsible for keeping an eye on the heirs to the throne, they could keep an eye on each other. They had reckoned without Dowager Duchess Elena, however. Within eighteen months they had been eliminated: she could be just as cold-blooded as they were. Glinski was packed off to prison, where he was forgotten and starved to death. Prince Ivan Belsky's fate was only a little better: Elena had him thrown into another prison where he remained until the dowager duchess's death in 1538; it was whispered she had been poisoned by agents of the Shuiskys. Once released, Belsky entered into a dominance struggle with the Shuiskys, which ended on 3 January 1542. His house was surrounded by a detachment of the Shuisky private army, and soon afterwards he found himself incarcerated in the bitterly cold and distant Kirillov monastery, far to the north-east of Moscow. There he lingered, the dreadful climate failing to break his health. Patience had never been the Shuisky family's strong suit, and even confined so far off he could have been a focus for rebellion organised by his relatives – so he was strangled during the following May. He was childless, so he would have no direct descendants. Cut off the head and the body will die, thought the Shuiskys; and the remaining Belskys, including Ivan's elder brother Dmitry, retreated to their estates, licked their wounds and bided their time for the next opportunity.

Politics were fraternal and strife was internecine. Many tails wagged two dogs. Ivan grew up suspicious of flattery, trusting no-one, always looking for hidden agendas and with an increasing conviction that his baleful, vengeful God was on his side. The brothers were kept short of food and clothing; their freedom was restricted because they were constantly watched; they did not know by whom or to what advantage. Many years later Ivan apparently recalled: 'our subjects saw their decrees fulfilled; they remained an empire without a master ... Yuri and me, they treated us like foreigners or beggars.' He was all too aware of his fragility in the hands of more powerful factions; and as he grew he realised that even though he was grand prince he was a tool in greedy, inferior hands; a pawn in others' games. He would have ultimate power in the future, if only he could survive. Princes Ivan and Andrei Shuisky effectively ruled Russia, but hardly in the name of the young tsar. As he grew close to advisors who genuinely had his best interests at heart, so were they made vulnerable because the tsar was too young to defend them. He was eight years old when his confidant and tutor Feodor Mishurin was captured by the Shuiskys. They could just have killed him, but, more as a demonstration that this rampaging family was above the law than anything else, they skinned him alive and hanged him, still agonisedly breathing, by his heels in Red Square for the boy to discover. This was the year when Ivan lost his mother and others whom he trusted. He was alone; and like Hamlet he had to smile on the villains who had perpetrated this appalling death on a man he respected, and maybe were involved in the rapid end of his own mother. No-one was safe – not even the seemingly all-powerful Shuisky family: on 29 December 1543 Ivan had Prince Andrei arrested and thrown into an underground cell, where a pack of starving street dogs was set on him. It is not recorded whether the thirteen-year-old watched, but we can safely assume that he did. At some point in these formative years he resolved to curb the power of the nobility once and for all. He would create his own pack of dogs to do his bidding. The oppressed was becoming the oppressor.

Ivan's frustrations were taken out on animals that he could control. When he was young he threw pet dogs and cats from the palace roofs and the walls of the Kremlin to see how they suffered before they died. He tore feathers from birds, gouged out their eyes and eviscerated them while they were still alive. As he grew older, some of his time was spent in outdoing his contemporaries in inhuman brutality. He roamed the Moscow streets with his own gang, assaulting folk who were unlucky enough to get in his way. He raped and robbed just because he could. When anyone had the impudence to complain they were strung up. Women were hurried into nunneries, never to escape. Some were buried alive; others were set on by bears that had been especially starved. Watching pain and anguish was an entertainment, as it had been for Commodus in the Colosseum in Rome or the Elizabethans at bear- and bull-baiting in London. When Ivan finally assumed power he treated subjects whom he thought had offended much the same as animals. In a huge contrast, he sometimes sat quietly, reading history, composing music or discussing theology – not unlike Henry VIII some years before in England. In his famous biopic of the 1940s the film director Sergei Eisenstein has Ivan, played by Nikolay Cherkasov, initially portrayed as a sacrificial bird and then, when he becomes tsar, increasingly as an eagle. The only person on his side with no hidden agendas was Ivan himself, so he knew that he had to rule by increased and intensified terror.

His inherited nature and life experience made him amoral. Because he could do anything he did not need to rationalise or justify his deeds. He was tsar: that was enough.

So when Ivan was crowned at the age of sixteen in January 1547 he had survived, he thought, almost certainly by the grace of God. He reflected his vast domain in naming himself tsar – the supreme leader of a northern centralised empire based on Roman lines. To the east there was no designated border and to the west his eminence was designed to intimidate the territories of Poland and Lithuania, who were always wary. Ivan's father had been the third named after the title given to the leader of the Byzantine (the Eastern Roman) Empire – *basileus*; his son assumed a greater title and responsibilities. In his veins flowed the blood of the last of the Byzantine emperors, Constantine XI, whose daughter Zoe had married Ivan's grandfather, Grand Prince Ivan III, changing her name to the more Russian Sophia; she had reportedly persuaded him to grant the succession to her son Vasili, rather than the son of his first marriage. The Russians had already adopted the Byzantine double-headed eagle as their emblem. Ivan was known as the Heavenly Tsar, favoured by the Almighty, and Tsar of all the Russias, emphasising the strength and extent of his temporal power and possessions. He was to govern from the new Rome – viewed by the Russians as the third reincarnation after the Eternal City and Constantinople, an idea given far more credence by his grandmother. To disagree with him would be opposing God, and therefore his Church. Ivan was Caesar, the personification of the nation. He was Russia – cold, cruel, barbaric, dreadful and awe-inspiring.

This is a description of someone larger than life;

someone who believed his own mythology. Ivan was capable of seemingly superhuman efforts. His indulgent cruelty was well known, but his behavioural extremes soon began to make themselves apparent. This was expected: his ancestors were capable of acts of excessive disinterested violence. Often the only way that they could keep control of this amorphous, chaotic country was by thuggery on a grand scale. As an example, his grandfather, Ivan III, called 'The Great' and feared rather than loved, ruled Muscovy with a rod of rusty iron for many years, and was rapacious in his personal acquisition of land, even from his close family. When the province of Novgorod allied itself with Lithuania it was defeated by him, all its notable citizens being compulsorily deported to Moscow. At the time of his death Novgorod possessed only a fraction of the land it had enjoyed at the beginning of his reign.

Ivan could appreciate that Russia was still not a centralised state; this was essentially an early medieval country. Although the bureaucracy was in the capital, domestic policy tended to short-term expediency. The boyars still ran their own affairs; their estates were essentially semi-independent provinces ruled by the families as their personal fiefs – much as was the case in England in the years after the Norman Conquest. They were over-mighty subjects, like the English John of Gaunt in Edward III's time. Ivan reformed internal law and established estates general to oversee land reform. They had their wings severely clipped.

To be a viable economy, this huge country lacked one vital element: it did not possess any ports that were navigable all year, so all significant trade came overland, even though road infrastructure was almost non-existent. There was a tiny port attached to the bleak St Nicolas monastery at the mouth of the Dvina river, some 600 miles north of Moscow, a site that is now part of the Severodvinsk city shipyard, some miles west of what became Archangelsk on the White Sea (so-called because of the sheet ice that normally covered it) in the far north. When this port was properly established under Ivan's orders it could only be open for five months of the year, so maritime trade was restricted. Any goods brought in by sea must have been impossibly expensive, with even staple foods regarded as luxuries. The tsar heard about the Company of Merchant Adventurers from London who had taken the terribly risky voyage to the north of Norway at the cost of many lives and ships, and met them in Moscow in 1555. Through this opening of trade with England the great tsar's reputation was enhanced in an increasingly intrigued and scandalised Western Europe.

From then on the drive for an all-year port never slackened until St Petersburg was established on the Baltic, 150 years later. Ivan's forces invaded Livonia (covering modern Estonia and Latvia), trying to expand westwards in 1558. Lithuania inevitably became involved and the war dragged on, sucking in Scandinavia and Poland, until after twenty-five years Ivan, now visibly failing, called a halt. This port building confirmed his far-sighted side. In many ways his personality spanned what Russia was and what it could be. To both Russians and outsiders the country was still essentially medieval, looking backwards to the past glories of the Byzantines and Romans, and primarily obsessed with internal security and rigid religious tradition rather than searching for innovative trading partners overseas.

Ivan was a man of enormous vision, and after the Merchant Adventurers' visit a Russian embassy visited the London of Mary I in 1557 with a view to fostering trade. There was no such thing as a Russian merchant navy, so they travelled in English ships and the trade relations were very much to England's advantage. The ambassador was left in no doubt of the perilous nature of the journey, as his voyage via the Kola Peninsula and the ice and rocks of the Norwegian seashore was delayed by bad weather, and eventually his ship was wrecked in a storm off the east coast of Scotland. Having lost several of his diplomatic colleagues to the elements, he was several months late presenting his credentials to the Court of St James. His expedition from Russia had lasted exactly a year. He left for home in May of that year, accompanied by more English merchants.

But Ivan was still hamstrung by conservative attitudes embodied in the Orthodox Church, which was where he went for salvation and shriving after bouts of excessive indulgence. As was reported by the chronicler Clement Adams, who may have been the scribe for one of the voyagers, 'The Emperour never putteth morsell of meate in his mouth, but he first blesseth it himselfe, and in like maner as often as he drinketh: for after his maner he is very religious, and he esteemeth his religious men above his noble men.'

In early 1553 Ivan was struck down with a serious illness. This unsettling event was not unexpected; it was rare for any Russian to live long, although his grandfather Ivan III died when he was sixty-five years old – almost unheard of; and he reigned as Grand Duke of Muscovy for forty-three years – unprecedented in those days. For many days he hovered between life and death, and the princes and boyars frantically prepared to become regent for his baby son. Ivan's cousin Prince Vladimir of Staritsa, the court chamberlain Adashev and the chaplain Sylvester, all part of his privy council, hatched a plot that would keep them at the centre of power. Surprisingly for them, Ivan recovered and the plot was plain to see. From then on there was a change in his attitude to his immediate advisers and subjects. We don't know what his illness was, although there is speculation that it could have been a syphilitic infection, or possibly encephalitis; but it is clear that from this moment Ivan became more polarised in his behaviour. He had never trusted anyone close – that was a legacy of his nurture – but his cruel nature was demonstrated now in his brutal and sadistic revenge on those who disappointed him. Although Vladimir was appointed regent for the infant prince in the case of the tsar's speedy demise, eventually Ivan's paranoia won. Vladimir and his children were obliged to take poison in 1569; a few days earlier his mother and wife had been forcibly drowned. Thus was the ignominious conclusion of the last prince in Russia, and the end of dynastic threat.

Whether it was the consequence of the disease or the constant, mind-boggling pressure of autocracy, the effect upon Ivan was profound. Physically he changed; in the next ten years he aged markedly. It was as if his body was undergoing accelerated development – rushing ever more swiftly towards old age. His hair had fallen out; he had wrinkled and grown ugly; by the time he was thirty-five he looked sixty – much like the great Heraclius, emperor of the second Rome and saviour of the second Roman Empire, eight and a half centuries before. Ivan's eyes stared maniacally; his emotions became ever more extreme. His anger became incandescent; it looked to onlookers as if he were becoming the devil. Bordering on insanity, his actions were precipitate and violent: he struck when he should have thought; he foamed at the mouth; it is reported that what little hair he had left was pulled out by the roots in his incandescent frustrations. But he was also as violent in his penitence and did himself harm after watching torture. People told how he processed to mass with a beatific smile on his face immediately after supervising the torture of a prisoner. Ivan's Rabelaisian excess formed a royal counter-culture, similar to the careers of African dictators more recently. It could be argued that Ivan's violent, divergent behaviour has contributed to the character of Russians today, combining bleak, black, fatalistic humour with huge, sentimental, naïve loyalty to their vast, pitiless, amoral motherland.

After his first wife, Anastasia, Ivan would not allow himself to become close to anyone. Everyone was a potential betrayer; his seemingly most reliable advisers had proved it. But this was Russia; the tsar had to exercise power and be seen to do so. The end justified the means. As Machiavelli said, 'Every prince should desire to be accounted merciful, not cruel; but a new prince cannot escape a name for cruelty, for he who quells disorder by a few signal examples will, in the end, be the more merciful.' There was no adequate bureaucracy to administer this; there were no institutions upon which the increasingly megalomaniac monarch could rely. His desires could only be reinforced by muscle, so on the advice of his second wife Ivan created a group of enforcers who had *carte blanche* to carry out his orders in whatever way they thought fit. They were mainly from the lower classes and depended on the tsar's personal sponsorship for their existence and power – so their loyalty was guaranteed. They were called the *oprichniki*, from the Russian word for 'apart' or 'exception'; they acknowledged no rule of secular or sacred law when carrying out the orders of their creator. They dressed in black, their robes resembling monks' habits, mocking their orders and motivations; their badge was an ominous combination of a severed dog's head, sniffing out rebellion and biting the ankles of Ivan's enemies, and a witch's broom, to sweep all potential dissidents away. It is said that some actually carried severed dogs' heads to further petrify their victims. Their reputation went before them; a famous 1911 set for Tchaikovsky's opera *The Oprichnik (The Guardsman)* shows townspeople fleeing in panic into their homes as the thunder of hooves increases. As perceived internal problems grew, so did this enormous band of ruffians of which Ivan was godfather, until it numbered several thousands. They were a secret police enforcement unit but more like a feudal private army, a huge elimination squad. As the *oprichniki* lost control and made their own rules, making examples of a few dissidents turned into wholesale eradication. Anarchy and appalling deaths characterised the few years when the *oprichniki* held sway, while Ivan glared balefully from the fastness of the Kremlin or an isolated monastery, where he had gone to shrive himself for the evils that he had perpetrated.

What happened in Novgorod was the prime example of violent pandemonium that Ivan personally perpetrated. Even after the depredations of Ivan the Great the once-great trading metropolis had hung onto its status as second city in Russia, home of the Rurikian dynasty. Ivan the grandson always remembered their leaders' betrayal of the ruling family. Revenge is a dish best served cold, and the winter of 1569–70 was freezing. During the late 1560s the Livonian war went from bad to worse. In the summer of 1569 a fort on the Russian side of the Livonian border was captured by a small Lithuanian force. An invasion of Russian sovereign territory, however marginal, was too much to bear. The cities of Novgorod and Pskov, traditionally founded by Rurik's brother, were situated not far away and Ivan needed little motivation to compel these old independent-minded communities finally to be under his control, even though there was no evidence of disloyalty. But his ever-deepening paranoia, imbalanced rage and manic imagination needed no excuse. Both cities received visits from thousands of *oprichniki* and their near-diabolic grand master. On 6 January 1570 Ivan arrived with his retinue and camped outside Novgorod. Before subjecting senior clergy and leading citizens to humiliation, his followers, led by his sadistic red-haired lieutenant and distant scion of the Belsky family Malyuta 'Baby' Skuratov, fresh from strangling a former Metropolitan Archbishop of Moscow the previous month, started robbing some and arresting others. Then they got bolder. Archbishop Leonid Pimen of Novgorod was paraded before his appalled flock sitting backwards on a mare, and his house and church were ransacked. Ivan then insisted on the senior clergy taking mass in his presence in St Sophia's Cathedral, despite the increasing chaos in and outside the church. In the middle of the service Ivan shouted orders and his hunting dogs were let off the leash. The struggling Archbishop Pimen was sewn into a bearskin and torn to shreds by them.

For the next month summary executions were committed. Men, women and children were slaughtered. Whole families were forced under the ice of the frozen river. Citizens were roasted on grids or torn limb from limb by horses. Others were turned out of their burning houses, starved and died of cold. Some were impaled on stakes. Hundreds had hands chopped off. Peasant women were stripped naked and used as target practice. Other peasants were mass-drowned in the local lake. Brave individuals who stood up against Ivan or whose loyalty he suspected were inevitably killed; sometimes slowly by impaling, others instantly by beheading. In one case an unfortunate baron was tied to a barrel of gunpowder and the fuse lit. Everything was looted. The surrounding fields and farms were burned. Novgorod never recovered. Far from maintaining its status, it declined into just another city with a celebrated past. Depopulated, half-demolished, financially ruined and logistically bypassed, it could only look back to an increasingly vague golden age. The historian Professor R.G. Skrynnikov thought that 'the sack of Novgorod is the most repulsive episode in the brutal history of the *oprichnina*. The cruel senseless slaughter of innocent people made *oprichnina* synonymous with lawlessness and excess.' The *oprichniks'* perversions knew no boundaries. The excesses of Ivan's mock monks have reverberated down Russia's long, grim corridors of dark memory to the barred rooms of the Lubyanka and beyond.

The mad will of the tsar could not be stopped. Tragically his eloquent demonstrations of man's inhumanity to man were nothing new; throughout history there are many incidents of mass executions of prisoners. Captured leaders of defeated armies during the Wars of the Roses were summarily and often brutally eradicated. Henry V had French prisoners killed during the battle of Agincourt. Thousands of captured Crusaders were ritually executed after the battle of Nicopolis in 1396, in retaliation for the massacre of Muslim defenders of a fort some months before; the killing took most of the following day. After his victory at Kleidon in 1014, the enlightened Byzantine Emperor Basil II, called the Bulgar-killer, commanded that ninety-nine of every hundred Bulgar prisoners should be blinded. The hundredth was left with one eye so that he could lead the rest home. All over medieval Europe unbelievers were burnt in the name of the Church. In 1208 the Cathar city of Béziers surrendered to French crusaders. Some Catholics in the city had chosen to fight with the heretics, and the crusaders' commander, Simon de Montfort the elder, asked the papal legate supervising the siege how he could tell Catholic from Cathar. The story goes that Arnaud Amalric, the abbot of Citeaux, replied, 'Kill them all; God will know his own.' Some 20,000 met their end in the following days. Whole races have been targeted for annihilation in the last hundred years – the Jews, the Biafrans, the Armenians. But rarely has massacre become the pitiless, macabre, inventive entertainments that Ivan organised.

Moscow's Red Square on a hot 25 July 1570 resembled a medieval hell, presided over by the sadistic Skuratov – a diabolical stage manager for the grim Gothic pleasure of his tsar, like Tigellinus for the Roman emperor Nero. Mass killings were nothing unusual – executions would be public entertainment in some countries for another 300 years. Only two years later on St Bartholomew's Day thousands of French Protestants and their supporters would be murdered, supervised (from afar) by Catherine de Medici. We are well aware of man's inhumanity to man and how we too often stand aside and observe seemingly helplessly. But nothing was quite as imaginative as the deaths in Red Square of those poor unfortunates whose only crimes were being who they were and being in the wrong place at the wrong time. The nineteenth-century historian Nikolai Karamzin described the proceedings with ill-disguised horror. Eighteen sets of gallows were constructed in the huge space. A huge cauldron bubbled and steamed. The edges of the huge space were thronged with frightened people. The tsar arrived on horseback followed by his entourage, who watched impassively. He encouraged the townsfolk to approach the scaffolds, promising that they would not be harmed – but they knew his promises were not worth the words. This was the tsar who made his own truth impulsively and convulsively; he could turn on them in a second. 'People, ye are about to witness executions and a massacre, but these are traitors whom I thus punish. Answer me: Is this just?' The terrified townsfolk knew that they could only agree, and praise their perverted leader.

Ivan accused his imperial chancellor and foreign affairs minister, Ivan Mikhailovich Viskovatiy, of having written to rival kingdoms – Sigismund of Poland in the west and the Muslim Khans of the east – inviting them to invade. As Ivan threatened him, he hit him with his steel-tipped staff. His helpless and bleeding victim swore that he had done no such thing; there was no evidence that he had been anything less than loyal. But Ivan was convinced that he was a traitor, and his every thought was law. Viskovatiy defiantly damned his emperor before he was silenced by a gag. Then he was dragged to a scaffold and his clothes were ripped off. Once strung up by his feet, he had bits of his body hacked off while he swung. Malyuta Skuratov began the ghastly ritual by slicing off the wretched man's ear, in a grotesque parody of St Peter's defence of Christ in the Garden of Gethsemane. Eventually he succumbed. The imperial treasurer, Funikov-Kartsev, Viskovatiy's colleague and friend, was accused of being a co-

conspirator, and was condemned by association. His protestations of innocence were similarly ignored, as were his curses of the tsar. He was dropped into alternate cauldrons of freezing and scalding water, so that bit by bit his skin blistered and he peeled like a flayed pig. He died as slowly as his friend, in unimaginable agony.

Hundreds more died through the heat of the day; the luckier ones were beheaded and so died fast. Others were impaled; many hanged; all tortured mentally and physically beyond endurance. It was a cataclysmic, apocalyptic scene, reminiscent of a triptych painted by Hieronymus Bosch. The walls of the Kremlin shimmered in the heat, which was intensified by steam from the viscera of still convulsing disembowelled bodies. Ivan spurred his horse with manic energy over that vast, slippery expanse, and from his equine eminence he lopped off heads and limbs with his own hand. The square streamed red. The Moscow mob, cowed and traumatised, chanted their approval and praise for Ivan, almost drowning out the cacophonous screams of the tortured. Everywhere, everywhere was the sweet, sour stench of death: crawling up walls, gagging throats, seeping in through closed windows, clogging nostrils, coagulating in eyes, burning into brains, curdling consciences. The tsar balefully gloried at the pain and terror he inflicted. He was the despot of Russia, so he owned these people; he was judge and jury, and he could do what he liked with them.

And in the background, almost part of the audience, half-way between heaven and hell, floated the joyous, gleaming, gorgeously decorated and patterned domes of the new St Basil's Cathedral. A dark myth was concocted later that the architect was blinded on Ivan's orders so that he could not design anything else as beautiful. The cathedral had been built only ten years before on Ivan's command, as a thank-offering to the God of victories for the defeat of the Khan of Khazan. It was dedicated to a contemporary saint called Basil the Fool; an eloquent commentary on and searing metaphor for the tortured, polarised mind of the tsar.

Karamzin relates how, when the butchery seemed at long last done and the stunned audience had crept away to their homes, the deranged, blood-glutted tsar decided he should visit some of the recently bereaved families – but not to offer condolences, as might be expected from one with such polarised emotions. No: under the influence of adrenalin-fuelled, diabolic delusion he mocked them, describing their husbands' last agonies with grim glee. He threatened Viskovatiy's fifteen-year-old virgin daughter with a fate worse than death – he had always been a sexual predator. He relented to her mother's frantic pleadings, and mercifully (for him) gave her to the hardly less tender ministrations of the crown prince. The next we hear of these unfortunate women is that they were immured in a nunnery. Karamzin was writing 250 years later, so he is relating legend and rumour as much as fact; he says they died of grief there, but implies that we must draw our own conclusions.

One of the extremes of Ivan's character was shown in his behaviour in terms of his conscience. Where some consciences pricked, his seemed to gouge. He often travelled 100 miles east of Moscow to the royal palace of Alexandrovskaya Sloboda, deep in the dark trackless forest, where he could feel safe from the capital's intrigues and indulge himself. This estate had been royal property for some time; the town of Alexandrov had been inaugurated by his father in

1513. Where Prince Vasili went so did the Church, so an appropriately huge cathedral dedicated to the Trinity (with forbiddingly apt schizophrenic connotations) and a monastery were built. Under Ivan the area was immediately fortified with a stockade and bastions in the event of an attack – for the obsessed tsar knew that he could never control the vast tracts of land within his fiefdom, which was populated with potential revolutionaries. The cathedral is a serene, soaring, blindingly white building (now a museum), surrounded by beautiful parkland. It is literally a whited sepulchre. When it was first built it was surrounded by endless dark forest, so the contrast must have been even greater. The tsar's attachment to the estate was so intense that it even became the state's capital city for a few months around Christmas 1564. Ivan's character intensified in its darkness; so did the complex of cells and torture chambers. It became a kind of sombre Versailles combined with the Bastille; an anarchistic court divorced from reality. It was where Ivan's sado-masochistic tastes could be given free rein. The Church hierarchy was too frightened to stand up against him; they had the Archbishop of Novgorod's fate to consider.

Only when he felt he needed relief from his dark desires could Ivan go to mass and confess. As much as the blood gushed from his victims, so he spilt his own. It is said that one of his favourite tortures was to rip out ribs with 'hissing hot' pincers; then, smiling at the enjoyment of a job well done, he might then wend his way to the church, where, to the accompaniment of the profound sonorities of the Slavonic mass at the Trinity cathedral, he would strike his head on the altar steps until his blood dripped onto the floor; it is said that he developed a permanent scab on his forehead. His followers would join likewise; some through their own perverted desires, others because they knew that this was what they had to do to fulfil their personal ambitions. The barriers between sacred and profane often blurred and orgies seeped between state and sacred rooms and condemned cells; one became another – a grotesque parody of the Christian symbol as a means of terminal torture. The church was the minster of the *oprichniki*. They had been inaugurated here, and to their hellish nest they returned. Blind drunk, their 'archbishop' sometimes delivered sermons to his equally inebriated followers on the errors of their ways in an extension of the ancient Feast of Fools, where time-honoured rituals were parodied. No wonder one of the more beautiful churches in Alexandrov is dedicated to the Crucifixion. The God of love was here calamitously mocked.

Ivan demanded automatic, mechanical, knee-jerk loyalty from every subject. Because he was Russia, everything devolved on him. Like most despots, he exhibited qualities and behavioural traits of what Manfred Kets de Vries calls a 'dark leader', the psychological consequences of a conflict-ridden childhood and youth. Kets de Vries says that such experiences generate excessive narcissism, a compensatory striving for power, a need for revenge, vindictiveness, excessive pride and feelings of rage, an inability to develop intimate relationships, paranoia and delusions of persecution. Whenever anyone appeared to fail Ivan, or loyalty was suspected, his revenge was graphic and out of control. Prince Nikita Odoevsky, a brave military leader and an *oprichnik*, somehow offended him in 1572, and Prince Kurbsky relates how he was impaled through his body, his shirt being shoved back and forth through the hole until he died. Prince Mikhail Vorotynsky, Prince Odoevsky's fellow general in the crushing victory of the Tatars at Molodi in 1572 (which ensured the end of the threat from the east), was stretched between two stakes and roasted over a fire lit in the middle. Another boyar, Ivan Sheremeteev, who may have been the father of the tsarevich's third wife Yelena, was stretched on a rough platform in a cramped, dark cell and heavy weights were attached to his body. The tsar threatened to load more weights if the boyar did not tell him where his personal treasure was; he continued to refuse. The tsar was true to his word, and the brave, stubborn captive died slowly and horribly. Jerome Horsey, one of the first English Russian speakers, the representative of the Russia Company in the early 1570s and the English envoy at the imperial court at Alexandrovskaya Sloboda, wrote how Prince Boris Telupa 'was drawn upon a long sharp-made stake, which entered the lower part of his body and came out of his neck; upon which he languished: a horrible pain for 15 hours alive, and spoke to his mother, brought to behold that woeful sight. And she was given to 100 gunners, who defiled her to death, and the Emperor's hungry hounds devoured her flesh and bones.' Horsey rescued a Dutch noblewoman from being sent to a brothel by the tsar, but despite this escapade seems to have enjoyed the tsar's mutable favour. He appears to be fondly remembered in the Russian annals, as is revealed by a famous painting of 1875 by Repin's fellow-countryman, Alexander Litovchenko, depicting Horsey being shown the Royal Treasury by Ivan himself. The scene is full of tension; although Ivan is centre stage he hardly dominates. Horsey is dressed in innocent white. The tsar is portrayed sitting; maybe this is the visit documented a few days before his death. Here is a sad, gaunt, distracted figure with a treasure box on his lap, surrounded by riches and aristocrats; a high churchman stares straight out into the middle distance and a couple of courtiers whisper in the background. A fool sits at his feet, showing more riches. *Sic transit gloria* ... Hardly anyone is looking at anyone else. Horsey seems to be admiring an embroidered saddle. The set of his companion's jaw demonstrates the discomfiture and tension felt by the two Englishmen: suddenly there might be an impulsive order and their fates could be sealed. One imagines the long sigh of relief once they had been dismissed, and passed out into the free, fresh air.

Malyuta Skuratov was killed during a siege on 1 January 1573. The crushing victory of Princes Vorotynsky and Odoevsky over the Tatar Khanate at Molodi the previous year meant that Ivan was safer at home; by then even the mistrustful tsar had seen that the *oprichniki* had outlived their usefulness, and he disbanded them. As we have seen, he had had many of his best soldiers killed, because of his suspicion of threats to his security, but the population were cowed and he felt that the opposition was controllable. The *oprichnikis'* atrocious activities in the few years of their existence have scarred their national memory. The 2009 film *Tsar* has constant visual references to the severed dogs' heads on the pommels of the saddles of Ivan's assassins. In one scene Ivan's second wife uses a birch besom as a weapon.

Any leader feels isolation to some extent, and Ivan was permanently alone. Even fate lent him only female companions. The custom was that a list of suitable wives was drawn up from a vast number of considered appropriate maidens. They had to be of noble family, of good child-bearing ancestry, of pleasant and modest demeanour – and virgins. Sadly, during Ivan's reign these lists had to be compiled far too often. If he had been fortunate enough to have a life-long companion perhaps his extremes of behaviour would have been mollified. But it was not to be.

In 1547, when he was barely sixteen, Ivan chose Anastasia Romonovna Zakharyina-Yurieva, a girl of much the same age and the daughter of Roman Yurievich Zakharyin-Yuriev, called *Okolnichi* or 'close adviser'. She proved dutiful, faithful and fecund. However, as it was in all countries in the middle of the sixteenth century, in the midst of life they were in death, either through natural causes or accident. Ivan wanted a son; the country needed a tsarevitch. Anastasia did her best: she gave birth to Anna in 1548 and Maria in 1551. Neither survived infancy. But on 11 October 1552 the Moscow church bells rang out wildly and masses were sung as the news spread that the tsarevitch Dmitry had come into the world. He seemed healthy; the succession was almost secured.

The following June, Ivan and his family travelled north, up the Sheksna river to visit the Kirillo-Belozersky monastery, the largest in northern Russia at that time. In sight of the huge edifice the royal boat was hit by a freak wave and capsized. Dmitry's wet nurse lost her grip of him in the chaos as the adults struggled to the shore. Desperately they looked for the tiny tsarevitch, but he was nowhere to be seen. When he was eventually found he was past help. The hope of the house of Rurik was gone. Anastasia must have been devastated; she was well aware that the lack of a male heir would make her vulnerable; after all, her husband was the product of a second marriage because of the barrenness of his father's first wife. At best a life walled up in a convent loomed, for Ivan had already proved himself the equal to his father in ruthlessness. God (and

143

therefore Ivan) must not be thwarted; as with Henry VIII in England twenty years before. Anastasia must have breathed a sigh of relief as she was brought to bed of a son, Ivan, in March 1554 at the age of twenty-three. There were no trips that involved him for some time. Two years later she had a daughter, who only survived eighteen months; but by then there was the young Prince Feodor to look after; born on 31 May 1557. He was the runt of the litter – puny and seemingly not as bright as his brother. Anastasia was already weak and she never recovered her full health. She died in August 1560, after lingering for months. Ivan was distraught, and of course poison was suspected. When some of her bone was analysed in 2000 it was found to contain large amounts of mercury, but this was used as a medicine in those days, so nothing could be proved. Anastasia had been a good wife and companion, and had provided a calm centre in her thirteen years of marriage to Ivan; no-one else had the same influence. Unknown to both of them she gave Russia an enduring legacy: from her is descended the Romanov dynasty – the only other family to have been tsars.

From this point there follows a sad chronicle of blighted hopes and ever more cynical liaisons.

Marriage and procreation became another royal obsession. In 1561 Ivan married a seventeen-year-old Circassian beauty, the Muslim Maria Temryukovna. She produced a prince two years later, but Vasili lived only six weeks. Maria proved as cruel and foulmouthed as Ivan could be; and her beauty could not compensate for her illiteracy and boorishness. Most men held double standards in those days: they could be brutal and often were, but their women needed to be continually compliant and demure. The royal couple grew further apart; she was hated by the people who thought she was a witch, and they never forgot her religious and racial roots. The new tsaritsa was regarded as a bad stepmother to Anastasia's boys and she was constantly pilloried; it was a relief to Ivan when she died aged twenty-five in September 1569. Again poisoning rumours abounded. Many suspects were tortured on suspicion, but the constant whisper was that Ivan himself had got rid of her.

The fabulously beautiful nineteen-year-old Marfa Sobakina, the daughter of a Novgorod merchant, was next, married in October 1571 in the Cathedral of the Trinity in Alexandrovskaya Sloboda. But something was wrong: she was already afflicted by some virulent disease that was consuming her body. By the end of the wedding ceremony she could hardly stand – perhaps the victim of over-ambitious parents who knew her condition. She died a few days later; the marriage was never consummated. This appalling tragedy turned the tsar's mind. His queen was dead. How could she have died other than by poison? Many reliable subjects were tortured and killed. The opportunity for further legitimate offspring, especially sons who could reign, had vanished, for the Orthodox Church would only sanction three marriages. He cast around for a noble scapegoat and found it in Prince Mikhail Temryuk, the brother of the recently deceased Maria. He met his end on a spike.

The next in this sad procession was Anna Koltovskaya. Although not of the very noblest birth (she was the daughter of a courtier), she was stunningly beautiful, and the ageing Ivan was smitten. They were married within six months of Marfa's death, on 29 April 1572, probably by a priest in fear of his life if he refused. Ivan knew that the marriage was illegal in the eyes of the Church, and he made a passionate speech in the Cathedral of the Assumption in the Novgorod Kremlin, advocating that he should be given special dispensation. Who knows what he said and how – but it is said that he moved the assembled bishops to tears. They agreed that the Church would legitimise the marriage on completion of stringent penitential conditions, and the tsar agreed – but he would have said anything.

The Orthodox Church was persuaded by Ivan's eloquence and ostensible sincerity, but apparently God wasn't. A year went by, then a second; an increasingly fraught Anna remained barren. Ivan, losing patience and almost certainly regarding her inability to conceive as disapproval from the Almighty, repudiated her, in much the same way as Henry VIII did Catherine of Aragon. She arrived at the Vedenski-Tikhvinski convent near Novgorod, perhaps with a sense of relief that the great procreative responsibility was off her shoulders. As Sister Daria she lived quietly there for another fifty-one years, and saw the Romanov dynasty established.

From then on the search for a life companion and a mother of more children became ever more desperate. Soon after Anna Koltovskaya's departure for the permanent veil, Anna Vasilchikova suddenly appeared as Ivan's fifth wife, in blatant violation of Church law: we can only speculate who she was and where she came from. The wedding was in early 1575. Ivan knew that any children of this marriage would be regarded as illegitimate by the Church. But Anna did not occupy the midwives, and vanished into a nunnery in 1576 as quickly as she had appeared. We do not hear of her again, and most commentators assume she died not long afterwards. The swiftness of her departure and the lack of information about her mean that her death was probably not from natural causes.

In 1579 Ivan entered into another Church-disapproved liaison, this time with Vasilissa Melentievna, a widow of a prince who had died during the Livonian War. She was more mature and Ivan was much taken with her charm and beauty; but she was also worldlier. Within a few months it was discovered that she had been having an affair with Prince Devletlev, as foolish a move as any tsaritsa could make. Although she might have been involved in the relationship before the tsar expressed an interest in her, it would have been sensible to stop it there and then. Ivan in his late forties would have looked as if he was twenty years older. He could not have been a prepossessing prospect physically, and Prince Devletlev was younger, more handsome and more vigorous – and she was in love with him. There is no fury like a king cuckolded. The prince was arrested, and the tsaritsa was brought to her bedroom and forced to look out of the window. There he was, her lover, being lowered, struggling, onto a stake. She was compelled to sit and watch for hours as he agonisingly slid downwards. When his suffering was finally over she was swiftly transported to a nunnery. Perhaps Vasilissa thought she would be forced to take the veil and spend the rest of her life in contrition for her misdeeds. In a way this was true. Made a nun, she was marched to a cloister and walled up, as the punishment for violating vows. She ended her days in total darkness, starving and dehydrating to death.

Maria Dolgorukaya swiftly followed Vasilissa Melentievna into the royal bed the next year. She had impeccable ancestry, being descended from the same twelfth-century prince as her new husband (Prince Yuri

I Dolgorukiy founded Moscow in 1147). On her wedding night it was discovered that she was not a virgin. She must have known the risk she was taking – or perhaps she was too young and inexperienced to think it through. Once her betrayal was discovered she was swiftly and unceremoniously drowned in the murk of the Moskva river. She took her burial place by the side of several of her predecessors in the Ascension church of the royal estate at Kolomenskoye. In 1929 many royal bodies were transferred to the Archangel Cathedral of the Moscow Kremlin.

Maria Nagaya must have viewed her fate with growing apprehension. When the now physically hideous tsar commanded her to become his eighth wife in 1580, she knew she could not refuse. She must also have been well aware of the price of failure in the deranged tsar's eyes. But she became pregnant quite soon, and son Dmitry was born in October 1582. Ivan was now fifty-two, and despite his gargoyle looks he was still full of strength, but his temper and vacillating moods were the terror of the court. Dmitry, although considered illegitimate because the marriage was uncanonical, was welcomed with enormous fervour by the tsar, because he was still in mourning for his firstborn.

Many neurotic leaders are suspicious of folk close to them, whether close colleagues or family. Ivan was crowned with the Cap of Monomakh, as all his ancestors had been from the fourteenth century onwards. The name derived from the Greek *monomachus*, meaning 'he who fights alone'; so he knew that all orders and reforms were expected to issue from him, and all responsibility devolved onto him. With that huge responsibility came the reward of enormous wealth, and much property was left to him;

the more he acquired the more he could give to favourites or keep for himself. When his younger brother Yuri died in 1563 without surviving children, his property reverted to Ivan. Yuri's wife, still of child-bearing age, was packed off to a convent where she could not be a focus for marriage and potentially produce a rival. Although physically more and more like a gargoyle, Ivan's self-love led to vicious ruthlessness.

Manfred Kets de Vries considers that paranoia in leaders is caused by narcissism. Ivan was certainly enamoured with his power and needed to demonstrate this; yet he also needed constant reinforcement of his power. He was obsessed with micro-management. Spies were set upon spies. The *oprinichi* were only loyal to Ivan because he made sure that there were no rivals. We have the tragic contradiction that the closer someone was to the tsar, the more suspicious Ivan grew of that individual. His brother Feodor was regarded as being of feeble mind, so he was no threat as a political rival, but there might be shadowy figures who would use him as a front for securing the ultimate power behind the throne. As he aged, Ivan became even more unreasonable, constantly interfering in his family's affairs. This was not just your normal curmudgeon. We have already seen how Ivan's amorality followed his father's example; but like his father, his marriages did not produce children. Ivan needed the legitimate succession and his patience shortened, as did his assessment of how long he would live. He forced the tsarevitch Ivan Ivanovitch to repudiate his first wife and then the second in quick succession. Of course they disappeared into convents, never to be heard of again – victims of an old man's impetuosity. Relations between father and son were strained both in military and social terms as the tsarevitch started to demonstrate that he was as intelligent and competent as his father. Although Ivan wanted the line to continue with as strong a ruler as himself, he was paranoid enough to believe that his son might become impatient and take the throne from him. They were like combating stags; the alpha male would win, but which one was it? Their rows were constant and ever more intense, with the father incessantly accusing the son of disloyalty.

As 1581 waned Yelena Sheremeteva, Ivan Ivanovitch's third wife, found that she was pregnant, and was proud to have achieved what her predecessors had not. If she was delivered of a healthy son her future was assured, at least in the medium term. Naturally she wanted to display her condition, so she wore only one garment instead of the three that were traditional for noble Russian ladies. Not everyone shared her happiness: her father-in-law was in despair. He took one look at her lolling on a seat and, always ready to strike before he thought of the consequences, started to beat her (some say he boxed her ears) for her inappropriate costume and carriage. Hearing her cries for help and pain, the tsarevitch rushed to her aid. It was reported later that he burst out: 'You sent my first wife to a convent for no reason, you did the same with my second, and now you strike the third, causing the death of the son she holds in her womb!' Alas, it was true: not long afterwards Yelena miscarried. Another hope of Russia had been destroyed by Ivan.

But far worse was to come. After the incident that led to Yelena losing her baby, relations between father and son broke down altogether. On the Orthodox Feast of St Matthew, 16 November, Ivan accused his son of defeatism, especially in his conduct of the siege of Pskov. Paranoia raised its ugly head again, and he also accused him of fomenting a rebellion against his own father. The son hotly denied it. Ivan, exasperated beyond reason, struck him, and Ivan Ivanovitch collapsed, blood gushing from a dreadful wound to his temple. The boyar Boris Gudonov was attending the tsar and tried to intervene, but the old man had lost control and lashed wildly in all directions with his long, heavy sceptre. Gudonov, the brother-in-law of Ivan's younger son Feodor, was struck to the ground, and the tsar fell beside his son, trying to stop the bleeding and wailing, 'May I be damned! I've killed my son! I've killed my son!' The scene is eloquently portrayed by Repin: Ivan's eyes say it all.

According to Gudonov, Ivan Ivanovitch mumbled 'I die as a most devoted son and your humble servant' and slid into unconsciousness – which deepened into coma. He died four days later, his father at constant vigil by his bedside. This horrendous series of events changed the history of Russia. Had the row not descended into fatal violence, the future Ivan V would have proved a worthy successor to his father; just as determined, just as ruthless and amoral, but perhaps without the extremes of temper. He would probably have consolidated his father's domestic policies and come to some military arrangement with Poland-Lithuania and Sweden. Perhaps Russia might have peacefully and permanently annexed the province of Ingria on the Baltic coast, and an all-season port like St Petersburg (Ivangorod?) might have been inaugurated a hundred years earlier. The Rurikid dynasty might have remained in power for the foreseeable future. But Ivan knew now that this could not be. His remaining son Feodor was of low mental capacity and his only passion was religion, especially when it involved bell ringing; and Dmitry, his son with Maria Nagoya, was too young for his competence to rule to be assessed. In any case, he was considered illegitimate in the eyes of the Church; Dmitry was therefore not entitled to rule, however suited he turned out to be. With this one blow Ivan had destroyed his family's future, and almost certainly condemned the country to civil war.

After this nightmare Ivan seems to have suffered a mental and physical collapse. We now know that he was the last effective ruler of the Rurikid dynasty, and he must have suspected that this would be the case. He was Russia; and as Russia started to look in on itself again and its corrupt families and institutions, so did the tsar. He was in deep despair of his life, and like many of his predecessors took the Byzantine way of preparing for death by being renamed as a monk. The name chosen was Jonah. Maybe in Ivan's mind was the allusion to the minor prophet in Matthew's gospel chapter 12 – 'an evil and adulterous generation seeketh after a sign; and there shall no sign be given to it, but the sign of the prophet Jonas ...' How significant the Church and Ivan thought this was is not recorded. Extraordinarily, many stages in Ivan's life were paralleled less than a hundred years later in the story of his remote descendant Peter I, the Great. He had similar nightmarish, life-threatening experiences when he was a boy; demonstrated the same wild strength and manic energy; trusted no-one; and was directly responsible for the death of his eldest son.

During 1583 Ivan's body rotted. He started to stink, suffering from what a contemporary called a 'corruption of the bowels'; we can hardly imagine what it must have been like to be near him. His body was decomposing while he was still alive, his decaying skin peeling off in damp, purulent shreds. He took long hot baths, which afforded some relief for both himself and his companions. As was the habit with his contemporaries, Ivan had long taken tinctures of mercury as a medicine; now he became addicted. He had a pot always bubbling in his private apartment, and the fumes killed his servants – although they were all unaware. Ivan had lost the will to combat his physical failures, and as the first signs of the spring of 1584 appeared his general condition further deteriorated; he seemed to recognise that 'decomposition of the blood' was to be his end. His robust constitution had coped astonishingly with a lifetime of excess, but the accumulated effects besieging his body were at last crumbling his resistance. Now bedridden, he knew he was dying. He ordered his will to be read on 19 March. Then he requested that his long-time servant and friend, some say lover, Bogdan Belsky (no relation of the powerful boyar family) should bring his chessboard. As the tsar of all the Russias was arranging the pieces he had a stroke, collapsed and died. The game was never started; the dark king keeled over, and Russia's stability died with him.

Feodor was duly crowned, as continuity had to be seen to be maintained; but father and son were chalk and cheese. He was twenty-three when he came to the throne, but a child among the noble brigands of the Russian court. His brother-in-law, Boris Godunov, ruled in Feodor's name. As the century drew to a close Feodor and his wife had only produced a sickly, mewling infant princess, Feodosia. She lasted two years, and after 1592 there were no more babies. Thus the central branch of the Rurikids withered. Even though he was not eligible for the throne, the illegitimate Dmitry was banished north to Uglich. On 15 May 1591 he was found with his throat cut – not yet nine years old. Rumours abounded that he had been assassinated by elements loyal to the Godunovs, and there were riots in Uglich, fomented by his mother, Maria Nagaya, and her family. Hypotheses about events abound to this day, one of them being that Dmitry was an epileptic who stabbed himself in a fit. Even if he had been legitimate and survived he might not have been competent.

There were three pretenders who aspired to be Dmitry in the next twenty years, much like Perkin Warbeck and Lambert Simnel masquerading as one or other of the murdered Princes in the Tower during Henry VII's reign. Feodor died in 1598 and Boris was elected tsar. For the first few years all went well. Godunov favoured trade with England, consolidated the border with Finland and expanded even further into Siberia, founding new towns. There was a strong intelligent son to succeed and the Godunovs looked to have cemented their hold on the tsardom; but Boris died suddenly in the spring of 1605, and his sixteen-year-old son Feodor II and his mother were strangled a month later. It is said that they put up a heroic struggle. The successor Dmitry II, who was not the tsarevitch, miraculously survived, lasting a mere ten months before he was murdered in his turn, and the throne was then contested by a Polish claimant and a Russian member of the Shuisky family, Vasili IV. He died in 1612; the last of the central male line of Rurik.

By then Russia was sunk deep into the civil war known as the Time of Troubles. The population was starving. Moscow was wrecked. There had been a disastrous famine in the early years of the seventeenth century, during which millions had died. Russia, so shortly before a powerful country under a ruler of gigantic reputation, was prostrate, and remained so until an initially deeply reluctant Mikhail I had been on the throne for some years – the first of the Romanovs. This entire tragic coda might not have occurred but for a flash of irrational temper on 16 November 1581 in a palace deep in the forest, when a suspicious, infuriated father lashed out at an able, misunderstood son. On such tiny incidents does the fate of the world turn.

Chapter 7
The Ottoman Sultans –
A Tarnished Age from a Golden Cage

The saddest thing ... is to get used to luxury
Charlie Chaplin

To us living in the twenty-first century on the fringe of Western Europe, the Ottoman Empire remains a fascinating and for some an almost forbidden subject. Schoolchildren are rarely taught anything of it; all I was told was that it existed. On further questioning I discovered it was utterly corrupt, brutal and marginally evil, and spent an interminable period in seeming perpetual decline until it finally vanished at the end of the First World War. Turkey-in-Europe, the area immediately around Istanbul, is the last vestige of the western part of an empire that spread over south-east Europe and the Balkans from the fourteenth to the nineteenth centuries. Much of the conflict in what was Yugoslavia derives from clashes of cultures epitomised by the Serbs' memories of the catastrophic defeats on the Field of Blackbirds in 1389 and 1448, which sentenced their nation to centuries of Ottoman dominance. Most of the British nation had no idea that there was an area of Islamic culture in Europe until the death of Marshal Tito, the strong man at the centre and a sultan in all but name, pitched Yugoslavia into internecine chaos at the end of the twentieth century. Turkey's recent application for membership of the European Union has aroused enormous controversy in the rest of Europe: is Turkey a European or an Asian nation? Do the Turks think like the rest of Christian Europe? The legends of Ottoman excess still inform our supposedly liberal attitude to the Turkish nation. Although many of us enjoy their hospitality and climate on holiday, nothing like enough of us are minded to discover their culture further so that we can understand them more. The stereotype is still easy to reconstruct and too prevalent.

There were thirty-six sultans of the Ottoman Empire reigning as absolute monarchs from its formation by its eponymous first sultan at the very end of the thirteenth century to the abolishment of the institution near the beginning of the twentieth. From the middle of the sixteenth century onwards for almost the next 400 years, almost none could be said to have turned or slowed the increasingly inexorable decline of this vast enterprise. The 'sick man of Europe' had been ailing for centuries before that slogan was coined in the 1850s. The sultans were never able to exercise the absolutism inherent in the office because of personal incompetence or reforms being opposed or neutralised by the very institutions on which the sultan depended. Rich beyond imagination, indulgent, inscrutable, increasingly self-regarding, the Ottoman Empire has been associated with cynicism and luxury since the Crusades in the Holy Land, before the Ottomans really existed as a military and colonial force. The sultans were inscrutable, unpredictable, ruthless and all-powerful: millions of their subjects existed just to obey their commands. They were swathed in silks and encrusted with jewels in incensed atmospheres; royal life was lethargic, hot and impossibly decadent. Yet the head was rarely connected to the vast body – few sultans had a pragmatic, realistic view of the world. Many Serbs, Greeks and Bulgarians, especially, still loathe and distrust them – an attitude often fuelled by the local, much more ascetic, Christian churches.

Our knowledge of the empire's civilisation was limited to sanitised children's versions of Sinbad, Aladdin and other stories of the Arabian Nights. British adults, especially the outwardly prudish Victorians, were in turn delighted and appalled at gossip of what went on in the harem. We knew nothing and were encouraged not to know. Muslims in this Christian Protestant country were few and regarded with suspicion. The first mosque in this country was not built until the nineteenth century to provide a place of worship for British Islamic converts, and Middle Eastern dress in public in the UK has only been a phenomenon of the last forty years.

The court of King Roger II of Sicily, which was visited by soldiers of the Cross in the twelfth century, was the envy and scandal of the Christian world, so deeply influenced was it by Muslim culture with its riches, harems and self-indulgent pleasures, and its tolerance of other creeds and ways of life. Islamic views on the nature of God, the role of women, slavery and the consumption of alcohol have enthralled and scandalised Western societies throughout the ages. Muslim civilisation's contradictory combinations of sophistication of thought and sheer barbarism have always fascinated and disconcerted the West. Muslims' normally tolerant view of other religions, including the other faiths of the Book – Judaism and Christianity – at times has been forgotten in the West, or more likely not taught. The Ottoman Empire became a series of dichotomies.

The activities of the harem delighted and outraged Catholic French culture especially, as the romantic 'orientalist' painters became popular during the nineteenth century, and the portrait of the *odalisque* became an object of polite erotic fantasy. Stories of white Western girls kidnapped and spirited away to be earthly houris in the harem of some alien, fabulously rich potentate were voraciously consumed by all classes of society. By that time the Ottoman Empire was in the terminal decline with which we are familiar, but it was still a vast and magnificent force to be reckoned with. The Islamic heritage of inventiveness, scientific research, exploration, architecture and the preservation of ancient 'pagan' literature classics, organisational genius and culture of philosophical scholarship was the envy of literate, liberal-minded people all over the world. We owe much to an Islamic world that by the eighth century was already cultured and sophisticated, when most inhabitants of the West were still illiterate, unenlightened and living at subsistence level. Many of the pioneering military engineering discoveries by which the Ottomans dominated the Christian nations in the sixteenth century had to be re-taught in the nineteenth.

Islam struck the early medieval world like a thunderbolt. Within two years of the Prophet's death in

632 in the east of Arabia, his followers had won their first battles against other countries' armies; a hundred years later they were campaigning on the plains of central France, northern India and the steppes of Asia, close to the Chinese border. The sultan was traditionally girded with the sword of the dynasty's founder, Osman, at a ceremony within two weeks of him assuming the throne, on a site that was traditionally the tomb of Eyub, a renowned Arab warrior and colleague of Mohammed, who died at the first siege of Constantinople by the Muslims in the seventh century. This ritual symbolised that the sultan was first and foremost a warrior. Alas, with a couple of exceptions the descendants of Osman were not equipped mentally or physically to emulate him. The Ottoman Empire started to expand in around 1300; the southern and eastern Mediterranean shore was already Islamic. The Black Sea became an Ottoman lake. Even Otranto, in the heel of Italy, had been occupied by the Turks in 1480–1; it was probably only the death of the sultan and an internal rebellion that curtailed the Turks' ambition to stable their horses in St Peter's Basilica in Rome, less than thirty years after the fall of Constantinople. The empire of Osman pushed seemingly relentlessly westwards from its tiny base in Anatolia, in what is now Western Turkey, engulfing the moribund Byzantines in 1453. A hundred years later the empire had taken over what are now Iraq and Iran in the east. The siege of Vienna in 1683 was not the first attempted by the Ottoman army, and it almost succeeded. Other followers of Mohammed traded in the Indian Ocean and converted the Indonesians in the Far East. There was no stopping them.

Although there were short respites, while Arab dynasties fought each other or struggled with invaders or the empire reformed itself, the Christian states in the West seemed largely impotent to prevent the advance of this massive military force, united in the zeal of religious conviction. However, the conquered peoples of Thrace and the Balkans were astounded that the Ottoman Empire was not especially interested in evangelising them; in fact a few churches were built with Turkish money. Some churches in Constantinople never became mosques. The Ottomans wanted their Christian subjects' loyalty, obeisance, their taxes and often their sons as tribute. When forcibly converted to Islam, these boys in time would join the infamous infantry regiment of Janissaries, the sultan's personal bodyguard. They were the enforcers of tradition and defended their privileges at any price.

The Ottoman sultans fathered many children by numerous wives and concubines from several other cultures, which meant there was always new blood in the family; thus they largely avoided consanguinity and its attendant dynastic difficulties, so prevalent in the West. It was whispered in Christian societies that some sultans numbered their children in hundreds, and at least one in the nineteenth century had family numbers in three figures. Nineteenth-century historians saw this profligacy as symptomatic of the terminal dilution of the warrior spirit of the early sultans. With so many children there were bound to be anomalies that may have been genetic; for example, Selim's youngest son was mentally handicapped, which barred him from consideration as a candidate for the throne. It is remarkable that many sultanic marriages produced no children at all. When primogeniture was introduced at the beginning of the seventeenth century, sultans who should not have been on the throne because of their unfitness to rule nevertheless wore the sword of Osman – because there was simply no other candidate.

The Ottoman policy of fratricide, instituted by Mehmed II, the conqueror of Constantinople (and also the author of the decree allowing religious freedom in the empire), culled all but one male claimant to the throne when the incumbent died. The tradition developed so that it was not the most ruthless of the princes who inherited, and this barbaric system was terrifyingly efficient. It meant that there was nearly always a strong sultan or (and sometimes this was more important) a reliable grand vizier to co-ordinate the empire and command further consolidation or expansion. It also ensured that there would be the minimum of internecine strife between rival claimants to the throne, with the consequent disruption of society, loss of life and loss of military potential. Of course this was more often than not a traumatic experience for the sultan. When Mehmed III assumed the throne in 1595, no fewer than thirty-nine royal siblings, twenty of them female, some suckling infants, were murdered. Jason Goodwin tells the story of the second eldest, a handsome and intelligent young man, pleading for his life before Mehmed. 'My lord and brother, now to me a father, let not my days be ended thus in this my tender age.' The new sultan is said to have torn his beard in grief, but replied not a word. The beloved brother was strangled in his presence; no royal blood could be spilt. The city wept for the waste of young life.

From then on, the tradition developed that princes of the blood would be incarcerated in a section of the harem, itself effectively a closed prison within the vast, rambling Topkapi palace, that became known as the *Kafes* or Cage. This meant that the assumed claimants to the throne became secular anchorites, watched by trusted staff day and night to make sure that they could not pose a threat to the current incumbent of the throne. The luxury in which they were kept was extraordinary, but they could not be free unless this was decreed by the sultan, and even then only under the closest supervision. They were deliberately made incompetent by removal from the world. Often they were almost forgotten. The practice of fratricide was increasingly abhorrent to all, including the rulers, and so it was abolished by Sultan Ahmed I in 1603. Primogeniture became the norm, as in much of the rest of Europe: the eldest son inherited, regardless of his competence to rule. The downside of this was that the theoretical successors had nothing to do; they were often intelligent and therefore potential rivals. Despite Koranic instruction they became frustrated and bored, and often their potential was thinned in disillusion and dissipation, as with some of the progeny of the autocratic Sun King, Louis XIV of France, reigning fifty years later. As Louis grew older he deliberately kept his competent and universally admired cousin, the Prince de Conti, away from interference in politics by not giving him a governmental post, which his many demonstrated talents deserved. Thus, with all other rivals falling on the battlefield, potentially the best military leader in France died in his forties without having been given the opportunity to prove his worth.

Three great Muslim-inspired civilisations reached their zeniths in the twenty-five years either side of 1600 – the Mughal Empire in northern India, the Safavist Empire, centred in what is now Iran, and the Ottoman imperium, based in Anatolia. The Ottoman Empire reached its apogee towards the end of the seventeenth century, but the first signs of its decline came near the end of the sixteenth. This coincides with the short but demoralising 'rule' of Selim II, called Sarkhosh or The Sot even by his fellow-countrymen, who were normally not keen to belittle their rulers. Selim was born on 28 May 1524 in the Topkapi palace in Istanbul, a city that with its new bridges, mosques and public buildings, thanks to his father, appeared very different from how it had looked forty-one years earlier, when it had been Constantinople, a bastion of Eastern Orthodox Christianity and the last outpost of the Roman Empire.

Selim's father was an unattainable act to follow. Suleiman I was not called the Magnificent in the West for nothing. He was fortunate that he had received a stable country and a full treasury from his father Selim I, called the Grim, but he built on that success exponentially. His forty-six year reign was the longest in Ottoman history, and during it the empire almost doubled in size. Huge areas of the North African coast were annexed; the western expansion of Persia was neutralised; Hungary was conquered; and Vienna besieged twice. Although they would not admit it, the Habsburgs realised that here was a dynasty that had proved their match. Suleiman is known as the Lawgiver in Turkey, but besides reforming the law he instigated much-needed internal social reform, especially in instigating the *madrasah* system in education. The Ottoman Empire would have come to grief a long time before it did had it not been for the administrative work of Suleiman and his viziers. Unlike many of his predecessors, Suleiman himself was highly cultured, and a gifted poet. Here is one of his best-known examples:

The people think of wealth and
  power as the greatest fate,
But in this world a spell of health is
  the best state.
What men call sovereignty is a
  worldly strife and constant war;
Worship of God is the highest
  throne, the happiest of all
  estates.

Suleiman died on campaign in Hungary, well into his seventies, admired and feared even by his enemies. His mausoleum is as magnificent as he deserved. However, in his old age and mistrust he performed filicide on his two intelligent sons (which robbed the Ottoman Empire at its zenith of two competent potential sultans), because of the civil war he thought it would cause. And so it would have done; but the alternative he bequeathed was worse.

Selim was already forty-two when he became sultan on 7 September 1566: no crown prince had ever waited so long. He was the only brother left, his father's favourite son by his fourth and favourite wife. One could surmise that the memory of his mother, eight years dead, was as instrumental in his accession to the throne as he himself, because it must have been known within the harem that he was not a successor to his father in competence. The mould was broken when Suleiman slept with his fathers. His ageing father had already suspected Selim's elder brother Mustafa of sedition, and pitilessly had his heir strangled in his presence. Suleiman's favourite and now only son had existed in a separate world within Istanbul, utterly cut off from the workings of the world and completely remote from the career and example of his renowned father, who must have seemed so distant from him that he could hardly have seemed to be from the same species.

Selim's mother, Hurrem Sultan, better known to Westerners as Roxelana, must have known of her son's weakness for drink. Reputedly the daughter of an Orthodox priest, she came from Ruthenia, now in Ukraine, as a ten-year-old captured slave. Once she became a royal concubine she exercised such a hold over the great sultan that she was freed by him and eventually became his legal wife. He was captivated by her joyful nature and her generous spirit, and was grief-stricken when she died in 1558. Her mausoleum is amazingly decorated with highly decorated tiles to show her ebullient personality. In contrast, her husband's burial place nearby is deservedly magnificent but reflects his increasingly forbidding character through its rather sombre nature.

Not even Suleiman could have controlled every aspect of administration of the empire, and his viziers performed the day-to-day management for him. In the same way, his son was not expected to control such a highly centralised system, but Selim ascended the throne incapable of controlling anything. His character was jovial, as befitted a son of Roxelana, but he was so inept and unschooled that his cabal of military, political and social administrators was indispensable to him from the start, so much so that he left the organisation of the empire to them; the first ever to abnegate responsibility for administrative process as well as decision.

His interest in what was occurring outside his immediate drink-based self-indulgences was so slight as to constitute deliberate ignorance. The contrast between father and son as effective rulers could not be more marked. Selim did nothing to prosecute the best interests of the empire. He did nothing; he was not able to, nor was he allowed to. He was so ineffective that his chief or *Valide* wife, the Venetian Christian aristocrat Cecilia Venier-Buffo, renamed Nurbanu Sultan when she became a Muslim, whom he married in 1545, acted as an unofficial co-ruler in the first instance of what became known as the Sultanate of Women. Despite her origin (she had been captured when a young girl), there is no doubt that she realised that it was in her interests to back the Ottoman Empire against the country and culture of her birth. There would be more indolent, indulgent sultans in the next century, leaving their vast empire to be ruled by their more capable wives and grand viziers.

Selim's father Suleiman died on campaign in Hungary; he spent many years of his reign away from Istanbul, one of the last restless wanderers of the nomadic tribe of Osman. True to tradition, the emperor's death was kept secret while messengers raced to Istanbul with the news. Selim, the new 'Lord of the Universe', emerged from the *Kafes*, blinking in the alien light of reality after over four decades of being silken-shackled in mysterious sumptuousness, with all his bodily whims and fancies catered for. Nothing was or could be denied him; Selim's was a completely skewed view of the world. Unnatural was natural to him. He hardly spoke, for so much of his court business was run using *ixarette*, the deaf and dumb sign language (many of his servants were deaf mutes), instigated by his father to prevent vocal distractions and, in his opinion, heighten the dignity of the royal family. No indulgence had been denied to him in his Paradise prison within a prison. As the Koran says, he was 'well provided for'. He was constantly 'served with a goblet filled at a gushing fountain'. Not surprisingly, on his accession he was already turned in on himself, a hedonist and an alcoholic; his intellect had been neutralised, and what talents he may have had were already well drowned. The Koranic assertion that wine 'will neither dull their senses nor befuddle them' did not apply to Selim, or to many of his successors.

Selim's period of occupation of the throne – it is not appropriate to call it a reign – started quite well. To the outsider, the Ottoman acquisitive juggernaut inexorably rolled on. In early 1568 Grand Vizier Sokollu, a Christian-born Serbian, concluded the treaty of Adrianople with Maximilian II, the Holy Roman Emperor, which secured Moldavia and Walachia (most of today's Hungary) and an annual 'present' – it would be bad form for the Habsburgs to call it a tribute or a subsidy – of 30,000 ducats to attempt to protect Venetian possessions from Ottoman colonial expansion. Speculation that Cecilia/Nurbanu had some input into the negotiations must be justified. In any case, the West was desperate to appease a military colossus which, despite its completely ineffective executive head, was far more potent and united than the often disparate, self-interested and temporary Catholic alliances. However, the Ottomans were not fully conscious of the fact that the Venetian republic was no longer the trade centre for Western Europe. *La Serenissima* was declining both politically and more quickly economically. The Atlantic-facing nations were becoming much more important, and they were too far away for the Turks to influence. The world had been circumnavigated with Western-designed ships designed for the open ocean, for which the Ottoman admirals simply didn't see the need, so obsessed were they with the Mediterranean. Europe's focus was increasingly towards the New World and its enormous wealth in silver, which was one of the causes of the Ottoman Empire's decline: the glut of mostly Spanish silver slowly but surely debased their coinage and the value of everything traded.

With the major powers in the West seemingly militarily neutralised for the foreseeable future, the Turks could look elsewhere for expansion. There had long been a plan to dig a canal between the Volga and Don rivers, thereby creating a strategic and trade bridgehead from the Crimea, in the north of the Black Sea, to the Caspian Sea, in what had been the disintegrating Astrakhan khanate. The cities of Astrakhan and Azov, both just occupied by the first Tsar of Russia, Ivan the Terrible, were besieged. A Russian expedition fought off the besiegers of Astrakhan and the canal builders; the Turks' supplying fleet was destroyed in a storm. The grand vizier soon realised that there was not enough to be gained for his inert master by prolonging hostilities, and called it quits with Russia in the following year. The Christian world was still a big place; there were still other tempting lands to take for the Crescent with not so much risk.

There were successful expeditions to the south of the Arabian Peninsula in 1569. Cyprus – a Venetian island for a hundred years, but completely surrounded by Ottoman vassals – was invaded in June 1570, to strategically secure the south-east Mediterranean. This must have tickled even the sodden sultan's passing interest, because apparently Cypriot wine was his favourite. Perhaps the expense of this invasion could be why the Ottoman Empire did not support the last revolt of the Moriscos in Spain, which was collapsing at that time. (These were the descendants of the Moors who had integrated with the Spaniards and accepted

Catholicism at least in title when the rest of the Muslims were expelled from Granada in 1492.) The great majority of the Cypriot towns capitulated without a fight, but Famagusta's citizens were made of sterner stuff. Under the captaincy of Marco Antonio Bragadin, a Venetian lawyer, the city held out for eleven months against overwhelming odds. During this time Venice feverishly tried to find allies to help defend her colonies. Pope Pius V was encouraged to plead to all concerned nations for aid. Russia wouldn't, because Tsar Ivan the Terrible had just concluded a peace with the Ottomans; neither would the Holy Roman Emperor Maximilian, who had been given valuable breathing space by his treaty with the Ottomans. Without military relief from the Serene Republic, Famagusta fell; Bragadin and his officers agreed terms with the Turks, but as soon as they emerged they were slaughtered. The Turkish general, Lala Kara Mustafa, had suffered over 50,000 casualties in the siege, including his beloved son; so his revenge on the Famagustan Venetians was sweet and slow. The captain had his nose and ears lopped off, and he was horrifically tortured over the next ten days, so the contemporary propaganda recorded, eventually dying in the process of being flayed alive upside-down from his feet downwards. His skin was stuffed with straw and sent to Selim. It is not recorded whether the sultan ever saw this ghastly trophy.

Bragadin's stoicism under torture and horrible death galvanised Venice to greater action. A loose confederation was formed to try and halt westward Turkish expansion, with Venice and Rome now feeling vulnerable. The sea lanes had to be cleared of allied shipping to facilitate a Turkish invasion of the Adriatic. Some 30 miles west of the Turkish fleet's base at

Lepanto, now Naupaktos, on the northern shore of the Gulf of Corinth, on 7 October 1571 the two fleets smashed into each other – the renowned last major battle between oared galleys in history; anachronistic even then. It was a stunning victory for the Allies of the Cross, with over 15,000 Turkish casualties. For Selim and Sokollu this was a serious setback, but it was only temporary; with a great effort the Ottoman fleet had made good its losses by the next summer. Perhaps Selim was so divorced from reality by this time that he hardly gave the defeat a second thought. There is no record of any royal reaction. But for perpetually declining Venice and her allies it was an amazing morale boost. The outwardly unstoppable Ottomans could be beaten. It was a proof that the God of the Christians could use Christian men to triumph over the anti-Christ of Islam. The cracks in Venice's military and trading reputation were temporarily papered over again and Lepanto was unjustly celebrated for the next four centuries.

And thus the story staggered on, with the empire still expanding, regaining what is now Tunisia from temporary Spanish control in 1574 but rottenly inert at the core. Selim grew even more turned in on himself. Sometime towards the end of 1574 he slipped on the wet floor of a bathhouse and hit his head. He must have been drunk at the time; he had apparently consumed a whole bottle of wine at a draught. His constitution must have been considerably weakened by constant indulgence. A fever set in, which claimed him in December – aged fifty. From the time he was born he had hardly stepped out of the Topkapi – in the same way that the Chinese emperors rarely left the Forbidden City.

His eldest son, Murad III, had his five siblings strangled straight away. One wonders what his

Venetian-born mother Nurbanu (born Cecilia Venier-Baffo) must have thought – but perhaps by then she was so imbued with the nurture of the harem that it was something she knew was inevitable. She still wielded enormous power over her eldest son as the Sultanate of Women perpetuated itself. She was regent for her ineffective husband and her disinterested eldest son. She, as Valida Sultan, and Grand Vizier Sokollu ran this vast, ramshackle empire like a corporate enterprise. When Sokollu was assassinated in 1579 she administered the realm herself – she was sultan in all but name. Almost certainly she chose her eldest son Murad's wife. She was another Venetian provincial – the daughter of the governor of Corfu, kidnapped when she was a child. Born Sofia Baffo, but renamed Safiye when she was converted to Islam, it turned out that she was also her mother-in-law's niece, so perhaps she had been targeted. This was keeping rule in the family in a big way. If the sultans weren't strong the sultanas had to be, to keep the *status quo*. Obviously Nurbanu favoured maintenance of good relations with Venice; as there was unrest on the eastern Persian border, another Venetian spouse would prolong the alliance. So the great replacement Lepanto fleet, constructed frantically in 1572, floated idly at its Greek moorings for years. On Nurbanu's sudden death in suspicious circumstances in 1583 (it was rumoured that she had been poisoned by an agent of Venice's trading rival Genoa), her niece/daughter-in-law took up the reins of government on behalf of her ineffective husband. He was far more interested in arts, especially illustrated books and miniature paintings. He was overwhelmed by his Venetian women and was pushed to the periphery as the figurehead and cipher for the sultanas. During his tenure the imperial borders began to shrink, and there were military reverses. One of his government's more intriguing accomplishments was that it nearly achieved an alliance with Elizabeth I of England, seemingly brokered by Valida Safiye. William Harborne, the English ambassador, addressed Murad as 'benign Caesar', and Anglo-Turkish trade expanded. Both nations had a mutual interest in curtailing Spain's activities: Murad is supposed to have favoured English Protestantism because, like Islam, it banned idols. So the years slipped by and Murad gently declined, until he died in 1595 at the age of forty-nine. His widow was very much alive, however, and as keen on dominating his first-born son as her recently deceased husband. Mehmet III succeeded his father at the age of twenty-five. He was a lazy, indulged glutton, perhaps just as his mother wanted him to be so that she could rule. However, he was shocked enough by military reverses (or was he obeying his mother's instructions?) to personally lead his forces in expeditions in Egypt and into Hungary, although at the battle of Keresztes he had to be persuaded at least twice from fleeing the field even when his troops were winning. There was an enormous triumph when the sultan and his entourage returned to Constantinople, and he enjoyed the celebrations so much that when the campaigning season came round again the next year he was considered too drunk and unfit to lead his troops. He never did again. Mehmet's mother was still in charge when he died in early 1603; no doubt her son's body gave up the unequal struggle with his appetite.

Mehmet's son Ahmed appears at this point. He was born in 1590, and so assumed the sword of Osman when he was barely thirteen. His grandmother Safiye disappears from the record at about this time; there is no report of her death, but she would have been in her mid-fifties. Ottomans rarely lived long, and so she might have died of natural causes – but there is a story that she was banished from the palace by Mehmet's mother; a Greek baptised as Helena, who converted to Islam under the name of Handan. Ahmed displayed some spirit and some original thinking under the regency of his mother, who proved to be not as effective a ruler in her son's name. She vanished in 1605, although she may have lived on in obscurity for several more years. People could be forgotten in the vast recesses of the Topkapi Palace. Ahmed abolished the traditional fratricide and sent his brother Mustafa away from the palace; he probably knew already that he would not be a threat.

The sultan was a poet and somewhat of an Islamic scholar, and tried to make living within the Topkapi more conservative, banning alcohol, trying to make Friday mosque attendance compulsory and destroying Western artefacts that he viewed as being un-Islamic, notably a mechanical organ sent to his father by Elizabeth I. There were some small initial attempts to change the running of the empire that may have originated from the young sultan. However, outside the soft *Kafes* of the palace there was another harder cage – that of the *status quo*. Any change to the way the huge, rickety empire was administered involved enormous personal risks to the administrators. It was suspected of being a house of cards. Either Ahmet was told that reform was not feasible or he eventually realised that there was little he could do. However much of an autocrat he was supposed to be, he could not beat the system. Perhaps he grew depressed, turned in on himself and washed less – for in 1617 he died aged twenty-seven, a victim of the human louse-borne disease typhus. Suddenly there was a vacuum in power. Ahmed was married twice, the first time to Mahfiruze Hatice, who gave him a son called Osman after the founder of the empire (perhaps they were hoping for a change to a much more proactive leader), and then to Kosem, with whom he had five children, including Murad and Ibrahim. None of Ahmed's progeny could assume the throne: Osman was considered too young. Who of Osman I's descendants could be sultan? There was only one candidate; and those in palace authority may not have slept easily in their beds when they considered alternatives. It had to be Mustafa.

It is difficult to know whether Mustafa I was deranged through nature or nurture. It is safe to speculate that if the fratricide policy abolished by his brother Ahmed had still been effective, his lifetime torture would not have been as prolonged. He was the inept brother of an almost competent sultan, though not quite as illustrious as their ancestor Suleiman. The vast personal power that he inherited disturbed him further. He ascended the throne, one imagines with the greatest reluctance, on his brother's death. His name means 'the chosen one'. Poor man, this was the most ironic of names. Ahmed had come to the throne aged thirteen in 1603 on the death of his father: he proved his own man very early in his reign, a poet, fencer, horseman and linguist. Mustafa was none of these things, and so he was sent away into a room in the *Kafes* for his own good, where he became institutionalised in that soft, quiescent world. There he would have remained, a tiny footnote in Turkish history, if his brother had not died so suddenly. This was a disaster for the Ottoman Empire; the hopeless Mustafa was sought out in the hushed gloom of the harem and brought to face very nearly the real world.

Alexander, eyes fanatically wide, charges towards Darius at the battle of Issus (333 BC). Detail from the Alexander Mosaic, discovered in Pompeii.

Queen Juana gazes distractedly at the coffin of her husband. Painting by Francisco Pradilla Ortiz (1848–1921).

A distraught Charles VI of France slashes at his own courtiers in a paranoid frenzy, 1 July 1392. Illustration by John Millar Watt (1895–1975).

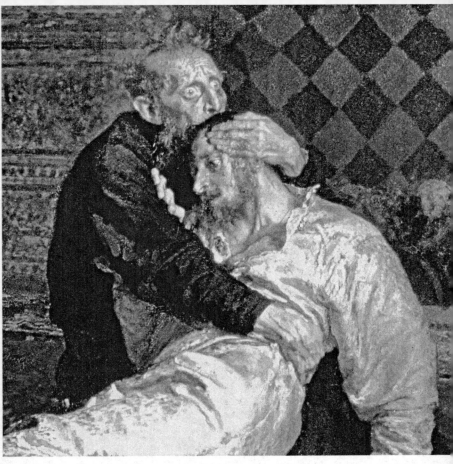

Ivan the Terrible holds his son and realises what he has done.
Painting by Ilya Repin (1844–1930).

A regal study of Christian VII in 1772 by the Swedish painter
Alexander Roslin (1718–93). Would we have suspected
mental derangement from this portrait?

The hopeless-looking descendants of the Portuguese Braganzas and the Spanish Bourbons, portrayed by Goya in 1800. Theophile Gautier thought that the royal family looked like 'the corner baker and his wife after they won the lottery'.

A naive portrait of the affable oaf João IV of Portugal by a
nineteenth-century unknown artist.

Ludwig II in all his finery as Grand Master of the Knights of St George. The romantic image has begun to bloat. Portrait by Gabriel Schachinger (1850–1918).

The scale of the disaster was immediately understood. Mustafa, his mother's 'little lion', had no will, no intellect; no real understanding of what was expected of him. He was certainly neurotic; he may have been mentally retarded or ill. His mother, Handan, tried to supervise him as she had his brother Ahmed, but never found the influence she had lost when Ahmed started trying to reform. Factions formed around Mustafa, each pushing him to favour them, but he was not able to make the smallest decision. As sultan, the personification of the empire, his was an empty head atop a vast, increasingly monstrous and dysfunctional body. He was supposed to be an autocrat; this was mockery of the office. Such things could not be allowed to carry on. His nephew Osman, despite his few years, was a true son of Ahmed in blood, enthusiasm and intellect. He was escorted into the inner court of the Topkapi palace, and the anomalous and, one can safely assume, extremely relieved uncle Mustafa was hustled away.

To the Europeans, the Turks looked as if they were beginning to fail; the empire was fraying at the edges. The empire lost significant territory to Hungary in 1606 and to Persia in 1612. Ottoman suzerainty shrank. The empire was rotten to the core. Sir Thomas Rowe, who was the first English ambassador to India and the seventh ambassador to the Porte in the 1620s, likened the Ottoman Empire to 'an old body, crazed through with many vices that remain when youth and strength is decayed'.

Osman II was fourteen when he was girded with the sword of his namesake ancestor and founder of the dynasty. Always called the Young, he set about reforms which, if he had been a little older and a more experienced politician, he would have realised that he could not achieve so rapidly. He went on military campaign (sadly not successfully); he began a consolidation of the empire; he instigated much-needed internal reform which had not been touched for decades under the Sultanate of Women. His principal target was the Janissaries, who in the succession of incompetent sultans had made themselves militarily, religiously and administratively essential and were bastions against any reform that would curtail their power and influence. The coffee houses where they met were abolished by Osman, who also sought to restrict their power in raising revenue. To the conservatives in the religious hierarchy whose relationship with the Janissaries had become symbiotic, any reform was anathema. Witness Sir Thomas Rowe's opinion again, predating the more famous remark of Tsar Nicholas I of Russia by over 200 years: '[the Ottoman Empire] has the body of a sick old man who tried to appear healthy although his end was near'. Both factions were astounded when this teenage sultan proposed a completely new army, independent of the Janissaries and largely composed of ethnic Turks. When the religious patriarchs and the Janissaries realised that the sultan would not be dissuaded they resolved to get rid of him. Osman didn't have enough powerful supporters. So on 20 May 1622 the young reformer was imprisoned, bludgeoned to the ground and, still struggling with his assassins, strangled, or, as some stories tell, finally dispatched by compression of the testicles, a death reserved for men of his status. He was a victim of his own vigour and lack of experience; he tried too much far too soon. The cracks were papered over again, but they became chasms. This was the first time that regicide had been enacted in the Ottoman Empire. Thomas Rowe thought that it indicated the empire's inevitable decline. It was not to be the only murder of an Ottoman sovereign.

Once the deed was done, the murderers cast about for a successor. The now late Sultan Osman had been only eighteen; he had only just married and there were no sons. A royal who would not reform was sought. It needed to be someone who would not be an independent thinker; someone who preferably didn't think at all. It had to be Mustafa: there was simply no-one else who would supervise the long-term ossification of the empire for short-term gain by the religious conservatives. Once more this pathetic creature was sought out through the labyrinths of the *Kafes*, and was found in a cell only accessible through the ceiling. He was dragged back to the throne that he had so loathed and feared four years before.

Somehow Osman's murderers were found and executed, but probably without the unhappy sultan knowing anything about it; this must have been on the orders of Kosem Sultan, the queen mother, who had tried to hold the reins of government since Ahmed's death. Mustafa believed that Osman was still alive: he was seen pathetically searching the Topkapi palace, knocking on doors and pleading for his nephew to come out and relieve him of the burden of responsibility. He cried to be let back into the somnolent world of the *Kafes*: reality was his nightmare. After less than two years the courtiers were again desperately searching for a successor to end the farce. The new candidate was another minor – Osman's brother Murad. He was big for his age and looked as though he was as vigorous, despite being only eleven. The experiment with a son of Ahmed was tried again, and Mustafa sank back into the sluggish, dreamy sub-society that he knew and in which he felt safe, slowly drowning in debauchery. He lingered in the sweet silence and deepening darkness until it closed in on him forever seventeen years later.

The pathetic procession carried on. Progress was stagnating; the status quo became the vital element in perpetrating self interest of the cabal of Murad IV's son Ibrahim, called Deli or the Mad. He is remembered with this epithet, but he was by no means the first Ottoman sultan to display mental instability; one could argue that many of the earlier sultans proved they were mentally impaired by condoning the fratricide custom. This certainly caused many sultans great anguish and must have profoundly affected them throughout later life. However, its abolishment and replacement with incarceration of the younger princes in the *Kafes* meant that many of the sultans displayed mental trauma from having been shut up in half-dark, half-silent interiors for years on end. Much as long-term prisoners reoffend because they are so institutionalised that they can't cope with the unregulated outside world and want to be sent back into an existence they understand, so did some of the sultans yearn for the stultifying atmosphere of the golden cage that they had known all their lives. If they were already on the mentally challenged spectrum, then the alien outside world must have been living torture; freedom to communicate with strangers would have been agony, even though these outsiders were their slaves and existed only to do their will.

Better any sultan than no sultan; but an alcoholic sultan with unpredictable mental behaviour – was this better than nothing? In fact nothing might have been better, as Ibrahim became yet another cipher for his mother, Kosem Sultan, who ruled in place of her third son. Under their joint supervision the empire juddered almost to the point of collapse. Ibrahim was probably completely unaware that anything was wrong; he was insulated from reality by continuous, unbridled hedonism, spending his time between the bottle and the harem. The story goes that when he needed some firewood for the harem he suspended a ruling council meeting in order to demand of the grand vizier why it hadn't been brought. On another occasion he suspected that a member of his harem had been spoken to, or unwittingly regarded by, an unauthorised man. This could not be allowed; the girls were his exclusive property. It was an insult to the (somewhat spurious) dignity of the Sultan of Sultans, the Lord of the Horizons. Ibrahim tortured some of the girls, but they wouldn't reveal the culprit. Maybe there wasn't one; perhaps they were all shielding the guilty party; possibly they were all cuckolding Ibrahim. He promptly had some 280 of them tied in shrouds up to their necks, weighted down with stones and thrown into the Bosphorus. Several escaped: one was exhibited in France where she caused a sensation; another was Turhan Hatice, the Ukrainian mother of Crown Prince Mehmed, the heir to the ever more disgraced and devalued throne. The tragic remainder traumatised divers for years afterwards as they rocked gently on the sea floor in the current, with only their ghastly grinning skulls poking out of the gloom. What were young women's lives to Ibrahim? The insult to his dignity was all. Suitable replacements were easy to find.

Eventually Ibrahim grew tired of the lissom girls of Thrace and Ukraine and demanded the fattest woman that the empire possessed. An Armenian (some say Georgian) maiden who apparently weighed well over 23 stone was discovered in the Caucasus; nicknamed Sechir Para, the Sugar Cube, she must have been practically spherical. Nevertheless she suitably absorbed the sultan, who showed his delight in her by giving her riches and honours (some say even the governorship of Damascus), so much so that she started to meddle in affairs outside the harem and thus became a potential threat to Kosem Sultan. Despite her dramatic dimensions she vanished without a trace. Ibrahim's mother showed no regret as she explained to her distraught son that the Sugar Cube had dissolved through a mystery illness.

The sultan developed an obsession for furs and ordered rooms to be lined with them. Jason Goodwin tells how he was observed galloping up and down the fur-covered corridors on the backs of harem girls, his beard stiff with ambergris and studded with pearls and jewels. Walls were covered in mirrors, so that he could see himself at all times from all angles in all occupations of the harem; apparently he was extremely creative. He was seen feeding coins to the fish in the pool in the Topkapi palace, much like Mustafa, who fed coins to the fish in the Sea of Marmara because he said they needed to buy food.

The grand vizier who had not organised the wood consignment was dispensed with, because he would not flatter Ibrahim and tried to discipline him. He was replaced by the toady of toadies; even the mad, indulged sultan could see that. 'How is it that you always so approve my actions, good or evil?' he asked the vizier. 'Thou art caliph,' came the silken, unctuous reply. 'Thou art God's shadow on earth. Every idea which thy spirit entertains is a revelation from heaven. Your orders, even when they appear unreasonable, have an innate reasonableness which your slave always reveres though he may not understand it.' He presumably grovelled his way out of his master's presence leaving an oily trail, although it meant that he lasted a little longer than his predecessor. But the sultan was out of control, and no advice that might constrain him was taken. He sold offices and privileges; he insulted the call to prayer by having his band play at the same time. He did not care how unpopular he was, and unrest grew so that military, religious and judicial leaders united in opposition.

By 1640 the prospect was that Ibrahim I would be the last of the Ottomans. Some said it would have been better if it had stayed that way – but his mother was determined that the dynasty should continue, and in a few years Ibrahim's lust had resulted in seven sons by at least three wives. The first-born was seven years old when the court finally had enough of the sultan's caprices. He had tried to involve himself in governance, raising and executing many viziers. No official knew where he stood, and some said that the times of Selim the Grim, the father of Suleiman the Magnificent, had returned – when viziers measured their terms of office in weeks. Military reverses in quick succession in the 1640s, especially by Venice, whose own empire's arteries were hardening fast, were insults to the empire's dignity and could not be borne; no more executions of high officials could alleviate the affront. The blame was the head of the organisation, and a new start had to be made. The sultan was judged to be mad and therefore had to vacate the throne. Patrick Kinross describes how when Ibrahim heard this he went into a towering rage. 'Traitors!' he screamed at the Grand Mufti of Istanbul, who was delegated to tell him. 'Am I not your Padishah? What does this mean?'

The grand mufti was made of sterner stuff than the grand vizier. 'You are no longer Padishah, since you trample on justice and holiness and have ruined the world,' he replied firmly. 'You have wasted your years in play and debauchery; you have squandered the treasures of the Empire on vanities; corruption and cruelty have governed the world in your place ... you have made yourself unworthy of [the throne] by leaving the path which your ancestors took.' Ibrahim's intellect was too sodden to argue further, and he allowed himself to be led back into the harem, no longer sultan.

Eventually the Grand Mufti of Istanbul, who interpreted Muslim religious law and by definition was an arch-conservative, sanctioned the ex-sultan's demise, because the Koran states that if there are two caliphs then one must be killed. The silken bowstring tightened around Ibrahim's fat neck in August 1648. He had been reading the Koran when he looked up and recognised the chief executioner, whom he had employed on far too many occasions. He died screaming for mercy, cursing the Turkish people for its ungratefulness to their sultans. No succeeding sultan was ever named Ibrahim, because of his appalling reputation down the generations.

He left the throne to yet another minor, inevitably dominated by his mother and especially his formidable grandmother. Three years later Turhan Hatice heard of a plot by Kosem to remove Mehmed and replace him with the son of a mother whom she could dominate more easily. Turhan acted first on behalf of her son. Kosem, now a toothless old woman of over eighty, was strangled, some say with a curtain, others a cord. Sir Paul Rycaut, an English diplomat who spent seventeen years in Turkey, described some years later how she fought the inevitable: 'There were four which strangled her, but being young Executioners, laboured long to dispatch her, till at length the Queen leaving to struggle lay stretched out, and was supposed to be dead, and so crying she is dead, she is dead, ran to carry the news thereof to his Majesty; but being scarce out of sight the Queen raised herself up, and turned her head about; upon which the Executioners being called back, the Cord was a second time applied, and wrung so hard with the haft of a hatchet that at length she was dispatched ...' The quiet surface of the government of the empire in the courts of the Topkapi palace split apart as the news leaked out. Any thought of the considered sign language of *ixarette* was forgotten; all the officials shouted the news in their own languages, unable to understand each other in the Babel bedlam. Although they did not know it, the Sultanate of Women was coming to an end.

Three days of official mourning were decreed. Mehmet soon bestowed his executive powers to his grand vizier, thereby reigning in the *Kafes* rather than ruling the empire. After this act of selfishness and folly the sultans never entirely retrieved their power. Some historians argue that this marks the start of the decline of the Ottoman Empire. Patrick, Lord Kinross dates it some seventy years earlier, when the dipsomaniac son of Suleiman the Magnificent gave his authority away through personal indolence; the first time an Ottoman sultan had abnegated his responsibility because he was unfit to rule. He was not the last. What Thomas Rowe saw as the beginning of the decline of the empire, in 1622 when Osman was murdered, was to continue inexorably. The 'sick man of Europe' was headed by inept and inappropriate rulers until the nadir of 1922, when Kemal Ataturk banished the last caliph from Turkey.

Chapter 8
Carlos II of Spain –
Royal Pond Life

Blind chance rules the World!
The Bewitched – Peter Barnes

A t the beginning of the seventeenth century many of the ruling Catholic houses of Europe were experiencing difficulty in finding members of other families of the appropriate status, religion and lineage to marry. The rise in the number of aristocratic Protestants, especially in Germany in the previous hundred years, had further diminished the number of mid-European Catholic noble families who could have provided candidates with suitable dynastic links for the next generation. There were beginning to be instances where an aristocratic inheritor's eight great-grandparents were declining in numbers, because of interbreeding.

Sometimes the products of this inevitable genetic bottleneck were mentally and physically bizarre. The French received Henri of Navarre, initially a Protestant, back into the Catholic fold as Henri IV because of the failure of the male line of the decaying house of Valois and the civil war that followed the violent death of a probably impotent Henri III. Henri's Valois predecessor on the French throne, his brother Charles XI, was increasingly delusional before his early death. 'Paris was worth a mass' as far as Henri IV was concerned, but religious allegiance was a secondary consideration; the limited bloodline he brought with his new house of Bourbon would not change the underlying problem of limited competence as a consequence of limited genes; and although Henri IV was an admirable, well-balanced king, well-loved by his subjects, his heir, Louis XIII, was born after the disappointment of four still-births. He manifested several physical anomalies, the most remarkable being in the lower part of his face: a double set of teeth, an over-large tongue, a stutter and a consequent profound difficulty in speaking clearly.

For most of the long-established ruling dynasties of Europe the gene pool was unavoidably shrinking, in some patrician families becoming not much more than a puddle; the instances of mental and physical incompetence in certain aristocratic progenies were becoming more frequent. Nowhere was this more apparent than in the great lineage of Habsburg, rulers of great tracts of land in central and northern Europe since the tenth century and Holy Roman Emperors, regarded as the apogee of temporal power, since the middle of the fifteenth. The gene count issue was not helped by special papal dispensations for niece and nephew marriages to aunts and uncles within certain royal families from 1550. These marital alliances were organised principally to keep property and wealth within a family, a special consideration that was only rescinded in the early years of the last century. At a time when life was regarded as transitory and sudden death was always to be considered, either by violence or disease, plans for marital alliance tended to be of short-term expedience, and the consequences for future generations were largely not taken into account.

Although sometimes first cousin and double-cousin marriages produced intelligent and competent rulers of an increasingly diverse and disparate subject base (for instance the Holy Roman Emperor Leopold I), it also meant that there were more royal children who were subject to increasingly noticeable physical and mental weaknesses, through no fault of their own. The most obvious is the Habsburg mandibular prognathism – the progressive lengthening of the lower lip and jaw as the victim matured; mostly evident in the males. The Holy Roman Emperor Maximilian I (d.1519), who was the first Habsburg who demonstrated it, extended the influence of the Habsburgs immeasurably over Europe less by war and more by marriage alliances, often dangerously close to his own genetic heritage. His policy merited the elegiac Latin couplet, some say coined by Maximilian himself:

> Bella gerant alii, tu felix Austria nube,
> Nam quae Mars aliis, dat tibi regna Venus

> (Let others wage war, you happy Austria, marry,
> for those kingdoms Mars gives to others, Venus gives to you)

This physical trait is supposed to have come from Maximilian's Polish grandmother, Cymburgis of Masovia. Little could the Holy Roman Emperor have anticipated just what a disastrous policy this marriage would prove to be to the family in the years after his death. In saving money through closer marriage alliances and so avoiding expensive foreign wars over succession issues during his and his son's lifetime, he was in fact ensuring the fatal undermining of just what he intended to preserve – the physical and mental competence of his descendants in the Habsburg dynasty. First cousin marriages among the great ruling houses were the norm rather than the exception, which eventually resulted in ever more serious combinations of genetic anomalies.

Mandibular prognathism is evident in his profile; but far more in his grandson and successor Charles V (d.1558) from an early age. His son, Philip II of Spain (d.1598), displayed it too, as did his direct descendants the Kings of Spain, culminating in his great-grandson Charles II. This unprepossessing prospect was the risk if the Habsburg babies lived; thankfully for them many did not. Recent research has found that only half the seventeenth-century Habsburgs reached their first birthdays, compared with 80 per cent of Spanish peasants, who were among the most economically deprived of populations at this time. The Austrian branch displayed the Habsburg jaw notably in Holy Roman Emperor Rudolf (d.1608) and most of all in Emperor Leopold I (d.1705), a direct contemporary of Charles and his half-brother-in-law. There is also occasionally manifested a thinness in the legs, shown in full-length portraits of Maximilian and Philip II; this may have been the product of genetic inheritance. If so, it is tragically manifested in Carlos's physical nature and was exacerbated by his nurture. The unfortunate Habsburg survivors of infancy were also often saddled with mental deficiencies, depression, increasing intellectual incompetence and obsessive eccentricity, especially appertaining to religious observance, which also marked out the Bourbon royal line, the successors of the Spanish Habsburgs throughout the eighteenth and nineteenth centuries. We are made intensely aware of their shortcomings because of the vicious satires in their portraits, especially those by Goya, executed at the turn of the nineteenth century, where they stare vacantly and complacently out of the frames – hardly royal.

Too-close marriages were organised all too often then – the first Habsburg Holy Roman Emperor, Frederick III (1452–93) was related to every other king in the area covered by what is now Germany – and it still occurred relatively recently: virtually every dynastic blue blood in Europe is descended in some way from the family of Queen Victoria (1819–1901), whose husband Albert was her first cousin. There have been some physical weaknesses displayed in nineteenth- and twentieth-century royals; especially the so-called 'royal disease', haemophilia, which has raised itself several times because the gene mutation was passed through two of Victoria's five daughters, and it tragically appeared in the British, Russian and Spanish royal families at the beginning of the twentieth century. Although there are almost no cases reported in children of royal descent today, the gene can remain dormant through several generations, carried by the female line; so one of the first fears of today's parents of royal descent must be that the affliction could manifest itself in their children. There is still no medical cure.

Autocracies in history seldom looked further than the next generation; it was keeping current temporal power that mattered. The Protestant Church specifically prohibits marriage closer than between first cousins; perhaps this was a reaction to what they had seen in their Catholic contemporaries in the sixteenth century, together with the general horror of incest reinforced in the Book of Leviticus.

Genetic mutations have always been more common in interbred families, whatever their social and economic background. Spanish Habsburgs tended to marry Austrian Habsburgs to reinforce mutual alliance, and to keep property and crowns within the extended family domain. This had been practised for well over a century, and threats of genetic weakness tended to lose out to contemporary pragmatism and what was expected of the children. Marriage among royals and aristocracy was principally political; the young person's personal feelings were of no more than passing interest. Catholic princes and princesses, especially if they were Habsburgs, must have had a fair idea of who their spouses were going to be. Many were apprehensive; there were very few marriages that were more than pragmatic alliances. What had love got to do with it? The royal women were brood-mares; it was the descendants who were important; political pawns for the greater and better to play marriage and alliance games with. A famous story tells of an altercation over an arranged marriage between the beautiful, popular and vivacious sixteen-year-old Marie-Louise d'Orleans and her uncle, Louis XIV, the Sun King of France. He negotiated the marriage of his niece to Philip's son, Carlos II. Politically it was a brilliant match for France, as it would prevent the Spanish Habsburg king marrying into the Austrian branch of the family. Carlos was the French queen Marie-Thérèse's half-brother. Any children of this union would therefore be more than half-French, and therefore French influence would take precedence over Germanic interest in what happened to a politically weak and divided Spain with her huge European and overseas possessions.

For Marie-Louise it was the prospect of a personal living death sentence. She had thought that she might marry the Dauphin. She must have heard rumours of what the monstrous King of Spain looked like and his eccentric behaviour; the rumours that he was too weak for sex; that in all probability he was impotent. This was a new version of *La Belle et la Bête*. Even if she could cope with this physical anomaly in her bed, she must have been aware of what the dull, sombre, rigid Spanish court was like, compared with the lively, outgoing brightness of the Sun King and his new palace of Versailles, which was within the year to accommodate the entire French court from Paris. Marie-Louise must have been told of the change in personality the second wife of Philip IV experienced when she arrived in Spain; there would be little compensation for what she must endure. This was all irrelevant to the great King of France. She was summoned into his presence, perhaps excitedly anticipating that he was to informally notify her that he had chosen her to be his daughter-in-law. An ecstatic Louis announced that she was going to be Queen of Spain and added, 'I could not have done more for my daughter.' To which appalling news, the hapless teenager replied, 'Yes, sire, but you could have done more for your niece.' There must have been tears, which the great king probably dismissed; he never could bear unhappiness in his presence. She had no choice – *noblesse oblige* – she had to go and embrace her fate. This was the price of aristocracy if you were female at this time, with few more rights to decide your future than a feudal peasant. We can feel for her when we hear of unhappy arranged marriages today.

Carlos's father Philip had inherited a sprawling empire from his indolent father, with an agrarian, underdeveloped mother country that did not possess any reformist bureaucracy to help it progress in an increasingly changing world. Spain had no industry to speak of and generated little domestic income. It became increasingly reliant on wealth from the New World, which was unreliable in its delivery and diminishing in value. The country was bankrupted by wars the Spanish could not win, especially in the Netherlands. Philip IV was forced to declare the country officially insolvent in 1662 and it was so again a year after his death. Corruption was rife at every level, presided over by the Catholic Church, which resisted any reform that might conceivably threaten its influence on politics, government and individuals' minds and bodies. The king had produced what was required of him and his Habsburg-related queen – a male heir, and another son in case the first-born heir did not survive. Queen Elizabeth of France was one of six children, all of whom survived to adulthood. Corrupt Habsburg genes combined with bad luck and medical ignorance must have contributed to the fact that only one of her seven with Philip would.

Portraits painted throughout Philip's life show him progressively displaying the Habsburg jaw; and the last portrait of his son, Prince of the Asturias Felipe Prospero, begins to exhibit the tell-tale sign of increasing heaviness of the jawline. Philip IV was the product of extreme selection in terms of his ancestry. His father was the product of an uncle-niece marriage and married his first cousin, albeit once removed. He and his first wife, Elizabeth of France, herself a near relative, had seven children, of whom only two survived infancy. Balthazar Carlos was created the Prince of Asturias and heir to the throne of Spain, with an empire the extent of which had rarely been seen before. He was to marry his father's niece, his first cousin Mariana of Austria, but to the shock of the whole nation the prince died suddenly, probably of smallpox, just short of his seventeenth birthday.

The succession was now disputed. Louis XIV of France, always ready to expand his sphere of influence, had several relatives whom he would have liked to promote; the Holy Roman Emperor was in the same position. The country was stripped of the legitimate heir, and it had to have the succession established – or else the great Spanish Empire would become the property of another part of the family; but they would be foreigners. Spain would have to resist being taken over against the king's dying will; a succession war would be ruinous. Philip IV had inherited a country that had lost its way under his father, who took less and less interest in government as it became increasingly obvious to him that he was not able even to begin to reform it. Philip had the energy to try but, autocrat as he was supposed to be, he was too often frustrated by the slow workings of the decrepit system he had inherited. His perceived failures haunted him throughout his life, and his depression and fatalism so often evident in his ancestors became cornerstones in his behaviour and his attitude to his role as king.

In 1649 the father and uncle at forty-four, and with a reputation as a fearful rake with dozens of illegitimate (and mostly healthy) progeny (he was not dubbed *El Rey Donjuanesco* for nothing), married the surely unhappy fourteen-year-old niece. In the next twelve years they had five children. Within eighteen months of their marriage his second wife Mariana had produced a healthy daughter, and then another who, true to Habsburg genetics, died in infancy. Then at last, to the great joy of the nation, Felipe Prospero was born in 1657. Another son followed a year later, who did not survive. Felipe Prospero's celebrated portrait by Velázquez, painted when the prince was little more than three years old, shows a pale but seemingly reasonably healthy child with his hand steadying himself on a chair, as one would expect from one so young. This was perhaps all the court saw of him; so it was with consternation that the nation heard of his death early in 1661. They didn't know that the dreaded self-destructive genetic curse of the Habsburgs had struck again; that the new Prince of the Asturias was epileptic and physically weak. They didn't interpret his hand on the chair as any more than the firm young hand of the next representative of God on earth, the hope of Spain who would lead the distracted country out of its self-imposed morass. His costume doesn't show his legs or his feet; they could not see whether his legs were supporting him or whether he needed the chair to keep himself upright. They didn't recognise the significance of the amulets strung around his neck and body, and the amber apple that was thought to give him immunity against infection. They saw only silver and light, hopeful colours in the portrait, and not the shadows surrounding him and the opaque darkness behind. Velázquez saw more than others were allowed to see: the portrait communicates the frailties of life and the surrounding difficulties that he knew this little Habsburg prince would have to face.

The tiny boy was gone; the succession problem had become a constitutional crisis. Foreign kings with expansionist ambitions, although some were closely related, quickly showed more interest in Spain and its empire's future; global power seduced far more powerfully than blood tie. They waited, and watched the distracted court of Spain, hawk-like, for something to happen. The ambassadors whispered with their supporters in corners and in the dark corridors of the palace, and checked on their couriers.

The king was in an unenviable position. Philip was already in his late fifties; his erstwhile strong physical disposition was failing, and given his long list of sexual liaisons he was probably suffering from venereal disease. He could not be expected to live too much longer. The queen had already produced four children, of whom only the firstborn had survived – and being a daughter could not inherit. Peter Barnes, in his play *The Bewitched*, portrays the prematurely old, raddled king having to 'do sheet duty' with his wife at every auspicious time in a desperate attempt to father an heir. We are not sure that Mariana knew she was pregnant at the time of Felipe Prospero's death, but the bells rang joyfully in the November of that year when she was brought to bed of a son who, although sickly, seemed to possess the will to survive. Many Habsburg babies didn't last a day.

Philip, as the leader of the nation, thanked God for looking favourably upon him in his old age. Carlos was a miracle. But he was a distinctly unprepossessing one. Philip's elder daughter, the Infanta Margherita, the tiny, glorious blonde princess in the famous Velázquez painting *Las Meninas*, is portrayed as having none of the physical attributes of her genetic heritage. She married Leopold I, the future Holy Roman Emperor, who was both her first cousin and her uncle. From his portraits it appears he was afflicted by prognathism as much as her half-brother and yet proved a successful ruler and father, despite his reported lethargy and unattractive physical appearance. Barnes, writing with typical grim gothic glee, has old, exhausted Philip taking one look at Carlos, portrayed as a gross corporeal freak of humanity, more like an alien phlegm-coated worm than an infant whom he had fathered, and keeling over dead from shock.

As a God-given miracle, Carlos was treated as if he was made of cut glass. No expense was spared in attempting to ensure his existence. By the time Philip died in 1665, supposedly of a broken heart over Balthazar Carlos's death, Carlos's feet still had not touched the ground. He was neither of this world nor of the next. He was carried everywhere, floating between existence and non-existence. His diet was strictly controlled; he was breast-fed by over a dozen wet-nurses until he was nearly five and rarely saw sunlight in the dark Real Alcázar palace and the bleak and forbidding El Escorial; consequently he suffered from rickets. Throughout his life he was afflicted by gastric complaints and problems with his digestion. He could not chew properly, a problem that got worse with the increasing gap between upper and lower jaw. A low fever seemed never far away and he was often seriously ill. Several times during his life his death was hourly expected, and the foreign ambassadors regularly collected like vultures at the sombre court to be the first to tell their voracious royal masters about the long-expected imperial vacancy. Carlos was never angered nor disciplined when young, for fear of what it would do to him. He could not speak until he was four; perhaps his over-large tongue prevented him. Philip died wishing that the boy's mother, who would be regent for Carlos, would have better luck than he did.

His son was destined to be king, but what a king! He had inherited just about as much genetic misfortune as was possible. Whereas most people have thirty-two great-great-great-great-grandparents, Carlos had but fourteen. There were documented cases of eccentric behaviour and madness in twenty-three of his immediate ancestors. One of his more infamous direct ancestors was the woman who been married to the first Spanish Habsburg; the last Trastámara ruler of Spain, Juana *La Loca* – the Mad, who was forced to abdicate the throne because of her obsessive, eccentric behaviour. Intellectually he was little more than inert, and therefore received almost no schooling. He displayed the unattractive combination of ignorance and arrogance because he was so uninformed. With apparently no ability to carry on a conversation, Carlos was as dull mentally as he was limited in his physical development: he couldn't read or write at the age of nine. He may have been epileptic, and his portraits show that he could have developed acromegalic tendencies (an excessive production of growth hormone), which would have further accentuated his physical eccentricities. He was not in control of his digestion and may have been incontinent, so he stank more than most. The world waited and watched with increasing fascination for decades as this pathetic human being fought to stay alive, sometimes despite his doctors' remedies. Philip's god had a particularly black sense of humour.

Philip IV had performed his prime function – he had provided a legitimate male inheritor at his death, and the Spanish Empire acclaimed another Spanish king; but as time progressed there were many Spanish, great and small, who wished they hadn't. This was their version of King Log, and they were stuck with him.

It is difficult not to feel sympathy for this wretched individual, the new King of Spain and the impossible position in which he found himself. We can assess with the benefit of hindsight the supreme irony that the Spanish Empire was at its greatest geographical extent during the reign of its most unfortunate and inept king, arguably the least competent of all monarchs. Carlos could not be described as clinically insane, but he was terminally multi-handicapped, and the cumulative effect of all his physical and intellectual ailments meant that he was always a shadow of a king; a gargoyle at the head of a corrupt, disorganised monster of an empire. As the austere Spanish physician, historian and polymath Gregorio Morreno y Posadilla (1887–1960) pithily described his reaction to the Spanish Habsburg kings, 'Charles V inspires enthusiasm, Philip II respect, Philip III indifference, Philip IV sympathy and Carlos II pity.' It is surprising that relatively little has been written about the end of the seventeenth century in Spain by anyone, let alone the Spanish themselves – almost as if this part of their heritage is an embarrassment. So many opportunities were missed to make Spain the greatest nation on earth; the country had the physical and economic resources, but what it lacked was individual talent, stamina and will.

Much of Spain's ambition foundered on the coagulating conservatism of the national ruling elite, epitomised by the Church and the temporal secular bureaucracy, and the escalating incompetence, indifference to and dependence on its royal leaders. The Spanish court above all others was renowned for its preternaturally sombre rigidity, hierarchy almost tantamount to caste and unyielding adherence to protocol. There were particular rituals, regulations and responsibilities that had to be honoured by certain individuals of a certain rank; there were apocryphal stories of domestic disasters occurring because there was nobody of the right status to perform a particular task, no-one being allowed to accomplish it. Concomitant with secular misgovernment was the impenetrable hierarchy of the Catholic Church: the two disorganisations complemented each other. This colossal, rickety subculture could be compared to the contemporaneous Turkish court, with its castes of civil servants and its concentration upon silence, or the vast, ritualistic, ramshackle organisation of the Chinese Forbidden City. Surrounding the old bones of the Spanish court, the flesh was a contaminated mass. The worms of intrigue and political mischief were always hard at work, with nobles constantly jockeying for position and changing alliances. If there was no strong hand on the helm of the Spanish ship of administration, and therefore of society, the winds of conspiracy would blow it in every direction. No-one could be trusted, so ultimate power was devolved to very few, whose energy was devoted primarily to keeping it.

If Carlos was not able to rule, and his father and grandfather had signally failed to do so adequately despite their initial good intentions, who did? His mother was appointed regent. She had no experience of governance and she was a foreigner, still with many German-speaking staff. Only thirty, and a dark, brooding presence, she tended to be morbidly over-zealous, obsessed by her religion and mortality, nearly always dressed in dark colours; sometimes she wore a nun's black habit. She had been noted for her high spirits and good company at home in Hungary, but marriage to her uncle was a traumatic experience from which she seemingly never recovered. She stares out of her Velázquez portraits a few years apart with almost exactly the same posture, garbed in old-fashioned sculptured farthingales and elaborate headdresses and a look of ill-temper, suspicion and intolerance. Her lack of judgement probably resulted in her Austrian confessor Father Johann Eberhard Nithard, one of the few that she trusted, being made a naturalised Spaniard as Juan Everaldo and being promoted to the post of inquisitor-general in 1666. This meant that he could meddle in the Supreme Council. As a Jesuit and *de facto* prime minister, he could represent the dead hand of the Catholic Church, which would resist any reform. We see a similar situation when Queen Anne relied too much on the advice of her great friend Sarah Churchill, Duchess of Marlborough, which led to Sarah's disgrace and voluntary exile until after the queen's death. Nithard showed his lack of political acumen when signing disadvantageous treaties with Portugal and France, and a plot to overthrow him began to be engineered by Don Juan José of Austria, the only one of Philip IV's illegitimate brood he recognised as his; but even then did not make him part of the royal family.

Don Juan was a complete contrast to the sickly legitimate males of the Spanish Habsburgs. Tall and good looking, with a dark complexion and masses of black wavy hair, he exuded vigour, charisma, strength and fortitude, unlike the pale, feeble, corrupted northern European stock of the royals. He looked like a Spaniard and must have taken after his mother's side, the actress Maria Ines Calderon, who retreated to a nunnery after his birth in 1629. Because he was recognised as the king's son and because of the dashing and mainly successful military career he embarked upon in Europe, he earned immense popularity with court grandees and commoners alike. This did not go down well with Queen Mariana, who knew that her son, although the legitimate heir to the throne, was no match for this half-brother. And so it proved: Carlos idolised this physical antithesis to himself. If Don Juan led a popular revolution there would be little internal opposition, and perhaps not much from his half-brother prince. This situation was exacerbated on Philip IV's death: Don Juan became the natural focus of opposition to royal policy dictated by the queen and her wily confessor. Nithard was ousted in 1669, because Don Juan placed himself at the head of a rising in Aragon in the north, and eventually retreated to Rome, where he was made a cardinal.

Why did Don Juan not take over the government on Nithard's dismissal? Aged forty, he was the obvious candidate, and the rest of the court seemed powerless to resist. But Mariana's opposition was implacable, and he seemed to be content with the granting to him of the Viceroyalty of Aragon. Perhaps he thought that he could be more effective as the greatest of the many powers behind the throne. Perhaps he did not trust his own supporters; such was the paranoia in the Madrid court. However, Mariana found her own version of Sarah Churchill in Maria de Uceda, one of her ladies-in-waiting, who became the wife of ambitious minor gentleman, or *hidalgo*, Fernando de Valenzuela; he in turn became essential to the queen dowager in advising how she should run the country on behalf of her son. She never wavered in her loyalty to him: rumours abounded in the rigidly controlled court that he was the queen's lover. Because of his relatively lowly background and his inexperience, his political activities caused consternation among the grandees. Rival candidates for the queen's favour developed into self-interested opposing camps, which became ever more estranged the more Mariana favoured the policies of de Valenzuela. In 1675, when Carlos was thirteen and only a few months away from the age of majority, a palace coup inspired by Don Juan forced de Valenzuela out of the country; in compensation he was created a grandee – the Marquis of Villa Sierra – and awarded the coveted post of ambassador to Venice. Within a few months he had inveigled himself back into Spain and was appointed *valido* – prime minister – by his faithful queen. This was a slap in the face for the other grandees, who were understandably outraged at the swift rise in power of such an upstart; but such was the mystique surrounding the royal family, coupled with the mutual distrust of all the court factions, that de Valenzuela was allowed to prosecute his office, 'protect' the feeble young king from other influences and, as was the custom during the process, line his progressively more capacious pockets.

At last the young king flexed his atrophied imperial muscles. On 4 November 1675, two days before he came of age, he refused to sign the document extending his mother's regency. Her justification for the lengthening of her time as regent was that her son would continue to function inappropriately for a king. Despite his inability to perform normally, he resented his mother's domineering attitude towards him. Her over-protection resembled patronisation from his perspective. He was certain that his half-brother hero Don Juan would come to his aid, and must have been aware of his mother's anger through fear of losing her enormous influence. He secretly wrote (or had written) a letter to Don Juan, who was in the process of being sent as an envoy to the Spanish possessions in Sicily. Mariana knew that Don Juan need not be close and available at this sensitive time. No doubt with increasing anticipation, Don Juan read, 'I need your person at my side to help me, and rid me of the queen my mother. On Wednesday the sixth [of November] at 10.45 am, you will be in my antechamber.' This was the invitation for which his half-brother had been waiting for so long; it was also the reason for finally showing his public allegiance to the son rather than the mother. Accordingly he presented himself, and accompanied the frail king to the mass to celebrate his coming of age, perhaps literally supporting him as the bizarre-looking adolescent tottered and lurched his way at his side, cheered to the echo by the Madrid mob. After the services the king, buoyed up with this public acclaim and assured of his half-brother's support, visited his mother, presumably to formally cut the ties of regency and reinforce his self-determination in thought and action. The court held its breath and waited.

Two hours later Carlos emerged from his mother's suite in tears. Mariana had won. Far from her acceding graciously to him, he had been persuaded, bullied, browbeaten and perhaps threatened with all sorts of retributions if he did not comply with his mother's wishes. We do not know if Mariana appealed to him as a mother does to a son or as a queen dowager does to a king; probably both. The queen had beaten him down with intellect he could not combat, weight of experience he was not old enough to have acquired and by sheer strength of mind and body he did not possess. The king's great act of independence, rebellion and abscission had lasted little more than half a day. Sir William Godolphin, the English ambassador to Spain and recent but still closet Catholic convert, gossiped that, 'Don Fernando Valenzuela whispered to me in the Ear and said that all this Stir will come to nothing.' It turned out to be his only revolt in the whole of his thirty-five years on the throne. Don Juan was not confident enough to move in the king's support – or his self-interest meant that he was prepared to wait for another opportunity to unseat de Valenzuela. The *status quo* seemed to have been resumed.

The opposition was not cowed. If Mariana's determination as regent could not be broken, her *valido*'s record could. De Valenzuela's subsequent administration was not a success; one can imagine that the rest of the queen mother's regency advisory committee were going to make de Valenzuela's life as difficult as possible. Towards the end of 1676 the disparate, dissenting groups of the opposition allied themselves again under Don Juan and attempted to destroy de Valenzuela with a petition to Mariana, demanding his dismissal. He realised that this time Mariana could not protect him because she would discover how he had been defrauding the government, collecting bribes and supervising false accounting. He fled to the grim monastery fortress of the Escorial on Christmas Day. He was arrested, demoted and exiled in close confinement to the Philippines, whence he was released some years later. He never saw Spain again. Some of his honours were restored and a pension was granted him, but the grandeeship was not restored. He retired to Mexico, where in February 1692 he was killed – felled by the kick of a horse he was trying to break.

At long last, in some contemporary opinions, Don Juan had the reins of power secure. Here, finally, was a man of talent who had the intellectual strength to promote desperately needed reforms and initiatives. One of his first acts concerning Carlos was to send his mother away, almost into internal exile, in the old, dark, forbidding Alcázar palace in nearby Toledo. Once she was out of the way he tried to show the young king what it really meant to be a monarch by sending him on royal progresses about the country, so that he could attend the regional councils or *Cortes*, meet the provincial aristocracy, who would not have been seen in Madrid, and learn more about internal governance and the strong regional identities and particular internal problems of Granada, Castile and Aragon, which had been incorporated into greater Spain for less than 200 years. Because of his frail constitution, Carlos had only lived in the capital city area, and provincials would hardly have been aware of him as a three-dimensional human being. Although physically he was still desperately inadequate, he had learned to ride and hunting was one of his passions; so he had breathed some fresh air and been seen by the local populace in an informal situation. However, while the king was in Saragossa – about as far away from the capital as he ever ventured – the weather conspired against him. There was another bad harvest in 1677, the latest of many, the price of bread rose dramatically and because of malnutrition among the peasantry plague broke out all over the country. For his own safety Carlos had to be recalled, to where his physical condition could be better monitored. While he was at home Don Juan supervised him in the taxonomy and drafting of official documents. Plague continued to spread and worsen, and public discontent rose, while the king remained insulated from and uninformed about the world in his imposed Madrid prison, with his mother in hers a few miles away. The vast returns of the treasure fleet convoys from the New World depressed the price of precious metals, and inflation skyrocketed. The money supply almost ran out again. Because the country could not guarantee the funds to prolong the war in the Netherlands, Don Juan had to sign the Peace of Nijmegen the following year, regarded as a humiliating climb-down by his dissenters and negatively affecting already shaky national morale. Mariana, fretting in her quasi-house arrest in the Alcazar, made the air between Toledo and the capital blue with her complaints about her personal treatment, and especially how she was not allowed access to her own son. Carlos was naturally sensitive to his mother's eloquence, and this put more pressure on Don Juan. Combined with the parlous national situation, this did little for his reputation among his fellow grandees, who saw him as a suitable scapegoat. All the country's problems were laid at his door because he had not been able, or more likely had not had sufficient time, to wield the magic wand of reform. There was too much long-established bureaucratic opposition and resistance to the inevitable restriction of privilege that reform would bring.

Although considered healthy for a half-Habsburg, Don Juan's body began to show the strain. In the summer of 1679 he collapsed with a gall bladder infection, and died in September. He was just fifty years old. Although the autopsy found two stones in the offending organ, rumours abounded that poison had aided his departure from this world; the accusing eyes of his dwindling number of supporters turned towards the erstwhile prisoner not far away in Toledo. This was where Carlos was summoned to a formal reconciliation with his mother a few days later. By undergoing this journey he symbolically submitted once more to his mother's influence, and from that day to the time of

Mariana's last illness he was completely in her power. The government of Spain reverted to complaisance and short-term financial fire-fighting – ever more dependent on the treasure fleet carrying silver from the New World. Seldom in history has such a great geographical empire boasted such an administrative vacuum at its centre. The continued decline of Spain was guaranteed.

However, personal destinies could be determined, and the doctors now thought that at eighteen Carlos was physically mature enough to marry. His choice was limited: a virgin from the Austrian royalty or the French. The queen mother's choice was obviously Austrian, but the only candidate was still a child and Carlos was considered not strong enough to be able to wait as long as ten years. Someone had to be found as soon as possible, and Louis XIV had an ideal candidate – charming Marie-Louise d'Orleans, the niece of Carlos's half-sister: practically family. We have already heard her initial response to the news that she would be Queen of Spain; and all the reservations she had were soon to be realised. She left France in a hysteria of weeping; she arrived in Burgos a few days later, where the young couple regarded each other. For her it was not love at first sight. With the courage that fatalism must bring, however, she endured, and did her best to make him happy. She did not speak the language; she had no French-speaking retainers to talk to – Spanish protocol dictated that she wasn't allowed to talk to servants, not even her loyal old French groom whom she had known since childhood and had volunteered to accompany her. She was unprotected in the sad, inflexible, brooding atmosphere of the royal court; all the older courtiers who visited the Spanish court she knew must be spies, as was the French ambassador

Rebenec, whose conversations with her were instantly relayed to Versailles. Poor girl, she must have been unspeakably lonely.

Carlos, however, was fascinated with this northern beam of light, and she lifted his spirits. Although he was simple and inadequate in many ways, he was genuine in his affection for his wife, and as the years went by he ever more desperately tried to conceive a child with her. All sorts of medicines and outlandish schemes were used to help him – even the biggest *auto-da-fé* in history in 1680 – a great public penance for sins committed, accompanied by torture and burning. In this ritual in the Plaza Major of Madrid, dozens of Jews, heretics, Moriscos and criminals were tortured and burnt at the stake, in the hope that by this cleansing of the Church, Carlos and his new wife might be looked upon favourably by the Almighty and a child, hopefully a son, would be born to them. James Stanhope, the soldier son of the English envoy to Spain, and a future Prime Minister of Great Britain, observed with disgust another in Palma in Majorca, in May 1691, where nearly fifty Jews (the richest men in town, he thought) and others considered heretics were burnt for the pleasure of Almighty God.

Louis XIV was extraordinarily interested in his dynastic investment in Spain, and wished to be kept informed of all the intimate details of the poor king's attempts to father the next generation of the Habsburg royal family. For the rumours seemed to be true; Carlos was probably not able to achieve proper penetration, and even if he could he almost certainly suffered from premature ejaculation. Even if he did achieve meaningful sexual congress with his wife, the unfortunate king could well have been infertile; many Habsburg marriages produced no pregnancies, let alone numerous dead infants; this might have been another physical manifestation of Habsburg consanguinity. Louis, a serial womaniser, with a swarm of illegitimate children to rival Philip's, demanded proof of the young couple's successful sexual activity. A pair of the king's drawers was procured and minutely inspected by doctors for evidence of any discharge. Diplomatically, they came to no real conclusion. Some years after the wedding Rebenec reported to the Sun King that Marie-Louise had confided to him that she did not think she was a virgin any more, but doubted that she would ever have children. The Sun King's French dynastic venture was not assuring any return. Louis was used to maximising his satisfaction, and if Marie-Louise could not produce she was ripe for abandonment. The French court was worried about her situation, but there was little that could be done diplomatically. Marie-Louise had lost her French national rights when she married Carlos II; she was Spanish property – beyond any influence of the land of her birth.

Could Marie-Louise have become pregnant by someone else and passed it off as a royal child? It was rumoured to have happened before. The French court was the scandal and, to some, the envy of the rest of Europe in the variety of hetero- and homosexual peccadilloes that were tolerated. Not so the Spanish court. There is no evidence that Marie-Louise ever had lovers; she was observed too closely for that; but as the years passed depression, frustration and loneliness must have had an effect on her mental state. She began to comfort-eat, especially sweets. Physical activity was not high on Carlos's agenda, although we have seen that he enjoyed hunting; so his queen stayed in her apartments, available for him as she must be. Although he liked her, he did not visit often enough, and so she fretted and binged and fattened. She had been left in an impossible position, and felt more vulnerable and paranoid by the day. Like her mother-in-law she may not have experienced a single happy day in Spain. As she ballooned in size she became less attractive to her husband, and her paranoia that she was being sidelined and cast away began to grow. She was well aware that she was a disappointment to her uncle, her husband, her mother-in-law (who never liked her because she was French) and to two countries, and knew what often happened to women who didn't produce children. They became irrelevant, and were divorced on any pretext or sent to nunneries, or both. There was a third alternative for her increasingly tortured mind to consider: that she would be pushed out of the way permanently.

As her fear grew she believed that she was being poisoned, and wrote to Louis telling him so. She might have had good reason: Olympe Mancini, the Comtesse de Soissons, who fled from the French court to avoid trial in a celebrated poisoning scandal among the French courtiers in 1680, in which she was certainly implicated, was now almost resident at the Spanish court. La Comtesse, who was still under suspicion for poisoning her husband, must have been a spy. Banned from the French court as she was, she could well have become an agent for the Austrians, who had always resented the French marriage and wanted their influence in Spain revived. As the years passed there were more Austrian Habsburg female candidates who came from large families, and might be more fecund than Marie-Louise was proving. But the French wife was in the way. So perhaps we ought not to be surprised when we hear that the young queen began to suffer from stomach trouble. She is recorded as being ill in August 1687 and again late in the next year. This could have been self-indulgence, but it could also be that the Austrians were beginning to lose patience and had encouraged la Comtesse to try her expertise again. In early February 1689 Marie-Louise had a riding accident. While not badly hurt, she was nevertheless confined to bed to recover; the next day she experienced more gastric problems and complained yet again of being poisoned. No-one was particularly worried, even though she vomited continually. This could have been bulimia; she had cried wolf before. But three days later she was dead.

Carlos was distraught. His wife had brought some delight to his joyless life, and with his physical and mental legacy that emotion was in short supply. His mother was already casting about for suitable wives before Marie-Louise was cold. Almost as the period of court mourning was completed, negotiations were underway for a new mother of the next generation of Spanish kings. Mariana searched the ranks of the Austrian branch of the Habsburgs and eventually found a suitable dynastic match in Maria Ana von Neuburg, a niece of one of her brother's sisters-in-law – so she was still within the (Austrian) family. Also in her great favour was that she came from a branch of the family that bred well: her parents had twenty-three children. Although their dynastic credentials were impeccable, Ana's family was relatively poor, as was their little fief. Marrying sons and daughters off into greater magnates' families was a father's greatest ambition, and so Philip William, the Elector Palatine, was more than willing to agree to the match, even though he knew the trials that his daughter might have to experience, and that he might not see her again.

Marie-Louise had died on 12 February 1689, but

Carlos wasn't allowed to be a widower too long. Maria Ana was married to Carlos by proxy the following August and in person in San Diego, near Valladolid, on 4 May 1690. The seventeenth century was not known for speedy dialogue, swift discussion or rapid journeys; either this was all done in haste for political expediency, or because the queen mother's Spanish advisors knew well that Marie-Louise's days as queen were numbered even before she could have been aware. Of course it also could be that Carlos's health was so poor that his life could have ended at any moment. Only two years before, as his first wife despaired and corporeally expanded, the papal nuncio described him to the Holy Father, Innocent XI:

> he is short rather than tall; frail, not badly formed; his face ... is ugly; he has a long neck, a broad face and chin, with the typical Habsburg lower lip ... He has a melancholic and slightly surprised look. His hair is long and combed back so as to bare the ears. He cannot stand up when walking, unless he leans against a wall, a table or somebody else. He is as weak in body as in mind ... usually he shews himself slow and indifferent ... and seems to be stupefied. One can do with him what one wishes because he lacks his own will.

Carlos was the tool of anyone who could use him,

especially his new wife. Pretty and determined, Maria Ana was no more successful than Marie-Louise in becoming pregnant, although there were constant rumours given out by members of her Palatine household, whom she had insisted accompany her – she no more knew the Spanish language and culture than her predecessor. However, she had been well briefed as to the restrictions and vicissitudes of the upper echelons of Spanish society, especially her mother-in-law, who despite being a fellow-national took to her as ill as she had to Marie-Louise. Therefore she may have had an inkling that her time as Queen of Spain might be limited, given Carlos's sometimes parlous health and the intensifying hysteria that surrounded him. She needed constant positive reinforcement of her public image, and her household performed her public relations campaign. She knew that she came from productive stock, and that if any woman could become pregnant by Carlos it would be her. Maria Ana let it be known that Carlos visited her often; it is unlikely that he did. She was nothing if not a woman of the world and knew where her loyalties lay. So while she kept the Spanish public waiting in anticipation of news of pregnancy, she voraciously ransacked the royal palaces and exported anything of value, especially works of art, back to Germany to ease her relatives' financial situations.

The Spanish Church was at a loss to explain to the faithful why Carlos was unable to father a child. They had gone through every penance and ritual, and so eventually the witchcraft issue would have to raise its head. The Inquisition had already been intimately involved in *autos-da-fé*, which seemed to have patently shown that God had turned His back on the king – maybe on the country. We must remember that 300 years ago medieval ideas of magic and the dark arts were much more immediate in uninformed minds. Not only was witchcraft a potent force in Spain, it had been a capital crime in England only since 1641, and in the early 1690s a future celebrated witch trial was taking place across the Atlantic in Salem, Massachusetts. French ambassador Rebenec had been reporting to Louis that the king was becoming delusional, and the Church was happy to collude with this idea. As early as 1688 Rebenec had told his king that it had been divinely revealed to a Dominican monk, a friend of Carlos's confessor, that both king and queen were bewitched. How seriously the French took this story is unknown; but given the source it is to be expected that there were many nudges, winks and raising of eyebrows when it was gossiped about in Versailles. Carlos, in his simplistic and bewildered thinking, convinced himself that he was under the power of the Dark One. Theologians of many religions had long agreed that impotence was a manifestation of demonic possession, and throughout the 1690s the king was convinced that he was pursued by demons. Often he blamed his mental suffering on his declining physical health, although there were times when his demeanour improved. In 1693 Alexander Stanhope, who was the English minister in Madrid from 1690 to 1699, reported that the king was in good health. Whether he was quoting the official line or what he believed it is difficult to say, but when talking about the bewitched king's healthiness one needs to recalibrate definitions. He was never vigorous in the accepted form of the word; just simple tasks were trials.

In May 1696 the dark Queen Mother Mariana died of breast cancer, 'in the odour of misplaced sanctity', having refused all medicines and with only her religious personnel to comfort her. She had been both a comfort and a scourge to her son, and initially he seems to have reacted well to being without her. But in

September 1696 he was seriously ill, so much so that he made his will. He survived, but two months later was poorly again. The country was racked with internal dissension, because there was no strong hand at the centre of government. Alexander Stanhope had commented in October 1694 that 'This country is in a most miserable condition; no head to govern and every man in office does as he pleases without fear of being called to account.' The French interfered in the north-east of Spain and the court was riven with factional plotting between the German favourites of the queen and the Spanish grandees. *Validos* and chief ministers came and went in depressing succession, at least one of them dying in office, overwhelmed by the problems of the dissolving country. Meanwhile Carlos was having trouble just taking food. Stanhope witnessed:

> his constitution is so very weak and broken much beyond his age … They cut his hair off in this sickness, which the decay of nature had almost done before, all his crown being bald. He has a ravenous stomach, and swallows all he eats whole, for his nether jaw stands so much out, that his two rows of teeth cannot meet; to compensate which, he has a prodigious wide throat, so that a gizzard of a liver of a hen passes down whole, and his weak stomach not being able to digest it, he voids in the same manner.

At the beginning of 1697 Stanhope heard that the

rulers of France, Bavaria and the Holy Roman Empire were staking claims for their protégés to be heirs to the Spanish throne. They at least were convinced that there would be no heir. Their conclusions were ratified when in the spring of 1698 the king's health took a definite turn for the worse. Stanhope observed that he was in 'a languishing condition' and that his doctors were only capable of 'preserving him some few weeks without any hope of recovery ... he fancies the devils are very busy in tempting him'. Public bulletins about the king's condition invariably decreed that he was very well; but whenever Stanhope and his colleagues requested a private audience he was said to be too ill to receive them. Of course this fooled no-one who knew anything provable about the king's condition, but the queen Maria Ana stubbornly kept up her public relations campaign in trying to preserve at least the *status quo*, with as many public appearances as his strength could manage. Stanhope wrote of the queen lugging him out into the open to 'make people believe he is well till her designs are ripe'.

The feeble king simply refused to die. How long he could stay in a state of perpetual deterioration was the subject of serious and frivolous discussion all over Europe. Huge decisions depended on this visibly degenerating creature. He collapsed in a gentleman's arms in the summer of 1698, and was observed several times to be experiencing some kind of fit. On 11 June Stanhope wrote his latest bulletin to his son James: 'his ankles and knees [are] well again, his eyes big, the lids are as red as scarlet, and the rest of his face a greenish yellow. His tongue is *travada*, as they express it, that is, he has such a fumbling in his speech, those near him can hardly understand him, at which he sometimes grows angry and asks if they all be deaf.' Yet Stanhope witnessed a recovery of sorts, Carlos acquiring the strength from somewhere to appear in public, because he wrote on 9 July that the king 'looks like a ghost and moves like an image of clock work'. Christmas 1698 came and went with Carlos much recovered, to the astonishment of everyone. But the following spring Stanhope was reporting a swift decline, and as June led into July he continued that the king was 'sensibly worse and worse'. Witchcraft was suspected as much for preserving him as afflicting; as Stanhope grimly remarked, 'not for the first time this game has been played'.

Yet there was a recovery even from this supposed nadir, because on 12 August we can imagine Stanhope, writing his report to London, shaking his head in disbelief that Carlos appeared 'well, almost by miracle'. In November Carlos had his thirty-seventh birthday; he was bald, shaking, emaciated and ready to depart this trial of a life. 'Many people tell me,' Carlos murmured to the Cardinal de Cordoba, 'I am bewitched and I well believe it; such are the things I suffer.' In his early life he was informally known as the Desired – and so he was both by the royal family and the people; he was the hope of the nation. Now he was officially known as the Bewitched, *El Hechizado,* and so he was believed to be. How else could he still live? How else could his degenerating body and mind so eloquently reflect the foundering state? There were bread riots, civil strife and mass unemployment. The Madrid mob bayed to be allowed to see the king and make their views known to him. There were barely controlled uprisings in the countryside and in the east of Spain in Gerona and Barcelona.

The Spanish succession was now developing into a far more important issue in European politics. If there was no Habsburg heir to this vast empire in Europe and the New World, who would inherit? Whoever it was would shift the balance of power in Europe, and both the Habsburgs and the Bourbons were determined that it should be them. The rest of Europe would ally themselves behind these families, either on dynastic or religious grounds, and hope to pick up some scraps in the form of small territories or trading rights. If there was no heir to the Spanish throne, war was inevitable. The effect of the Thirty Years War, which had utterly devastated northern Europe, including Maria Ana's father's little domain, and ended some forty years earlier in 1648, was still horribly vivid in some memories; some parts of Germany were only just becoming repopulated, Philip William's territory included. The Spanish lands were truly colossal: besides the home country there were the disputed Spanish Netherlands; much of Italy and the Balearics; there was all of South America but Brazil, which had reverted to Portugal after the Braganzas had wrested their independence back from Philip IV; virtually all of central America under the vice-regency of Mexico, and an as yet undisputed claim to all of the south and west of north America. In the Far East floated the Philippines, a Spanish colony since 1565. In Africa Spain owned much of what is now Morocco, and trading posts on far-flung coasts of all continents but Australasia. There was plenty of scope for expansion for every nation that had the fleet to service them and the treasury to fund reorganisation. Unfortunately because of the stasis and vacuum at the head of government many Spanish ships were in disrepair, as was much of the bureaucracy. Through corruption and self-interest phenomenal amounts of money were wasted, and the organisation of overseas colonies was at best ramshackle.

At home, the French and Austrian-backed factions

at the Madrid court were constantly at each other's throats. Machiavelli would have been at home here. The Spanish Church favoured the French, as much as anything because Pope Innocent XII leant towards the French. The Austrian faction collected around the queen, who made herself extremely unpopular by trying to create many national nobles who would back her claim. William II of England and the Netherlands and Louis XIV decided to support the young Joseph Ferdinand of Bavaria, grandson of the princess Margaret Theresa of Spain, the main subject of Velázquez's *Las Meninas* and Carlos's half-sister. Carlos was persuaded (presumably by the queen) that this would also be a good choice. Accordingly Joseph was created Prince of the Asturias in 1698, as are all heirs to the Spanish throne. This would be a boy who would need a regent for Spain, and Louis could provide one. This must mean that by this time even the deluded royal family had realised that there would be no heir from Carlos's loins. Intriguingly, Joseph's inaugural portrait, in which he is dressed largely in red – one of the Spanish national colours – also features a half-veiled globe in the right foreground, implying that he would rule the undivided Spanish overseas empire. The main elements of the partition treaty were that Louis, the Dauphin of France, would receive Tuscany, Naples and Sicily, while Holy Roman Emperor Leopold I, Joseph Ferdinand's grandfather, would acquire the Spanish Netherlands. However, all this scheming was left null and void, as the little prince succumbed to smallpox the following February. Another partition agreement with another candidate had to be ratified and that quickly; this treaty was rushed and unsatisfactory. The main terms were that Philip of Anjou would receive most of the Spanish empire, while the Dauphin of France would get the Duchy of Lorraine. This time Leopold was only peripherally involved; he was not a signatory and naturally objected to the alterations, which would radically change the balance of power in Europe in favour of the French. The incumbent King of Spain had not been informed; it may be that the other European powers did not think that he was capable of any meaningful contribution. Carlos's advisors refused it on his behalf. The European powers, mistrusting each other's motives, warily watched each other and waited for the inevitable in Spain.

For at long last even Carlos's remarkable powers of survival were beginning to break down. The first year of the new century was one of enforced political stasis for southern and western Europe while the pitiable King of Spain fought his last battle. It lasted months, every day passing slower as the poor man sank. On 28 September he was given extreme unction by Cardinal Portocarrero, Archbishop of Toledo, who was the leading Spanish grandee of the Church supporting the French claim, purely to gain more personal influence. On 3 October, under Portocarrero's supervision, the decrepit king slowly and painfully dictated his last will and testament, bequeathing his empire to the dauphin's son and Louis XIV's grandson, Philip of Anjou, 'without allowing the least dismemberment of the Monarchy, founded with such glory by my ancestors'. This meant that all other claims were invalidated. It would have been beneficial for the Bourbon succession to have acquired the endorsement of the pope; but as fortune would have it on 3 October 1700 there was no pontiff. The French-favouring Innocent XII had died on 27 September, and the convocation to elect the next was only just forming.

The pitiful king's death was expected every day, as it had been so many times before. The month of October dragged on to its conclusion, and on 1 November, just before three o'clock in the afternoon, Carlos's tormented and increasingly marginal existence finally petered out. He didn't quite achieve his thirty-ninth birthday. The new pope, Clement XI, who initially adopted a neutral political position between France and the Holy Roman Empire, was not elected until the 23rd.

Part of Carlos's will decreed that his wife should be treated well by his successor and should be given a good pension. Maria Ana of Neuberg had hardly endeared herself to the Spanish people, and was loathed by the court because of the barefaced way she favoured Germanic causes during her ten years as queen. However, Philip V had commanded that she should leave Madrid before he arrived, and so she followed in her mother-in-law's footsteps to the Alcázar palace. She wrote to her German relatives for aid, but her brother refused, saying that she had brought her misfortune on herself. She was resigned to staying in the old dark palace, and during 1704 complained to her mother how badly she was being treated. However, two years later, when the ensuing civil war was raging, the troops of the Holy Roman Emperor occupied Toledo. She still hadn't learned her lesson and she welcomed them with open arms, which was a contributory cause for her ejection from the country by Philip V a few years later. She didn't go home; perhaps she realised that she was too much of an embarrassment to her family, who could never have politically afforded her. She settled just over the Spanish border in Bayonne, where she lived much more quietly for well over thirty years. In her seventies, too tired and ill to be an aggravation any more, she was allowed to return to Spain, and died in Guadalajara in July 1740.

The sixteen-year-old Philip of Anjou was acclaimed in France as Philip V and, having renounced all claims to the throne of France for him or his successors, arrived in Madrid a few weeks later. Not only did his succession politically unbalance Europe, but it was not universally acclaimed in his adopted country. There followed a disastrous civil war in Spain and the first global conflict, with theatres of war in Europe, North America and the Caribbean, lasting from 1701 to 1714. The War of the Spanish Succession may have cost over 400,000 lives. Louis XIV used his influence to try and secure his northern flank by taking over the Spanish Netherlands, and Leopold declared war in their defence. England (Great Britain from 1707) realised that if the Netherlands became French her borders would be threatened, and entered the war on the emperor's side. There followed the great land battles in the Netherlands, Germany and Bohemia that would seal John Churchill's reputation as the greatest land commander of his generation and the successful expansion of the English battle fleet, which would ensure Britain's dominance as a trading nation in the next hundred years. It is in this war that Gibraltar was captured in 1704 and became British in perpetuity in 1713. When it was all over, because both alliances were economically exhausted and vast tracts of land had been devastated, causing untold misery, the Spanish had lost most of their European possessions; but Philip was finally established in law on the throne of Spain. He had been there in effect for the past thirteen years.

The Bourbons have remained there, off and on, ever since. King Juan Carlos I (1975–), the first king of the third restoration of the Bourbons to the throne of Spain, is a direct descendant of Philip V. Alfonso XIII, the last of the Bourbon kings of Spain of the second restoration before he fled the country in 1931, was the son of a queen who had been a Habsburg grand duchess. His photographs show the tell-tale signs of the developing Habsburg jaw. Juan Carlos is his grandson. The regressive genes of both the Bourbons and the Habsburgs are in his bloodstream.

The seemingly perpetual decline of Spain as an international power throughout the 350 years from the beginning of the seventeenth century is reflected in the lack of leadership and successive aberrant and self-destructive personalities of its rulers. From the apogee under the second Habsburg king Philip II – he of the marriage to Mary Tudor and the Armada – Spain began a long social, economic and political deterioration, only reversing after the accession of King Juan Carlos in 1975 and the rapid modernisation of the Iberian Peninsula, funded by the European Union. Under General Franco after the 1930s civil war a Spanish peasant's situation was not that different from what it had been under the Habsburgs.

The descendants of the Spanish Habsburgs were never again claimants for the throne in Madrid; there were almost none left to claim. Consanguinity had done for them. Their genetic heritage reached its physical and mental nadir with the culmination of all the interbreeding that had been committed to secure the family possessions – the cumulatively degenerate runt of all the litters, the hapless Bewitched King.

Chapter 9
Charles XII of Sweden and Peter I of Russia – Personal Obsession versus National Fixation

Oh, it is excellent to have a giant's power
But it is tyrannous to use it like a giant
Measure for Measure – William Shakespeare

The date is 1 July 1709. The place is Perevolochna on the river Dnieper, in what is now western Ukraine. In the previous three days the Swedish continental field army, the most potent force in northern Europe at that time, has been annihilated by the reformed army of Russia at the battle of Poltava. The Swedish army's supply train has been ambushed and the soldiers are starving. The Swedish besiegers of Poltava are now threatened by a

227

relieving Russian army three times the size. This had happened some years before and the Swedes had been victorious, but now the boot is on the other foot; this is a different Russian army – organised on Western lines. No-one, least of all the two leaders, realises how significant these last three days will become in the history of Western Europe.

Offering battle against a much bigger army, with updated weaponry and better led than before, was an act of Swedish desperation, but there seemed no alternative. Utterly defeated, when earlier in the conflict it seemed they would triumph yet again over Peter the Great's numerically superior forces, the stupefied remnants of the Swedish army retreated south towards Cossack territory, where they hoped for succour. Charles XII, the Swedish king, was still in his twenties and a mercurial, stubborn, brilliant and inspirational leader. He had been wounded in the foot in a skirmish a few days before, and had not led his army from the front as he usually did, motivating his forces with his sometimes reckless bravado. These few days marked the turning point in the balance of power in northern Europe, the beginning of the decline of the Swedish Empire and the rise to European prominence of Russia.

Charles forded the Dnieper with an escort of 1,500 cavalry, mostly Cossacks, into what they hoped would be friendly Ottoman-occupied territory, leaving orders that his general Adam Lewenhaupt would follow him with the rest of his battered forces, including the shattered remnant of the Swedish infantry that had loyally followed him for so many years. Knowing that the victorious Russians must be approaching, Lewenhaupt, commanding Charles's demoralised rearguard, concluded that his position was hopeless. If he offered battle he would have to fight with his back to a wide river, utterly isolated, against a highly motivated and much bigger army bent on revenge. He was hundreds of miles away from Swedish territory and any help. A meeting between the senior officers concluded that fighting would be futile. All they could do was surrender and hope that Peter's forces would be merciful. In the event the Russians didn't massacre his forces. They were interned and mostly vanished into the vast hinterland; some became slave labour in the building of St Petersburg, the very thing Charles was trying to prevent. Very few found their way back home. Some ten years later the faithful general died, still a Russian captive, deserted by his king.

Charles XII was left with almost nothing of the extraordinary army that he and his father had created, and with which he had overwhelmed Peter's forces at Narva in 1700. But was he discouraged? Here was a man whose occupation, to almost the exclusion of anything else, was fighting. The Ottomans welcomed him, and thought that he would be an asset to the Turkish forces in future campaigns against Russia. The Janissaries attached to him revelled in the constant action of their restless, charismatic leader-cum-prisoner, whom they called Iron Head. 'With a king like this, we can conquer the world', one of them is supposed to have exclaimed. Whether this was reported to the sultan, Ahmed III, is unclear, but Charles's constant scheming for his personal military agenda tried the Turkish court's patience. Even in a potentially hostile area Charles wouldn't curtail his intrigues, and he badgered a reluctant Ahmed into declaring war on Russia in late 1710. Despite the sultan's misgivings, the Turks defeated the Russians a year later; any more military reverses and Russia was more in danger of being overwhelmed by the Turks than at any subsequent time in Peter's life. However, Ahmed had had enough of the war and quickly came to terms with Peter, to Charles's evident exasperation. After five years as an increasing irritant to the sultan, a plot to kill Charles was attempted. An Ottoman army contingent forced its way into his redoubt at Bender (now Bendery in Moldavia) on 1 February 1713, and after a desperate fight with fewer than fifty companions against several hundred Turks he barely escaped with his life. The king was now kept under house arrest in Constantinople.

Eventually Charles succeeded in obtaining his release; we can assume that the sultan was relieved to see him go. Crossing hundreds of miles of now hostile Europe, on horseback and in disguise in less than three weeks, he found that his military adventures had bankrupted his country, both monetarily and in manpower. By the time it ended in 1721, the Great Northern War had cost Sweden as many as 200,000 men out of a total population of less than two million; a whole male generation sacrificed to the Swedish king's nationalist, military and expansionist obsession, which some contemporaries said bordered on madness. Even with these crippling losses obvious to him, he was not deterred, leading his forces in raids against Norway. Yet even Charles's charmed life had to come to a violent end, as it did at the siege of the fortress of Fredriksten in the south-eastern Norwegian town of Halden in November 1718. This was Charles's desperate attempt to take pressure off other parts of the Swedish empire, which were being threatened again by Denmark. It is unclear whether the holes in his head were created by a bullet fired by the enemy or by an assassin on his own side. The king was thirty-six years old and had been militarily active for over half his life. As soon as his death became public knowledge within the army, the Swedes gave up their hard-won blockade and took their dead leader home. They saw no point in prolonging their agony.

Charles's death signalled not only the end of Sweden as a significant economic and military power but also the beginning of the end of the Swedish monarch's role as driving force in the country. Charles refused to marry; there were not even illegitimate heirs. His successor, his sister Ulrika Eleonora, although wanting to continue her brother's absolutism, had to concede some regnal powers to the national parliament; she become more of a figurehead, and in the end she abdicated in favour of her utterly ineffectual husband, Frederick I. It was the end of the line of strong Swedish monarchs and their empire, which had been expanding for a hundred years, and the end of the attempt to keep the eastern Baltic as a Swedish gulf, against which most other countries with a border on the Baltic had allied themselves.

In 1700 the thinking was that Sweden as a military power would be fatally weakened by such a young and inexperienced leader. This was proved wrong by the first decade of conflict. Charles had come to the throne at the age of fifteen on the death of his father in 1697. At the precise moment of his coronation he is said to have taken the crown from the Archbishop of Stockholm and crowned himself. From that day to his death he would not be told what to do; he ruled as a complete autocrat and no-one could disagree with him. The Swedish population, especially the men, were his, almost in a feudal sense – utterly subject to his preoccupations, whims and fancies, with ultimately appalling consequences.

His modern-style portrait shows a lean young man in dress uniform without the traditional armour, with a determined and shrewd face. He proved intelligent and a quick learner; he had been well trained in the social and military reforms of his father, Charles XI. He was a forward-looking king, interested in scientific research and fascinated by mathematics; but those talents were sacrificed in favour of his military adventures. Being possessed of a whirlwind energy, reminiscent of his hero Alexander the Great, within three years he had embarked on a series of continental campaigns against Denmark and Norway, Saxony, Poland and Russia, which became known as the Great Northern War. He was not to see his capital again for fourteen years.

Charles demonstrated that he was a master military strategist even in his teens. By August 1700 Denmark and her ally, Norway, had been knocked out of the war. Immediately Charles turned his attention to Peter I of Russia, whose forces had invaded the Swedish territories of Estonia and Livonia, not expecting that Denmark/Norway would succumb so soon. On 20 November at Narva (still today on the Russian-Estonian border), after a long, swift voyage from Denmark, Charles's 8,000 tired Swedes routed the huge Russian army, which was besieging the city, in a blinding snowstorm. The Russians lost over 17,000 men at a cost of less than a thousand to the Carolean army. There were so many Russian prisoners that the Swedes couldn't guard or provide for them. They kept the Russian officers, the ordnance, the treasury and the banners, but they had to let the rank and file go. It was an utter humiliation for Peter the Great, who had absented himself from the fray, and one from which he learned much about military organisation. The Swedish soldier was confirmed to be the best trained and the most efficient fighting man in the Western world at that time, and Peter resolved to make root and branch reforms of his army and navy.

Charles then turned his attention to Poland, seeking total victory. He had already declared to Voltaire, 'I have resolved never to start an unjust war, but never to end a legitimate one except by defeating my enemies.' There were always more enemies and continuous unfinished business; he was impervious to the social and economic suffering he was causing. This was Charles, and therefore Sweden, against the rest of the Baltic nations. Wherever he campaigned in the first years of the eighteenth century he was successful, but his supply lines became too long and dangerous and he was never able to control what happened in his newly conquered territories: he couldn't be everywhere at once. Charles may have achieved a smashing success in his relief of Narva, but Peter the Great's Russia was overwhelmingly rich in manpower; and while Charles was busy elsewhere in Europe, Narva fell to a new Russian siege in 1704. The small Swedish garrison fought hard and gallantly and sold their lives dearly; a third of the besiegers were killed, but there was nothing that Charles could do about it. Nor could he stop Peter's establishment of his 'window on the West' – the port city of St Petersburg, a few miles from Narva.

So we come through the years of increasing success and rising national morale, then the predictable decline to Charles's seemingly inevitable violent death: unmarried, childless and apparently uncaring about the long-term future of the country with which he had reached his zenith in 1700 and nadir nine short years later. All the spectacular work of his illustrious military forebears, like King Gustavus Adolphus, killed at the battle of Lutzen eighty years before, and the careful reform of his father had come crashing down. The treaty of Nystet in 1721, which largely concluded the Great Northern War, conceded many of the lands that Sweden had won over the last hundred years, mostly to Russia. The balance of power in north-east Europe was now heavily weighted on Peter the Great's side; the eastern Baltic, with St Petersburg growing fast on its eastern shore, was now Russian-dominated water. So it has continued to be.

As an absolute ruler, Charles XII may be considered to have been 'a victim of his own fate', according to Urban Swahn. He was more a victim of his own initial success; it turned his head, and his country lacked the resources in manpower and reliable allies to sustain it. He may have been 'the most remarkable man in the world so far', as maintained by Voltaire in 1731, but his obsession with the aggrandisement of his country caused that same country to bleed to near-death, never again to rise to the same potency. By his military obsession Charles XII sowed the wind, and he and his eventually bankrupt country reaped the whirlwind.

The main author of the whirlwind was Tsar Peter I of Russia, now universally hailed the Great. Voltaire completed his biography in 1763. Many Russian monarchs have been given epithets; one thinks of Peter's predecessor, Ivan the Terrible. Only one other ruler before him was called Great – Ivan's grandfather, Ivan III, who although styled the Great was only Grand Prince of Muscovy. No other Russian royal leader ever has merited that sobriquet by his country. One of the most massive statues in the world is that of Peter by the Moskva river, standing on a life-size seventeenth-century frigate. It was constructed in 1998 and is regarded as one of the most overblown pieces of vulgar kitsch ever constructed. In a strange way it is rather appropriate for such a larger than life character, who changed his country more radically and rapidly than perhaps any individual in history has since.

He was born in 1672, the third generation of the Romanovs who were to rule Russia until the Revolution of 1917. He was thus ten years older than Charles XII, and was to survive him by nearly seven years. In his reign Russia received the reform that the country had needed since 'The Time of Troubles' nearly seventy years before, when the Rurik dynasty, which had ruled an expanding Muscovy since the twelfth century, died out and the inheritance was in dispute; there was no tsar between 1610 and 1613 and the country was ruled for a time by Poland. Peter was to inherit a country still medieval in its institutions and eastern in its regard. The shadow of the eastern nomads who had devastated the Grand Duchy loomed long in Russia's collective memory. By the time of his death Russia was firmly pointing towards Europe, with a port on the Black Sea and one on the Baltic; a reformed army and navy; and was internally more secure, because many of the noble families had been shorn of the feudal power they had wielded for centuries. In the 400 years that they were to rule Russia, the Romanovs provided their country with some inspired leaders, as well as often being ruthless autocrats; but as much as there were many talented rulers, there were also some pathetically ineffective individuals.

Peter was the only son of Alexis I's second marriage. Peter's father died in 1676. The four male children of his first marriage were feeble, either dying early or being mentally unstable and sickly. Ivan V was twenty-nine at his death; Dmitri hardly lasted a year; Alexei was fifteen when he died; and Feodor was twenty-one. Even in an age where Russian adults rarely passed the age of fifty, this was a disaster for the royal inheritance. At the age of ten, although he remained fond of him, Peter had to endure his half-brother, who might have been epileptic and was certainly mentally unbalanced, inheriting the throne from his elder brother, who had had mental difficulties himself and whose health was marginal. The two elder brothers were not able to rule on their own (contrast the adolescent Charles XII) and so regents were appointed. Feodor was nominally on the throne for six years. When he died there were riots on the streets; the young Peter witnessed some of the brutalities. This experience must have had an effect on his future conduct.

Because Ivan was older he was therefore senior, but it was obvious even at the age of ten that Peter was far more competent to rule, and they were crowned as joint tsars: Ivan, reluctant as the first tsar, and Peter, frustrated as a subordinate tsar. Ivan's regent, his elder sister Sophia and Peter's half-sister, could see that the young man was becoming far more incompetent physically and mentally as the days progressed. If the tsar died then her future in power would be in serious doubt.

Peter was restless, lively and physically arresting. He is supposed to have been well over 6ft tall, but was described as having a head too small for his height and tiny, thin feet. His health, like that of many of the Romanovs, was never robust, and he did not help it by the way he punished his body through hard manual labour, long periods with little sleep and alcohol-fuelled orgies. He was a victim of venereal diseases – certainly syphilis and possibly gonorrhoea, and all the cumulative complaints brought on by years of an unbalanced diet. Even if he displayed facial tics and evidence of *petit mal* epilepsy, his intellect was certainly in no doubt. In stark contrast, by 1694 poor Ivan was described as senile, paralytic and almost blind; and Peter had managed to get his half-sister immured in a nunnery. However, his mother took over the reins, and when Ivan finally gave up the struggle for his pathetic life two years later, to Peter's obvious distress, there was another riot by the Moscow military elite, the Streltsy, against his mother's family. This, the second Streltsy uprising, cost two of Peter's mother's relatives their lives before his eyes. His revenge was swift and brutal. Many of the Streltsy were rounded up and executed under Peter's supervision; some say he wielded an axe on bowed necks with unbridled enthusiasm. He was twenty-one years old. He was going to be in charge.

The Russians have always respected physical strength, often manifested in acts of excessive, sometimes bestial cruelty over potential rivals in their leaders. Iosef Vissarionovich Dzugashvili, a Georgian peasant who controlled the Soviet Union for twenty-five years until 1953, assumed the sobriquet Stalin – a combination of steel and Lenin – and included torture, terror and mass murder in his portfolio of weapons that kept him in power. To this day many older Russians remember the Soviet regime with affection, and regard that paranoid monster as 'Uncle Joe', the genial, sagacious, patient patriarch who thought so much about them and did everything for them.

Peter, like his distant ancestor Ivan the Terrible, displayed a dark, psychotic side to his character, which manifested itself in extremes of personality, uncontrollable anger, unpredictable behaviour and sometimes bad judgement. This may have been because both were seriously ill with brain fever in their youth. It could have been encephalitis. As an intelligent boy with incompetent brothers on the throne, Peter must have been a focus of many power struggles between the great families – the Romanovs, his father's family, and the Naryshkins, his mother's. In the Streltsy riots of 1682 she lost two brothers and had to hide Peter, who not for the first time in his short life was in fear for his existence. His mother died in two days in 1694, which even in those days of crude medicine must have aroused suspicion.

These traumatic events must have made Peter more impervious to mental and physical pain, both given and received. He seemed to enjoy watching torture, enjoying thinking up inventive ways to cause agony before death. Glebov, a lover of Peter's first wife, was impaled outside her bedroom window so that for hours, perhaps days, she could hear his agonised screams; he was dressed in a fur coat to prolong his suffering in the depths of a Russian winter. Willem Mons was hanged, drawn and quartered for being on too good terms with Peter's second wife, Catherine. Peter caused his son Alexis to be tortured and beaten to death, because for years he would not comply with his father's wishes.

Like Ivan the Terrible, Peter enjoyed extremes of behaviour, often involving religious parody in long orgies, and always fuelled by enormous quantities of alcohol. His body was never as resilient as he thought it was (again like Ivan), and could not cope with such sustained punishment. He was old before his time. In later life Peter suffered severely from bladder stones; his post-mortem revealed gangrene of the bladder, disease of the urinary tract and cirrhosis of the liver.

Many of his entertainments were gross in nature. As a child, Peter was drawn in a sleigh by a team of dwarfs and physical freaks, which made farmyard noises and broke wind to his obvious delight. Bizarre behavioural excess developed in his adulthood into anti-Church ceremonies – where clerics and their rituals were mercilessly and ever more crudely lampooned. Peter formed the Synod of the Most Drunken Fools and Jesters in 1692 and drew up this bizarre organisation's rules, the first of which was 'to get drunk every day and never go to bed sober'. The synod was presided over by Zutov, Peter's old tutor, who was slipping into undignified senility. Peter organised a marriage for the bewildered old man with a young widow some years later, and managed to find an even older, blind and deaf individual to 'marry' them. This was Peter's way of amusing himself; he didn't consider that it was uncivilised to bully, denigrate and otherwise make fun of his subjects. This was just what a Russian autocrat did. Ivan had declared, eighty years before, 'The monarch can exercise his will over all the slaves whom God has given him ... God Himself orders that you obey your prince blindly.' It was not unusual in Russia in Ivan's time, or Peter's: serfdom was not abolished until 1861. This Rabelaisian burlesque savagery is often considered essentially Russian; the philosopher and philologist Mikhail Bakhtin, writing during the Stalinist tyranny in the 1930s, surely a time for black humour in Russia, links affirmation through degradation in his theories of the 'carnivalesque'. Peter reviewed the rules for the synod a couple of years before he died, showing that this satiric humour remained important to him.

Peter's drastic reforms and his iron will hauled a reluctant Russia from its medieval Asian coils and laid the foundations of a modern European state. He personified the change. A picture of him in the 1680s shows him in his traditional coronation robes, which were Eastern, traditional and medieval; the famous

Kneller portrayal of 1697 on his visit to England, where he saw the development of a constitutional monarchy, show him symbolically in medieval armour but with a modern face – demonstrating the transition from the old approach to kingship to the new. Subsequent portraits show him as a Western gentleman – not even royal – in a largely unadorned contemporary frock coat and sporting a clipped moustache, reminiscent of a young Louis XIV of France or Charles II of England.

The army was reformed on the Swedish lines of Charles XI and XII; Peter's statement after Narva that he was 'well aware that the Swedes will defeat us for years to come, but eventually they will teach us how to defeat them' was prophetic. However, he could overreach himself, as he did after Charles's defeat at Narva and was very nearly overcome by the Turks in 1711. The ramshackle state bureaucracy was forced to be more accountable and efficient. He was the first ruler of Russia to travel abroad extensively to improve his country internally; he visited Holland, Germany and England and was feted in each place; he learnt practically, from first principles, how to build ships, organise docks and trade (and pull teeth). He earned his rise in the ranks of the army and navy on ability alone. However, he remained the king; therefore a despot, like his ancestor Ivan and his own descendants; the responsibility and relative success or failure of each restructuring devolved utterly upon him, in the face of constant conservative opposition. The relentless pressure must have been intolerable. Perhaps it is no wonder that the stress and fatigue accentuated some of his more bizarre recurrent mental conduct.

Charles and Peter were contemporaries. Voltaire wrote their biographies in 1731, thirteen years after Charles's death, and in 1759, thirty-five years after

Peter's. He compares them at the time just before the battle of Poltava: Charles is famous because of his nine years of victories; Peter is renowned because he has learned in those nine years how to completely defeat him. Charles has a personal agenda; Peter's agenda is to improve his country. Voltaire understood the theory of benevolent despotism as advocated by Diderot, but he was aware of what would happen to a country, especially of limited resources, when that power was invested in one man. Charles was the seeming expansionist saviour and eventual destroyer of his country; Peter saved his country by changing its geographical and philosophical focus to the West.

In defeating Charles at Poltava, Peter demonstrated how his ruthless will had resurrected Russia to Sweden's permanent detriment. At different times both were thought mad in their single-mindedness and bizarre behaviour. Charles had too much power and too few resources to sustain his personal ambition; just like Alexander, his country could not sustain the position his military genius had won. It was doomed to eventual failure. Peter's powers were his seemingly limitless personal and national resources, and his dominance of national institutions and customs, combined with his ruthless will to wrench his country from its moribund self-regarding traditions into what he knew could be the premier power in Eastern Europe. After his death Russia continued to expand until it became known as 'the sleeping giant'; Sweden's decline as a military power ensured the complete curtailment of the power of the monarchy with regard to its direction of foreign and domestic policy, and its future extraordinary concentration on the defence of its political neutrality.

Chapter 10
The Spanish Bourbons –
A Royal Disaster

A family with the wrong members in control
George Orwell (speaking of the British Royal Family)

When Spain's version of God's representative on Earth, the mental and physical incompetent King Carlos II, finally met his maker in November 1700, after over thirty years of hovering close to death, he willed his Spanish throne to the Bourbons of France. He was not even able to father an heir – the prime function of anyone, let alone any king – and with his long-anticipated demise, the moribund life of the Spanish branch of the great Habsburg family guttered out. The inheritance of the Bourbons was inevitably disputed, leading to the War of the Spanish Succession which, from its outset in 1701, was a military disaster for France. Time and again, France and her allies were beaten on battlefields in Europe by John Churchill, the Duke of Marlborough and his confederates. When all sides were exhausted and nearly bankrupt, human misery had cut a swathe through mainland Europe and thousands of military and civilian lives had been extinguished. The Treaty of Utrecht in 1713 confirmed many British colonial gains and that the thrones of France and Spain should be forever separate. This confirmed Philip V of Bourbon on the throne that he had already occupied for the past thirteen years.

If Carlos II, the runt of the Spanish Habsburgs, was inept, Philip was little better. His ancestry was also questionable in its physical and mental capacity. However, he was extremely highly sexed, if not very physically attractive; the Spanish were sure that there would at least be some continuity in the new royal family. How competent as a ruling dynasty they were to be they did not know. Philip V was Duke of Anjou in his own right, through his Bourbon ancestry. With family connections to the ancient Capetian dynasty, he was part of the oldest ruling family in Europe. But the Bourbons' genetic heritage was close to collapse and the family was often plagued by psychological instability and physical shortcomings. No-one knew it more than his grandfather, Louis XIV; he is reported to have told his grandson on his accession to the Spanish throne: 'No other person will tell you what I can say to you. You yourself are witness of the nervous disorders originating in the indolence of the Kings, your predecessors; take warning by their example and remedy, by an opposite conduct, the ruinous effects which they have entailed in the Spanish monarchy. But I confess to you with concern, that while you freely expose yourself to the perils of war, you want courage to combat this odious vice, which overpowers and prevents you from applying [yourself] to business.'

It was all too apparent, if he observed his immediate relatives. Philip's intelligent cousin, Louis II de Bourbon, Prince of Conde, called Monsieur le Duc in his lifetime and a Prince of the Blood, displayed graphic eccentricities of physique – little more than a dwarf in height, with a yellow-complexioned head far too big for his tiny body. In the early years of the eighteenth century he was to become increasingly deranged, and he died early in 1710, making frightening facial expressions. Conde's father was considered insane for much of his life and had gone the year before, howling like a wolf. Louis' sisters were also very small in stature: some say that they were hunchbacked. In her 1968 biography of Louis XIV, Nancy Mitford calls them 'little black beetles'.

Philip, although not insane in the strict clinical sense when he ascended the throne, soon displayed signs of manic depression and delusion. He was vain, solitary and retiring; he did not like company and depended on a tiny coterie of relatives, family and advisors, notably the formidable French Marie-Anne de la Tremouille, Princesse des Ursins (or Orsini), who made herself indispensable to Philip and, by doing so, mentally emasculated him. Philip was also unfortunate in his marriages. His first wife was his sister-in-law, Maria Luisa of Savoy, an intelligent and lively girl. She was horrifyingly young when they married in 1701, and she persuaded him to play some of her nursery games, which distracted him from his routines in the dark, austere and enervated Spanish court; but she died in 1714 aged only twenty-six. She was very popular among the Spanish and deeply mourned, even by her husband, who by the time of her funeral had been persuaded back to his routine of the chase. 'The king of Spain was much moved, but somewhat in the royal manner,' observed the Duc de Saint-Simon, French ambassador in Spain. 'He gazed after it [the funeral procession]; followed it with his eyes and then went back to his hunting. Princes, they are human.' Philip had depended on her; despite her tender years, she had been his regent (advised by Marie Anne) when he was involved in the war of the Spanish Succession.

Philip was not destined to be single for long. Another princess was arranged for him as a marriage partner – Elizabeth Farnese, Princess of Parma. Completely contrary to her publicity as a plump, docile country girl, she summarily dismissed the Princesse des Ursins as soon as she had set foot in Spain, on Christmas Eve 1714. It was out of the frying pan into the fire for Philip: he depended just as much on his powerful new wife as he had on his first wife and Marie Anne. Regarded by many in Spain as mentally unfit to rule, he began to believe it himself: at no time was he given the opportunity to contribute to the government of his adopted country, and so he turned in on himself and his confessed inadequacies. His mental illness manifested itself in hypochondria. In 1717 Philip thought that he was on fire, as a forerunner to being punished for his mortal sins in hell. He thought that only by his own death would he discover his real torments. His chief minister and one of the instigators of the Parma marriage, the hated Italian Cardinal Giulio Alberoni, observed that 'he has been showing symptoms of insanity, his imagination inducing him to believe that he is destined to die immediately'. When they began to hear this, the crowned heads of Europe started to think that another situation similar to that in 1700 might arise, with the two surviving sons from the king's previous marriage still small children – and no notion of how they might develop, if they survived. But like Carlos II, Philip did not die soon. His life was hell on earth – and the torments increased as his self-esteem diminished.

As the years progressed, the king's depression deepened. Philip's sombre religiosity became another obsession, and he still constantly blamed himself for the ineptitude of his contribution to government. The pain and remorse became so acute that he did not feel he could continue as head of state; and so, at the beginning of 1724, he made a statement of abdication in favour of his sixteen-year-old son Luis, in similar words to another monarch in London over 200 years later: 'I have resolved to retire from the heavy burden of governing the monarchy, in order to concentrate my mind upon death during the time that remains to me and to pray for my salvation in that other and more permanent kingdom.'

The obscure and remote king retreated even further into the shadows in his magnificent new palace of La Granja at San Ildefonso, north of Madrid. Interference in state affairs, especially by the now dowager queen, never stopped. Both the new king and queen were far, far too young and irresponsible to take on governmental 'heavy burdens'; they were party animals and relied exclusively on ministers to administer policy (Alberoni had been dismissed for provoking too many wars to Spain's detriment in 1719). Queen Louise-Elizabeth of Orleans, at just fourteen, never expected to be thrust into the limelight so soon; she simply didn't have the education or the training to cope with her new role and withdrew emotionally, sometimes demonstrating antisocial behaviour: she liked being naked, and burping and farting in public. A mortified Luis had to have her confined at one point, and the royal family increasingly became the laughing stock of the country. This threw his father Philip into renewed flagellation of his conscience; the farce being acted out in the dignified, formal Escorial was God's punishment for his act of cowardice in abdication. Could his son's marriage be annulled, he wondered, even though it should by now have been consummated?

Philip's dilemma was over sooner than he could possibly have thought. God worked in a mysterious way, but the wonder He performed was cruel. At the end of August Luis died of smallpox, just past his seventeenth birthday and after a reign of a mere seven months – one of the shortest legitimate occupations of a throne in modern history. Philip had been punished twice. He had lost his first-born son and heir, and he (or rather his wife) had to take up the reins of government again. The self-restored, self-centred king was still tortured by his inability to rule; his periods of manic depression lengthened and grew more frequent. The teenage royal widow, ridiculed by the court, was banished back to France, where she died in obscurity many years later. She never married again. The queen used her influence to promote her eldest son, the eventual Carlos III of Spain, and his interests abroad, while the domestic economy, never very energetic, foundered. Reform was desperately needed, but the inspiration didn't come from the king.

Philip's mood swings became more pronounced. In 1727 he was ill again, beating his wife as she tried to curtail his religious mania. His weight dropped alarmingly; he thought his feet were different sizes and he could not walk; he refused to have his hair cut (which made wearing a wig, as was the style, well-nigh impossible), change his clothes, or shave for months at a time. He slept less and less and started to re-organise his day during the night. The king's interest in government ceased altogether for a time in 1732, when he took to his bed for several weeks. Sir Benjamin Keene, the British envoy, wrote to the Duke of Newcastle that 'we are now properly without any government, for he has not seen either of his ministers, or his confessor for twenty days past'.

However, by the spring of the next year Philip seemed to be functioning much better, thanks to his young son Ferdinand, who persuaded him to observe rules of decent public behaviour. It was not to last. Some months later he started howling like a wolf at mealtimes, which meant that the queen needed to clear the royal apartments because, as the English envoy put it, 'the queen cannot be sure of his behaviour, she does not keep him within doors, insomuch as they do not take the air in their favourite garden of S. Ildefonso as they used to do heretofore'. His court singer, the famous castrato Farinelli, might have provided some relief; he sang the same four songs to Philip daily for nearly ten years – he thought that he chalked up over 3,500 performances. Sometimes the king accompanied Farinelli's sublime voice with wails and screeches of his own. Often he threw himself on the floor after the performances, yelling and writhing to the acute embarrassment of his family; they were at a loss as to what to do with him. And thus did the appalling story continue, as the king moved inexorably towards permenant disconnection from reality.

Suddenly Philip's torment ended; he dropped dead from a cerebral haemorrhage on 9 July 1746. At that precise moment Elizabeth Farnese's personal influence on the government of Spain stopped. She was to promote her own children from her position as queen dowager for another twenty years. She had seven children with her husband, perhaps as a consequence of them sharing a small bed – presumably to alleviate the king's insecurity. Five of them lived to good ages for the times. None displayed extended eccentric behaviour, but some of their many children did.

Ferdinand VI ascended the Spanish throne under a personal and public cloud. He had experienced a dreadful childhood; his mother had died when he was only months old, and his dominant stepmother regarded him as the obstacle to her royal ambitions for her own children. He had tried hard to maintain his father's mental equilibrium when only in his teens; the inevitable consequence was that he earned his stepmother's further opprobrium because of her perception that Ferdinand's influence with the king was superseding hers.

The new king had a better understanding of what Spain needed, which was a period of internal and external consolidation. His chief minister, the Marquis of the Ensenada, initiated internal modernising reforms. However, Ferdinand could never deal with his painful shyness and lack of confidence in his own abilities. When complimented on his abilities as a good shot he is said to have replied, 'It would be hard if there were not something I could do.' He married Barbara, of the royal house of Braganza in Portugal, a talented musician, when he was only sixteen. She tended towards unsubstantiated neuroses herself, and he depended on her judgement far too much. There was too much of his father in him. Both king and queen were afraid of sudden death, which the queen's chronic asthma and the memory of Ferdinand's father's demise furthered. They were a devoted, too interdependent couple, both suffering from their own psychological problems and each re-infecting the other with their psychoses. Farinelli's glorious voice continued to soothe them both.

When Barbara died on 27 August 1758, probably from an asthma attack brought on by her increasing corpulence, her doting husband came apart spectacularly. He would not sleep and hardly ate, and withdrew into a black despair in the furthest reaches of his palace of Villaviciosa de Odon. This ineffectual monarch, called the Learned because of his patronage of music and the arts, began to be violent to his personal servants. Utterly distracted, he wandered in his garden dressed only in his nightshirt. Like his father when he descended *in extremis*, he refused to be washed or shaved. He would not lie down and hardly slept, believing that he would die if he did. Afraid as he was of death, it did not stop him from trying to commit suicide with a pair of scissors. Prevented from physically damaging himself, he pleaded piteously for someone to administer poison to him. Less than a year after his wife's death, Ferdinand joined her. There seems to be no evidence that he was assisted in any way. He died of inherited melancholia; some would call it a broken heart. There were no children of the union of these unhappy people.

The country had groaned under incompetent royalty since 1661 and similarly languished for another forty years. Despite attempts to reform led by noble ministers, a century of royal ineptitude did much to hasten the vast Spanish Empire's fragmentation and decline. The reign of Ferdinand's successor, Carlos III, is a beacon of benevolent despotism in a moribund dynasty. Louis-Michel van Loo's 1743 study of Philip V's family, with Queen Elizabeth Farnese sitting controllingly in the centre and the abstracted king pushed to one side, shows a set of gentle but not very bright royal expressions. Francisco Goya's 1800 portrait of the family of Charles IV shows them as bored, dim, myopic, disinterested and unfocused. This was an excoriating satire on a despised family – visual proof of dynastic morbidity, if any were needed.

Yet they have survived. Many of the Bourbon descendants physically show the genetic bottleneck of the Habsburg jaw as well as a deep tendency to depression. King Juan Carlos I's rule of Spain as a constitutional monarch since the dictator General Franco's death in 1975 has been characterised by his liberalising of a rigid, backward-looking society with a firm, shrewd and benevolent hand. He is a Bourbon, but not from the genetically exhausted main family. He is from a cadet branch, with much Saxon blood in the ancestry – but is still a direct descendant of Philip V through Prince Felipe, the fourth child of his marriage with Elizabeth Farnese and the founder of the family of Bourbon-Parma.

Chapter 11
Christian VII of Denmark –
The Masochist King

All things can corrupt perverted minds
Tristia – Ovid

The crowns of Britain and Denmark have been dynastically close for hundreds of years. Separated by a few miles of the North Sea, England had been raided by Danes since the eighth century and was part of a Danish empire for a few years in the eleventh. There have been several alliances involving both countries since then, and some have been cemented by royal marriages. Edward VII's long-suffering Danish wife Alexandra made herself enormously popular through her charitable work, coupled with the dignity and forbearance with which she tolerated her husband's many amorous peccadilloes. If Prince Philip, Duke of Edinburgh, now towards the end of his long life, muses on his Danish ancestry, he must journey back over 900 years to when the first of the great North German ruling house of Oldenburg, Elimar, the first count, made his appearance in 1101. From its base on the coast of north-western Germany, the family grew in prominence and influence from that point, and Elimar's distant descendants include all the current crowned heads of Europe. As one of his direct successors, the present British Prince Consort can look back to the time in 1947 when he formally renounced his title of Prince of the Hellenes and Denmark in order to marry Queen Elizabeth II. He must also be aware of the scandals that have affected his branch of the Oldenburg family. Famously crusty, socially unpredictable and acerbic, his demeanour is nothing compared with some of his ancestors, whose behaviour was the embarrassment and sometimes the laughing-stock of the whole of Europe. One of his ancestors married one of George III's sisters, and was demonstrably insane for much of his reign – if it could be so called.

This unfortunate monarch was Christian VII, a member of the German Oldenburg dynasty when they were rulers of Denmark. They had been kings of Denmark since 1448, when his ancestor Christian I was elected to the throne (many of Europe's northern monarchies began as elective). His story is both sad and pathetic, but a lesson to all over-ambitious folk. His tale involved very many people, some of whom were dragged into intrigues and treasons against a publicly admitted mentally incompetent king, who was considered hopelessly unstable for thirty-six years, yet remained head of state until his death. This was a country with many medieval institutions, many of them involving the status of the monarch. There was every opportunity to adopt the ideas of the Enlightenment and provide a far-sighted liberal government, such as exists there today, but because of ossified attitudes among the Dano-Norwegian nobility and the incompetence of its kings in the eighteenth century, it didn't manage to struggle out of its backward-looking coils until much later. An ineffectual autocrat was the nightmare scenario in all countries; Christian VII was just that.

Denmark occupies the northern peninsula and most of the islands that provide a natural barrier between the North Sea and the Baltic. Although part of mainland Europe, it has always regarded itself as culturally a Scandinavian country and has looked north and east, with navigable routes rather than land connections south to the German states. Indeed, for many years Denmark, Norway and Sweden, which in those days included Finland as a province, loosely allied themselves in the Union of Kalmar, despite many international strains and traumas. This alliance lasted over 140 years from the 1390s. At their greatest extent Denmark and her possessions, Iceland and Greenland, Norway and Sweden, were coalesced. At the time our story begins, Denmark still possessed suzerainty over Norway, but to the south lay the rising power of the German states under the Holy Roman Empire. Germans increasingly settled in the southern Danish provinces of Schleswig and Holstein, and the German language and customs increasingly influenced Danish politics. Many of the powerful courtiers in Copenhagen were German-born, and the German and Danish languages were interchangeable at court in Copenhagen, much to the irritation of the native members. The great foreign affairs reformer Count Johann Hartwig Ernst von Bernstorff came from a long line of Hanoverian administrators, and effectively governed Denmark for well over twenty years in the middle of the eighteenth century without learning the native language.

Christian was born in January 1749, the only surviving son of Frederick V of Denmark and Norway and his first wife, Louisa of Great Britain, who was a daughter of George II but of course culturally more German than she was English, and overwhelmingly German in her ancestry. The prince was not physically like his father; he took after his petite mother. Frederick was a stout, rather unresponsive but quite impressive individual with a weakness for mistresses and drink; perfectly normal for eighteenth-century absolutist monarchs. Louisa proved enormously popular in Denmark, lightening the strict religious atmosphere of a rather grim German-dominated court with theatrical and operatic performances and encouraging her stolid husband to be more interested in the performing arts. He founded the Danish Academy of Arts in 1754, perhaps in her memory. She also endeared herself to the Danish court by attempting to speak Danish, when it would have been so much easier to revert to the German that she had known since her childhood; her conversational skills were especially noted. She married at just nineteen and died miscarrying her fifth child, who also died, a fortnight after her twenty-seventh birthday in 1751. Christian was not quite three years old and can hardly have remembered much of his mother, but he must have realised the affection in which her memory was kept. His father had grown to depend upon Louisa; her sudden death left him distraught. He quickly married again, as was the custom, but it was not a success. Christian never liked his stepmother, Juliana Maria of

Brunswick-Wolfenbuttel, a patrician of impeccable German heritage. She never ingratiated herself with the Danish court and unashamedly promoted her son by Frederick, styled the hereditary prince and also called Frederick, who was apparently physically disabled. She was cold-hearted, domineering and sadistic. Frederick V, unable to deal with the change in his fortunes, not so slowly drank himself to death.

As in all cases of insanity, we must consider whether Christian's madness was a natural occurrence. After all, his British cousin George III was regarded as mad, although this may have been the physical manifestation of porphyria (possibly exacerbated by the arsenic given him to supposedly combat it). Were there cases of mental disability in Christian's immediate ancestry? It seems not. His ancestors seem for the most part to have been dull and pious; some did not like company, but at no time is there any evidence of mental instability other than the behavioural traits that came with being male absolute monarchs. All his male ancestors had mistresses, but this was the norm. His female ancestors married because of dynastic duty rather than through any emotional attachment, but essentially seem to have been intelligent, ambitious for their children and generally quiet living. Christian's father was a hard drinker, which over-indulgence led to his early death at forty, but he died claiming never to have harmed anyone deliberately, and was proud to have kept Denmark out of wars and expense through strife and unwise alliances. There are suggestions that he may have had some sort of nervous collapse before his death; he certainly lost interest in running the country.

So we must look at the way the prince was brought up. Royal children were not expected to have normal family lives. A child with a remote father and, at best, neutral stepmother, Christian depended on servants and his first tutor, Detlev Greve zu Reventlow, who was from a distinguished Prussian/Danish diplomatic family and had infamous German Nazi descendants. He was a sadist who treated the prince cruelly, calling him his 'doll' and beating him unmercifully. Christian took the hint: pain was something to which he became accustomed and which he could endure; from which he even derived some pleasure. The regime he endured was dark and oppressive; he was under the impression that he was in prison rather than in a royal palace. Because of his relative physical insignificance he took to playing practical jokes on courtiers to get their attention. He frightened his aunt by blackening his face, jumping out from under a table and screaming at her, and pelted distinguished and grave clergymen with food. This was not behaviour to endear Christian to the court or to his immediate family; perhaps there were some beatings that he deserved. But it is well known that if a physically stunted individual tries to make himself better recognised there will be some conflict of personality. This was certainly the opinion of Elie Saloman Francois Reverdil, the Swiss tutor who was engaged in 1760 when Christian was eleven. He found the prince not unattractive physically or intellectually; he was quite intelligent and demonstrated a penchant for languages. Reverdil's memoirs of his time as royal tutor and then companion and secretary to the young Christian understandably suggest that psychological damage had been done to his charge before he arrived.

Christian was easy prey for his degenerate and irresponsible pages, who led him into hedonistic sexual and alcohol-fuelled binges on the streets; he whored his way round Copenhagen, supposedly in disguise, accompanied and encouraged in his excesses by his new companion, the boisterous young Count Conrad Holcke. The protests of Reverdil fell on deaf ears. There were the expected sado-masochistic elements in the prince's behaviour: he liked to see pain being inflicted, sometimes on himself. He fantasised about an execution he experienced while in disguise, and imagined that he was the victim – having a rack made and ordering Holcke to strap him onto it, then beating him until he could bear no more. He and his fellow roisterers rampaged through Copenhagen's streets in drunken mobs, insulting passers-by and breaking windows. Christian was well on the way to becoming completely physically corrupted when he unexpectedly succeeded to the Danish throne aged just seventeen, on his father's unforeseen death. There followed a period of over forty years where the Danish government was in continual crisis, because of the king's intellectual immaturity and his increasing estrangement from reality.

Young, inexperienced, impressionable, Christian desperately wanted to be regarded as someone overtly masculine. He wanted to be significant: the representative of his country and therefore due respect. The humiliations of his early childhood had already turned his mind. Although he had expressed the desire to govern absolutely, as his father had attempted to do, his heart was never in it. Now that he had power he was able to explore sensuality and depravity without fear of immediate censure or reprisal. His testosterone-fuelled urges were often assuaged by physical combat. Often he was no match for his opponents, and only won impromptu fist fights and wrestling matches because it was worth his opponent's while to lose. The king became more violent and less predictable, occasionally striking out at a courtier, whether or not he had said or done anything to cause offence. At first this was regarded as indulged behaviour and adolescent petulance; the court knew that many princes have been guilty of more and worse at an earlier age, so there was no real cause for concern. A wife and family, including at least one male heir, would give him responsibility and calm him down; Christian would have more than himself to think about. Courtiers hoped that as he matured he would begin to regard his country as an extension of his family, and would therefore give more thought to matters of state.

Christian had been engaged to Caroline Matilda of Wales, a sister of George III, since she was thirteen. Many commented on the similarity in colouring of the young couple – understandable, considering how close the families were. After Frederick V's untimely death he was hurriedly married to her by proxy, to ensure that the British connection was reinforced. This was a good match for Britain, an attempt to guarantee that Denmark would not be hostile in Britain's dealings with France, and also maintaining British political and trade influence in the Baltic. This would change. In the previous fifty years Britain's powerful mercantile marine backed up by a fast-developing navy had proved her the most influential maritime nation in Western Europe. Her colonial possessions, coupled with the huge rise in her influence in India, since Clive's victory on behalf of the British East India Company at the battle of Plassey in Bengal in 1757, was overwhelming Denmark's small coastal trading forts in Africa and India. Perhaps Denmark should be siding more with Britain than with France, which seemed to be on the wane after the exhausting Seven Years War, which ended in 1763 and was as near to a global conflict as the world had seen, with separate American, European and Indian battles.

Caroline was another royal child who had had her future decided by others, because of family and political justifications that she was too young and inexperienced to understand. Many were the family tears when she left London for Copenhagen, never to return. Danish royal protocol meant that neither British servants nor companions accompanied her; it is certain that she spoke very little, if any, Danish, and we can only imagine her apprehension. She and Christian were married as soon as was possible, in November 1766, and afterwards they were forcibly bedded to ensure a succession; she was barely fifteen. Were there already questions about her husband's competence? George III had expressed concerns about the marriage; could he have known about Christian's instability, or was it the unseemly haste of the match, or the princess's age? However, Christian proved his manhood, and in January 1768 the future Frederick VI was born to the sixteen-year-old mother.

To some courtiers Caroline was a breath of fresh air, not experienced in Copenhagen since the death of her aunt Louisa. To others she seemed a dangerous free spirit, scorning the rituals and codes of conduct of the rather stern Danish court. She walked when she should have ridden, although she enjoyed riding and she liked wearing a man's riding habit. She was a good linguist, so we may be sure that she soon picked up enough of the native language to make her needs known. Her singing voice was much admired. As a foreigner, it was natural that she should grow close to a few of her personal servants; a favourite was Louise von Plessen, a relative of minister von Bernstorff (her family had introduced the count to the Danish court) and a lady-in-waiting. She did not approve of the king's excesses with his wild companions, and advised the young queen to remain aloof.

Now a legitimate heir to the Danish throne had been born, Caroline had performed her prime function, and Christian's interest in her diminished in favour of mistresses – especially Anne Cathrine Benthagen, the daughter of a female boot maker and known to the Copenhagen mob as Støvlet Cathrine – Boots (or Gaiters) Cathrine. She was procured for the king by Holcke, having already been appreciated for an extended period by both the British and Austrian ambassadors. Her natural father may have been a member of minor German nobility, while her mother was said to have come from Africa. There were several immigrants from Danish trading posts on the Gold Coast in the capital, and Cathrine was as dark, enigmatic and exotic as Caroline was fair and open. Christian was fascinated with her. Louise von Plessen made it known to Christian's secretary that she disapproved of the liaison and his treatment of Caroline; so did Reverdil, probably directly to Christian himself. Both were summarily banished. Cathrine was subsequently pensioned off and married well – twice.

The practice of the ruling monarch taking a mistress (or several) was not formalised in the northern kingdoms as it had been in Louis XIV's day in France, where there was an official *maitresse en titre*, but it was accepted practice – however much moralists and the Church may have frowned on it. Many of the peerage of Britain can trace their ancestry back to the progeny of Charles II (who spent some formative years in exile at Louis XIV's court) and his mistresses. When the head of the new dynasty, George I, arrived in Britain from Hanover, having imprisoned his wife eight years before for her adultery with a Swedish count, he had two mistresses in tow, one fat and one thin, nicknamed the Elephant and the Maypole. Unusually for the time his grandson, George III, did not take a mistress. Although he met his wife for the first time only on their wedding day, it proved to be a brilliant emotional as well as political match, and they seemed to be extremely content with each other.

With the heir to the Danish throne seeming healthy, Christian's advisors decided that he should take a trip abroad; not a Grand Tour to the Mediterranean to view classical architecture and immerse himself in enlightenment philosophy, but a visit to countries closer to home where he needed influence. So he travelled to Germany, Britain, the Low Countries and France during the latter half of 1768, accompanied by an entourage of over fifty. Among his court were Count Holcke, the chief minister, the able and loyal von Bernstorff and the king's physician, Johann Friedrich Struensee, all of German extraction. As normal, Christian travelled nominally incognito as the Count of Travendal, a district in Schleswig. He did not stay in England long but he certainly made up for it. Not since the licentious shenanigans when Peter the Great visited decades before had so much damage been done. George III was anxious at the beginning of the trip, but the slender king was feted and spoiled by Londoners, with a seemingly endless round of theatre visits, parties and masked balls. Of course he visited the lowlifes too. There is a story of Christian, in disguise, taking a fancy to a dark girl in a London market. Perhaps she reminded him of Boots Cathrine, whom he had tried and failed to see while he was away. Her neckline was low and she was selling cherries. Her lover, a huge Irishman, took exception to this well-dressed dissolute and his familiarity and slapped the king, not knowing who he was. Christian realised that, even though he enjoyed hurting and being hurt, he would be no match for this giant, and apologised. To the great amusement of Holcke, he was extravagantly reconciled with the Irishman, and shoved a handful of money down the girl's cleavage in recompense for the mistake. No doubt he beat a hasty retreat, nursing his bruised ribs from the Irishman's forgiving embrace – and a wounded ego. Although he tried to promote a macho image, Christian was a coward and a bully.

The weeks the king spent in England, far from being enlightening, were unruly and lewd for the most part; the growing anarchy in his indulged mind was mostly given free rein. The lodging first provided was not to the Danish party's liking; Holke remarked that they were too poor to house 'a Christian'. Better accommodation was provided in St James's Palace, which the Danes vandalised in an orgy of drunken mayhem – propelling furniture from balconies onto the street below, like the rock star cliché of throwing televisions out of hotel room windows. George stayed away from his wild brother-in-law and kept one-to-one conversation to a minimum. The royal-sponsored entertainments where Christian was guest of honour were restricted, confined to a ball, a dinner and a farewell entertainment for the king and his retinue. Not that Christian would have been much affronted; he did not care for formal occasions, because it meant that he could not do as he wanted. He liked to be the centre of attention, but (like Peter the Great before him) not always consistently. He was young and immature, and to English eyes he was uncultured and inexperienced; he could be boorish and bad-mannered, but he was not entirely unprepossessing. Many of the courtiers took this into account when making their assessment of him; one liberal-minded lady dubbed him the Northern Scamp. When he went to the opera he leant over the balcony in the theatre with his head in his hands, and stood instead of sitting down; he picked his nose in public and yawned without putting his hand in front of his mouth towards the end of the show. But there were times when he tried to be polite and engaged in conversation with court ladies. Lady Mary Coke, the renowned correspondent of the eighteenth century, thought that the Danish king was able to behave himself and 'act properly when he pleases'. What he was pleased to do was to be popular with the ordinary people, which he ensured by his profligate dispensation of the fruits of the Danish treasury to the London mob. The popularity was not confined to London: on visits to Oxford and Cambridge, where honorary degrees were bestowed upon him (the main purpose of his expedition was supposed to be educational), he continued to distribute royal largesse to all and sundry.

The Northern Scamp was certainly an imp and could act like an urchin. He was a rascal and, although obnoxious at times, had no real harm in him. We hear it now when perpetrators of petty misdemeanours come up in magistrates' courts: 'He's easily led; he's not a bad lad.' But the vast majority of antisocial activity today is perpetrated by those with none of Christian's social status, and although their activities are inconsiderate, there is probably little harm in them as people. But here we are discussing the activities of an absolute monarch, in the medieval sense, over 250 years ago. Although Denmark was not the richest country, Christian had direct access to more money and therefore much more power and influence than the great majority of individuals in Europe. The country depended on a king whose behaviour was becoming increasingly erratic. But because Christian was the king, however incompetent, to most ordinary Danes he was still God's representative on earth and therefore whatever he did he was due appropriate respect and loyalty.

The tour continued across the Channel, and was a social triumph. Feted in France, Christian was allowed to give his sensual passions full rein, but he was not always comfortable in the company of the never-ending stream of actresses and sophisticated courtesans that an indulgent Louis XV provided for his delectation. He began to make less sense in his speech, and the physician Struensee became more important as a companion as well as a protector.

Christian and his exhausted retinue returned in Copenhagen in early 1769, and his relationship with the queen seemed to have been somewhat repaired. As life went on he took less and less interest in matters of state, despite his initial promises, and depended more and more on an increasingly small coterie of companions. The court was effectively alienated and power was held by very few, with the court physician being pre-eminent. Von Bernstorff, despite having governed well for close on twenty years, found his position under increasing attack. The queen fell ill at the end of 1769, perhaps partly because of the strain of seeing that her husband's behaviour was changing for the worse. She loathed his companions, because she could see how they were taking advantage of a mind that was beginning to fail. The British envoy of the time hinted that the queen's condition, while not giving cause for concern, was dependent on that of the king. The queen dowager, all too well aware of her personal unpopularity because of her naked ambition for her son, and the continued public esteem for King Christian, collected a little coterie around her. This group of plotters included the hereditary prince's tutor, Ove Guldberg, and Count Schack Carl Rantzau, whose family the young doctor Struensee had originally ministered to. The queen mother awaited an opportunity to strike for her son.

Struensee was nothing if not ambitious. He could pull the strings of the Danish government by making Christian his puppet. He was a handsome and charming character; this might have been how he acquired the court position in the first place. Caroline Matilda was well aware of this, and submitted to examination for her illness with great reluctance. He seems to have cured her, and successfully inoculated the crown prince against smallpox. He was a good physician, and her regard for him as a professional grew. But such was his magnetism that she soon found herself becoming just as dependent upon him as was her husband; she had fallen head over heels in love with him. As she had never much cared for what the court had opined about her behaviour when she first arrived in Denmark, she was open in her public adoration – to the court's impotent outrage. Struensee had no opposition; the king and queen were quite literally in his hands. Von Bernstorff, despite his exemplary track record over many years, did not last much longer and was forced to resign by late 1770. Ousting opposing commoners and minor nobles from court was easy; Christian's mother-in-law, disliked though she was by the court and still scheming for her son's succession, was a different matter. She was royal; a race apart. She could play by other rules.

Struensee's rise in influence was meteoric; the nine months on tour with Christian made him, and also sowed the seeds for his downfall. He had proved his worth as a doctor and as a student of the Enlightenment. The old autocratic rules were being seriously questioned, especially by philosophers like his contemporary Immanuel Kant, and the rights of ordinary people were beginning to be seriously discussed. This philosophical movement would lead to revolutions all over Europe and the Declaration of Independence in America, much of whose text and sentiments was written by Englishman Thomas Paine. Struensee took the Danish royal couple's welfare seriously, and Bernstorff encouraged them to become more reliant on him because of the increased stability that he seemed to bring them. He did more than that; he became indispensable to them.

As opposition faded away, the young doctor realised what a position of power he had inherited – almost without realising it. He was now the country's sole mover and shaker, not the prime minister. He could do anything and not be censured; everyone had to ask his permission or opinion before anything was done. The student of the Enlightenment had become an autocrat almost by default. Power went to his head, but he knew it was not his own power. The queen was to be his conduit: she could influence the king, and with the king's support, no matter how incompetent he was, Struensee could rule just like an autocratic king. And so, with the assistance of his friend Count Enevold Brandt, an enormous amount of legislation was enacted, some based on the ideas of the Enlightenment. He reduced court spending, cut religious holidays, abolished torture as a form of extracting information, and abolished the death penalty; he also founded orphanages. There was no opposition, because Struensee persuaded the king to dismiss the cabinet. He became the Director of Requests, which claimed authority over all other governmental departments. Nothing was to be seen by the king except via Struensee (who was ennobled on his own suggestion) and Brandt. On 15 July 1771 the king signed a decree appointing Struensee his privy council minister (there was now no privy council) and giving him the same authority as his royal self. This was the pinnacle of Struensee's ambition; he had the king dependent upon him legislatively and the queen emotionally.

For the queen had succumbed to him. Their affair was the scandal of the Danish court, and soon the gossip of the rest of ennobled Western Europe. Struensee gave her extravagant presents and she allowed him unprecedented (and unacceptable) access to her royal company – he travelled in her coach and she walked alone with him. She wore his miniature round her neck in full view of the rest of the court. Even the cuckolded king, distracted as he so often was, was aware during 1771 that the queen's attention was diverted elsewhere – although he was not sure where. He imagined that the King of Prussia was having an affair with his wife; at other times he mused that it might be his privy council minister. Meanwhile, the queen was growing round the waist. Juliana Maria, the queen mother, continued to watch and wait.

Struensee had all his eggs in one basket; he was dependent solely on the king's support for his power. Christian needed Struensee as a barrier between himself and the real world, with which he was finding it increasingly difficult to cope. As long as the king was indulged and not angered, Struensee could do whatever he liked: whether it was legal or illegal or what the king wanted mattered little. The German was *de facto* ruler of Denmark. However, one of his reforms was about to rebound upon him. True to his discipleship of the Enlightenment, he had abolished censorship, which allowed the Danish press to mount a constant satirical tirade against the gross manipulation of their sovereign.

Christian was beginning to doubt who he was. Although he often thought he was a god, as he imagined the French and the English had perceived him during his tour, his slight build sometimes made him think otherwise. He contemplated suicide, but could not decide how to do it. His concentration worsened, and sometimes he believed himself in some parallel universe. He listened to no-one, and became furious if he felt he was being humoured or that someone was not executing his wishes. His world had shrunk to his wife, his doctor/prime minister and his assistant, his chamberlain and occasionally his tutor, who had been recalled as secretary, perhaps to help re-establish some mental stability. Struensee wanted Christian to be weak and dependent on him, so stronger opium-based sedatives were prescribed. These seemed to make little difference: the king's violent episodes against others and against his own person became more frequent, as did his wanton destruction of property. He struck himself and rubbed ice and snow on his body; he tortured himself by pressing burning wood onto his skin. He banged his head against stone walls until the blood dripped into his eyes, and ran around the gardens, seeking to build up his body and make himself a real man. He destroyed furniture, and when rooms had been cleared to prevent more vandalism, he ripped shutters off their hinges and threw them outside. He fought with anyone; there were no holds or rules barred, but mostly he had to win. Once at dinner he offended Brandt and threatened him with violence. Brandt said nothing, although his honour had been slighted, but despite both the queen and Struensee defending him, the king continued with his insults. Later Brandt, without the queen and Struensee to prevent him, challenged the king to a duel. Christian, ready to attempt a trial of strength rather than skill, agreed to a fist fight and was knocked down immediately. Brandt's blood was up: it did not matter that this was the king – and he gave him the drubbing of his life, leaving him grazed and bruised, and as verbally insulted as Brandt had been at dinner.

The doctor's reforms were creating deepening hostility among a deeply conservative Danish population, as was his arrogance. Reverdil, who had known him the longest, felt that Struensee's control of the king constituted an insult to the whole nation. Sir Robert Murray Keith, coming to the end of his time as British Minister in Saxony, wrote in 1771: 'The populace love the King and are extremely averse to the delegation of power to a man whose rise is so unbecoming.' Lady Mary Coke was in Vienna that summer when she heard rumours of a national insurrection against the upstart doctor. The nineteen-year-old queen was delivered of a healthy daughter on 7 July 1771; no-one from the gutters to the court of Copenhagen was in any doubt that the father was not the king, and the French court was alive with delighted gossip. The Danish press had a field day. Even Brandt was becoming disaffected, frightened of the consequences of the chief minister's conduct. In a letter to Struensee, in which he threatened his resignation if his salary was not raised, he declared: 'No despot ever arrogated such power as yourself, or exercised it in such a way. The King's pages and domestics tremble at the slightest occurrence; all are seized with terror. They talk, they eat, they drink, but they tremble as they do so. Fear has seized on all who surround the minister, even the Queen …'

Far from extending the embrace of Enlightenment tenets, Struensee had espoused the autocratic process, which had been the accepted means of dispensing rule, and applied it with great cruelty when he thought it was appropriate. He was hypocritical in the public mind because he was attempting sweeping reforms and forgoing privileges while he was at the same time retaining many of the outward trappings that should have been solely accorded to the king. It looked as though the monarchy was his target, so it was only a matter of time before someone stood up and became the legitimate rival to the usurper's power. Sir Robert Murray Keith commented that Struensee had become 'vulnerable from every quarter, and some who did not dare to look at him now shake off their deep submission, together with the awe which was so necessary for the support of his unbounded authority'. The press fomented rumours that Struensee was contriving the king's abdication or, even more fantastically, engineering his murder in order to marry his widow and start a new dynasty. By freeing the press, the chief minister had been hoist with his own petard. The situation had blown up in his face. The people had turned against him; the king was regarded as being under undue influence, and despite his personal record royal popularity soared; there was no escape for Struensee. The royal couple and its little group of dependent adherents awaited the inevitable.

It came at 4am on 17 January 1772 after the first masked ball of the winter season at the Christiansborg Palace in Copenhagen. It very nearly didn't happen. The king's bedroom door was always kept locked, so when the queen mother, the hereditary prince and Guldberg, together with several others, arrived to arrest Struensee, Brandt and Queen Caroline Matilda, who was implicated in the affair, they were shown a secret passage. The king's personal valet took fright at the conspirators and refused to admit them. They had no authority to arrest the German; the order had to come from the king. If he could be manipulated by Struensee and the queen, he could just as easily be manipulated by his step-relatives. The conspirators were in despair: the queen mother was close to collapse, and her son was in a state of stupor, lying in a nearby chair. Guldberg, in a panic, dropped a candle, reducing everything to half-darkness. The potential new government of Denmark had not made a very auspicious start. Eventually Count Rantzau, once Struensee's sponsor, and apparently the only one of the plotters with any courage left, gave the king's valet his guarantee that no personal harm would come to his master. The valet relented and the door was opened. In hysterics when he was awoken, the king was ushered upstairs into the hereditary prince's room, where papers for the arrest of the principals, including his wife, were signed by him. He could hardly have known what he was doing. Thus the ten or so months that had begun so loftily as an Enlightenment-inspired governmental experiment and in later times became known as 'the time of Struensee', another form of degenerate autocracy, came to a grubby, shabby end in a *coup d'état* that was as amateurish in its execution as it was self-interested in its purpose.

The next day Christian was paraded through the streets of Copenhagen, locked in his state coach, to reassure the people that the royal family still continued. There were four others in a different kind of prison – at

Kronborg, in the far north-west of Denmark, close to the sea and almost within sight of Sweden; the assumed site of Hamlet's Elsinore. Brandt and Struensee were fettered to their beds. Caroline and her baby daughter were not subject to that deprivation but were incarcerated in a poor, damp, cold environment; perhaps her captors thought that she and her daughter might die of disease when the conditions weakened their constitutions. The end came quickly for Struensee and Brandt. Despite Caroline's spirited defence of her lover, Struensee knew that ultimately he was doomed and, while he initially put up a vigorous justification that he was acting in the king's best interests, a hostile court was to inevitably find him guilty of *lèse-majesté*, and Brandt culpable of aiding and abetting treason. He had abolished capital punishment and torture, but in this case his proclamations were ignored; they were deemed unconstitutional. Once Struensee realised there was no possible hope for his life, he implicated the queen. The death warrant was signed by the king, who had been well schooled in the new anti-Struensee propaganda. Struensee and Brandt were sentenced to have their right hands cut off and then to be beheaded on 27 April, the next day. Brandt suffered first, so that Struensee could witness what was to happen to him. The bodies were drawn and quartered. Juliana Maria was said to have watched the horrible ordeal with grim satisfaction, and thousands ringed the place of execution. Christian attended the Italian opera on the night of the sentencing, seemingly unaware that his erstwhile protector was about to be executed. Some years later he sketched some naïve profiles of people in his life, all looking much the same. On the 'portraits' of Struensee and Brandt he wrote: 'died at the behest of Queen Juliane and Prince Frederick and not through my will or the will of the council of the State'. There is also a pathetic inscription that encapsulates his helplessness: 'I would have saved them if I could. It was all done at the will of the Queen and Prince Frederick.'

Within a month (on 10 May 1772) Caroline Matilda was summarily divorced from the king and sentenced to life imprisonment in Aalborg Castle in Jutland (now picturesquely restored as government offices) in the port city at the northern extremity of the Danish mainland. Although her conduct could not be condoned, this was viewed abroad as too harsh a punishment, and George III had to threaten reprisals before the Danish court relented and banished her. George was not prepared to receive his disgraced sister again in her homeland, so on 28 May she was taken by a British ship to the castle of Celle, north-west of Hanover, to live on a British pension of £5,000 a year. Here she succumbed probably to scarlet fever, possibly typhus, three years later; she was not quite twenty-four. She never saw her children again. There is a profile 'portrait' of her by Christian, very much like those of Struensee, Brandt and other courtiers, only distinguishable from the males by her earrings. The date of her death Christian added is erroneous by many months: he writes 9 June 1774; she actually died on 10 May the following year. Nothing is written to tell us how he felt about her.

At the age of twenty-three Christian was still king, but only nominally. The eighteen-year-old hereditary prince became regent for the incompetent monarch, and tutor Ove Guldberg was ennobled and assumed the role of chief minister (although he was not appointed). The real power behind the throne, however, was Juliana, the queen mother. An arch-conservative, she largely rescinded the Enlightenment-inspired powers bestowed on the Danes by Struensee. The nobility kept their privileges – the crown, its absolutism – and Denmark was not to experience a constitutional monarchy until 1849. Christian's son by Caroline, the future Frederick VI, loathed her, and at the age of sixteen was involved in a coup to become regent for his father (now almost entirely sunk in his own catatonic world) instead of his stepbrother. Guldberg enacted legislation (the Act of Citizenship, 1776) to ensure that only Danes should have public office of the monarchy, but the style of rule was much like Struensee's; and he remained indifferent to the teenage Frederick's growing opposition. In 1784 Frederick somehow persuaded his father to attend a council of state to sign a document that dismissed the current administration and appointed him regent. Christian may or may not have understood the document's significance and implications. As soon as he had signed, he hurried from the room in an uncontrolled emotional condition, followed by his stepbrother, who was in the same emotional state because he understood all too well the consequences. As the king had signed the document everyone had to obey, however powerful they were. Both the dowager and her son had to accept the dynastic precedence: Juliana retired from public life, as did her son; and the ennobled Guldberg was demoted.

Despite his lack of comprehension, and the physical degeneration that his mental condition and physical excesses earlier in his life had brought about, Christian was still treated with the honour and dignity accorded to a member of the house of Oldenburg. In the 1770s Sir Robert Murray Keith wrote: 'I was much struck by the venerable appearance of the monarch as by the marked homage and respect with which he was treated ... While in the midst of the most cheerful conversation and when apparently quite collected, he suddenly ran across the apartment and the first person he met he saluted with a violent slap in the face.' Twenty years later not much had changed. The Rev. Thomas Malthus, he of the *Principle of Population* controversy, observed that 'the king is very fond of the parade of royalty, and appears extremely displeased when any thing like a want of proper respect is shewn to him. He is to be answered only by a bow.' In his diary for 30 May 1799 he commented: 'It seems to be agreed that the King of Denmark, tho' by law the most despotic monarch in Europe, has the least power of exercising that despotism.' By now Christian had been king for thirty-three years, but there was no move to dethrone him or cause his abdication – although this was not unknown in Scandinavia, and Frederick as the natural heir could have justified his promotion. The real reason must have been that the government under von Bernstorff's nephew, Andreas, was progressing, and there was no perceived need for change.

The last ten years of Christian's increasingly tenuous grip on the world coincided with the rise of Napoleon in France. Danish neutrality was under strain. The country needed to trade with France, and the Russian tsar Paul, once an ally of Britain, tried to organise the League of Armed Neutrality, involving Russia, Prussia and Scandinavia, in order to ensure free trade during time of war. The British needed access to the Baltic to ensure timber supplies for building warships. Christian's brother-in-law George was still on the throne, although subject to increasingly frequent bouts of unpredictable mental behaviour, and the British navy was the only armed force preventing an invasion of his country by France. The Dano-Norwegian navy was a threat because it could protect trade with France, and Napoleon could appropriate it and combine it with the French and Spanish navies for an invasion force of overwhelming strength. The Russian Baltic fleet would constitute a major threat if it managed to get out of its ice-bound harbours to combine with the Dano-Norwegians. So Christian, befuddled as he was, must have heard the cannonade outside Copenhagen's harbour on 2 April 1801, as the British navy pummelled the Danish fleet into submission.

Christian's ever-more twilit existence faded away at last in the early morning of 13 March 1808. He was fifty-eight. Perhaps it was as well, for the British under Sir Arthur Wellesley, soon to be Lord Wellington, had invaded the previous year with a small but battle-hardened force to neutralise forever Danish potential naval power, as they had the Franco-Spanish navy at Trafalgar in 1805. The Danish army, starved of resources, was easily defeated in the field, and the capital was subjected to severe bombardment before it surrendered. If she deserved one, Caroline Matilda had had her revenge on the Danish nation. Her brother George III might have rejoiced, but he was degenerating fast into his own incurable insanity.

As Christian VII succumbed, his countrymen knew that they had been humiliated by the British. Yet forty years before he had been feted in England; the Northern Scamp had charmed court ladies and roistered in the streets. Much of his ancestry had British connections: his wife had been born in England, and his descendants would marry into the British royal family. How ironic that his country declared war on Britain in the last year of his reign. Because of his aberrant behaviour, Christian should never have remained king, but because of the legal system in

Denmark he did. It was on his watch that the country was disgraced at the hands of his wife's relatives: Denmark would never be the same again. Norway achieved independence, but the Danes were militarily hamstrung and turned in on themselves. The Danish colonial empire was largely bought by the British in the next forty years. The nightmare scenario of the incompetent autocrat had manifested itself.

The British monarchy was already subject to the power of parliament; it took a revolution in Denmark to bring about the same thing. If Prince Philip as the Prince Consort renounced his claims to a throne of Greece and Denmark, to which others also had claim, he can also remember that if it was not for the incompetence of his ancestor Christian VII his story might have been very different; he might not have had the opportunity to wield global influence as the husband of the most respected of titular heads of state. The naval victory over the Danes in 1807 had ensured British dominance of the waves on which her empire depended, and on which much of her diplomatic prestige is founded.

Chapter 12
Maria I of Portugal –
A Victim of her Ancestry

The evil that men do lives after them
Julius Caesar – William Shakespeare

Monarchs, especially those who claim long ancestries, have always been considered as something unlike us – a race apart, blessed by God and wielding God's power, which would brook no contradiction. It is one of the prime tenets of the Catholic Church in its infallible head the pope (although the principle of papal infallibility had been discussed since the ninth century it was only codified towards the end of the nineteenth), and it is thus one of the reasons why Henry VIII made himself head of the Church in England. He could rule with much greater domestic influence, almost in an absolutist manner, when he had the Church, with its enormous worldly wealth, under his power. Before the Protestant Reformation most European monarchs bowed to the overwhelming power of the religious orders who represented the Holy Father, a prince in his own right. Other than him, the medieval monarchs recognised no superior.

One of the consequences of monarchs holding rule by right of succession rather than by conquest was that the succession was paramount – reinforcing the mystique of the monarch and his supreme influence on matters temporal and spiritual. It meant that increasingly Europe was dominated by smaller and smaller numbers of families. This had advantages in that there were fewer rivals for a throne internally and from outside borders, but the disadvantage was that the gene pool shrank, so later generations ran the risk of being flawed in many ways. The situation was not helped by the papacy, which granted dispensations for marriages between uncles and aunts and their nephews and nieces from 1550 – as previously mentioned. Charles Butler, the distinguished Hampshire clergyman, educationalist and apiarist, called the Father of Beekeeping, wrote a religious justification of the marriage of first cousins in 1636. This meant that the risk of genetic malformation was raised geometrically; the bottleneck was awarded papal approval. The practice was abolished as late as 1913.

Consanguinity was and is understandable but, in our society, a heinous practice. There are tribes in other parts of the world who have practised keeping the family blood pure; it gives the members of the tribe a greater sense of identity and reinforces the familial bonds. The practice has been satirised in many works of fiction, in the last few years probably most famously in the Harry Potter novels, where the pure-blood, aristocratic Malfoys (bad faith) are portrayed in the films as having a certain Anglo-Saxon/Viking/Teutonic colouring and physiognomy – father and son being almost too pale and blond – compared with the miniature United Nations of the half-blood magicians in Hogwarts. Geneticists think that the reason there is a relatively small human gene pool, considering how long modern humans have been on the earth, is because our remote ancestors were few. It is thought that a relatively small number of humans moved out of Africa in the first human diaspora. This small genetic resource was perhaps limited further by natural disasters that decimated flora and fauna, like the Toba supervolcanic eruption in Sumatra some 70,000 years ago, when the species was not yet numerous because of the effects of an Ice Age. Like all species that become critically reduced in numbers, humanity is susceptible to genetic dysfunction. As an example, the Ancient Egyptian religion had a tradition of close relatives producing children: the deified nature of the pharaoh meant that he had to produce an heir from his sister or closest relative, also regarded as gods. The contradiction is clear: by attempting to keep the blood pure, the family was risking mental or physical genetic weaknesses, which could perpetuate or intensify in future generations. Tutankhamen's skull was thin at the back, as were those of several forebears, almost certainly because of this, and he was generally physically weak; he had a club foot and his DNA shows that he was susceptible to disease. Tribes in certain areas of Pakistan, where traditionally marriage among first cousins is encouraged, also perpetuate many physical and mental weaknesses.

Endogamy (consistent marriage within a particular class or social group) was practised by the crowned heads of medieval Europe to maintain property and alliances, and ensure a controllable succession. The crowned heads of Iberia were no exception: Maria herself married her uncle; her eldest son, José, married his aunt; and certainly within the Habsburg branch of the Spanish royal family its pathetic results were all too clear. Charles II of Spain was a victim: he had less than a quarter of the potential genetic divergence that he should have had, and yet he struggled on, physically and mentally impaired for decades, with the rest of Europe awaiting his demise any day. Maria I Francisca of the house of Braganza, sometimes called the Pious at home, now more often called the Mad, and the sad subject of this chapter, could not avoid her genetic legacy nor the personal disappointments of her life. Fate was cruel to Maria.

The Portuguese Braganza dynasty was not free of incompetent rulers. Their gene pool was smaller than it ought to have been. They had been Dukes of Braganza since 1443 when Alfonso, the illegitimate son of King João I of Portugal, was given the title. The family assumed the kingship in 1640, with the accession of João II of Braganza as João IV of Portugal, after the country had been dominated for many years by Habsburg Spain. They inherited the crown of a wealthy country. At the turn of the sixteenth century Portuguese sea-captains were exploring and then securing the first global trading empire of the modern world, with possessions and influence all over South America, south-east Asia, India and Japan. Wealth in luxury goods from those far-flung exotic places increased the small country's economic power base – as it was to do for their old island ally in the north a century or so later. It would have been fortunate if the strong economic power base had been matched in wise and strong kingship, but it was not.

Maria I's grandfather, the fabulously wealthy João V, demonstrated increasing incompetence and religious obsession during the last ten years of his life; his father-in-law was Leopold I, the Holy Roman Emperor, whose overlarge jaw caused by long genetic paucity in the Habsburg family earned him the epithet Hog's Mouth. Maria I's mother was Mariana Victoria, daughter of Philip V, the first Bourbon king of Spain, who as we have seen was a melancholic and, as he became older, subject to bouts of severe depression. Philip abdicated in favour of his son Luis I, but had to take up the reins of power again on Luis's unexpected death from smallpox seven months later. The Bourbons had already produced their fair share of oddities in Louis XIV's court, a contributory cause possibly being that they married close relatives. Maria's husband Pedro, who was also her uncle, was a dolt whose mother had been a manic depressive. He was crowned king but took no part in government.

At the time of Maria's accession in February 1777, as the seventh Braganza on the throne, the first queen-regnant and joint-monarch with her ineffectual husband, Portugal was enjoying an unprecedented economic boom which had lasted for some decades, fuelled by enormous wealth from the new goldfields and diamond mines in Brazil. A fifth of all gold mined was reserved for royalty – riches beyond the dreams of avarice. Maria's grandfather had accumulated a vast artistic wealth and now had the money to indulge his mania for extravagant building in Lisbon and elsewhere in Portugal. However, because so much could be imported (as it could be promptly paid for), inflation rose, and the economic infrastructure and the merchant marine were neglected. At home the agrarian classes lived a subsistence existence, while the nobility luxuriated. Brazilian gold could pay for everything, and everything had its affordable price. Old-established institutions like the Catholic Church, especially the Jesuits, exercised rigid control over practically everything, particularly over the Braganza monarchs, whose predilection for religion especially as they aged might be evidence of their depressive nature. But natural resources are finite. As soon as the money supply began to diminish, Portuguese society began to show signs of strain.

Maria's father José was another depressive who was as passionate about opera as he was with his religious devotions. He left the running of the country to Sebastião José de Carvalho e Melo, better known as the Marquis de Pombal. Born in 1699, as minister of the kingdom (a prime minister equivalent) he was responsible for wide-ranging reforms, some learnt from observations of economic reform when he was his country's ambassador in Britain and Austria. These included the abolition of slavery at home and in the Portuguese possessions in India, and the suppression of the categories of pure blood, the *Limpeza de Sangue* – almost a caste system based on the 'purity' (in terms of nationality and Catholicism) of the Portuguese bloodline. He was also involved in the expulsion of the ultra-conservative Jesuits, who had a remarkable hold on how people conducted their formal education and what they learned. Their alleged political meddling culminated in accusations regarding their involvement in an assassination attempt on José in 1758. This also involved the powerful Tavora family, most of whom were arrested, accused, tried and sentenced to be executed in quick time, whether they were implicated or not; only special pleading from the queen and Maria saved some of them. The marquis's most important reforms were the regulation of companies and institutions, in the English mould. He was hated for his tax reforms, which affected all strata of society, but the money supply, once so plentiful, was lessening as the gold and diamond mines became exhausted. Spending had to be curbed and revenue acquired in other ways, especially personal incomes, trading and land. Of course these reforms and innovations were unpopular with the powerful nobles and magnates who might have formed an effective opposition to Pombal. In France, the nobility and the clergy were historically exempt from tax, and further similar reforms led to wholesale revolution within half a century. If Pombal's reforms had not been successful there might have been a similar upheaval, and Portugal would not be the country it is today.

Probably the marquis's most obvious contribution today is his organisation of the reconstruction of Lisbon, after the flooding and fire caused by the calamitous earthquake and tsunami of 1755. Indeed, the Portuguese architectural style in the second half of the eighteenth century is named after him; and the Pombaline Lower Town of Lisbon possesses some of the first earthquake-resistant buildings ever constructed in Europe. With the money supply dwindling, the infrastructure around the capital all but destroyed by floods and fires and the workforce being much reduced (estimates of the casualty list vary but as many as 100,000 Portuguese may have lost their lives), there were many buildings that remained unfinished or where work proceeded only slowly. It is unlikely that the king regarded his minister of the kingdom's buildings with any great enthusiasm. After the earthquake his mental weakness manifested itself in several nervous complaints that included claustrophobia, making his stay in any enclosed space torturous. He and his family, including Maria, had escaped the earthquake on All Saints' Day, 1 November 1755, because he had been persuaded by one of his daughters to spend much of the day away from the capital. He lived, as far as he was able, in a tented encampment at Ajuda, to the west of the devastated capital, for most of the rest of his life. Pombal's new city was forward-looking and far better planned, using Enlightenment ideas – much like the rebuilding of London after the Great Fire almost a century before. Lisbon became a modern edifice with a clear architectural vision, unlike many other European cities that still remained medieval mazes. However, the cost was many of the fabulous artefacts that the royal family had acquired in previous years, which were destroyed in the flood, collapse and fire. The sense of traumatised loss must have permeated the psyche of the king and his successors, and inevitably exacerbated the sense of melancholia from which they all seemed to suffer.

As the minister of the kingdom's power grew, so did the number of his conservative enemies. He would countenance no resistance and so became a virtual dictator, with the king, who had given him the power because he could not handle it himself, as much under his thumb as anyone else. The minister collected titles given by José: Count of Oeiras in 1759 and Marquis de Pombal in 1770. The Tavora scandal and the public execution of their Jesuit confessor, Gabriel Malagrida, effectively cowed the old, powerful, conventional nobility and their Jesuit backers. For the next nineteen years Pombal was supreme. However, he was well aware that his power was only given him through the king, and when José was pronounced incapable of ruling through his many mental deficiencies in 1774 and the queen took over as regent, he must have known that his days in charge must be numbered. During the regency Pombal was ordered not to come within 20 miles of the heir apparent, so allergic was Maria's reaction to him. When José died three years later, Pombal's fall was inevitable; the queen mother and her eldest daughter loathed him for his dictatorial ruthlessness, and especially the way he had handled the Tavora affair and broken the power of the old aristocracy. Maria was proclaimed the first Queen of Portugal and, together with her mother, she summarily dismissed Pombal, who was still vigorous even at the advanced age of seventy-eight. He retired with considerable dignity to his estates and died peacefully five years later. There have been few men with a comparable effect on their country.

Daughter and mother were inseparable, and the queen was much under the influence of her parent. When Maria was not confined before the birth of one of her children, they were always seen together. Maria's father had made her Princess of Brazil, the title of the heir, after her third sister was born in 1746, when Maria was ten. He despaired of having a son; it was fortunate that the Portuguese like the Spanish and British, and unlike the French, did not practise Salic law, which prohibited princesses inheriting the crown; there could have been a succession crisis otherwise. Portugal during Maria's reign was still a rich country, fiercely independent of her neighbour Spain despite the two royal families sharing common ancestors.

Maria was devastated when her mother died in January 1781. Her death was 'such a painful blow', she wrote to her uncle Charles III of Spain, 'because she was a precious companion in every way'. It would have been expected that her husband Pedro would have taken some of the governmental responsibility, but he was not made for ruling. He was not in the least intelligent; some say he was illiterate. There was no doubt that Maria was the dominant member of the family, and Pedro was left to his own amusements of hunting and religion. There was nearly twenty years between them (he was also her uncle, remember), but they seemed to live cordially together and had six children in some fifteen years.

Aged thirty-nine when she ascended the throne, Maria took her role as Queen of Portugal, Brazil and the Algarves seriously. No-one could say that she was a brilliant, inspired leader; but she was sober and conscientious, took her advisors' views and tried to rule as best she could. The surviving Tavoras who were still in prison when she acceded were released, but some refused to leave their appalling conditions until they had been legally exonerated, which in some cases took time. How much help her husband was is difficult to say, but he probably provided the domestic stability she needed and took her mind off affairs of state. He lived a bland, conventional, deeply religious, inoffensive life until his death in his seventieth year in 1786. Pedro was obviously dear to Maria and she reacted in a histrionic manner, mourning her dead husband much as her distant Spanish ancestor Juana the Mad had, banning any court entertainments. The rich court was dressed in black for months and the old nobility, including the Tavoras, some of them subject to odd behaviour because of their imprisonment, lurked in corners like spectres. The court scene had the seeds of proto-Gothic horror. One night Maria collapsed and was observed being carried away from public gaze, almost insensible. That night bloodcurdling screams, including pleadings to Jesus, were heard from the royal apartments.

Two years later in September 1788, her misery was compounded by the death of her first-born – Prince José Francisco – of smallpox at twenty-seven; he had married his aunt, fifteen years his senior, when he was just sixteen. Although he could have been vaccinated against the disease the queen had refused to allow it. Her daughter, Princess Mariana, followed him to the grave in November; she was nineteen. By this time Maria had just one child living out of the six she had produced – Prince João, an awkward, lumpy, good-natured oaf. He would succeed her as King João VI, but at the end of 1788 she was not to know that. For a natural depressive these losses must have been unbearable, a personal and national disaster. Her confessor died in this year, as did her chief minister and advisor on state matters. She felt increasingly alone, despite her religious ardour and devotion to the point of obsession. God had turned his back on her; she did not recognise the few who attempted to comfort her.

The royal family lived apart from the rest of the population, as the special family called by God to supervise the rule over the country. This geographic and political isolation had been encouraged by Pombal as he became the *de facto* ruler of Portugal in the name of the passive king; but from the end of 1786 Maria was publicly seen less and less as her grip on reality loosened and she began to be utterly uncontrollable. By the end of 1790 it was thought she was beyond medical help. In the next year some of the royal doctors thought there was a similarity between the illnesses of King George III in Britain and Maria, so the king's specialist physician, Dr Francis Willis, was sent for in 1792. He stayed for some months, and under his ministrations (notwithstanding the humiliating treatment to which he had subjected George III) there may have been some stabilising of the sick queen's condition. While he was there, the council asked her surviving son João to take on direction of national affairs. Dr Willis returned to Britain in 1793 with little improvement being noticed. João was affable and seemed concerned, but had neither the intelligence nor the insight to provide the country with the leadership or even the figurehead that Portugal needed.

A royal palace had been built on the site of Maria's father's tent-city at Ajuda, in which she took up residence; when this palace burnt down, the whole court decamped to the Queluz palace. Distracted to be in a place which her late husband had enjoyed, and she and he and their family had lived in happily during Pombal's administration, the queen at times refused to get up from her bed. Her screaming was heard often from her light and airy bedroom through many closed doors, notably by the English traveller, writer, politician and Gothic Revivalist William Beckford in 1794/5. At other times she ran distractedly through the rooms of her apartments constantly crying 'Ai, Jesus!' seemingly without hope of consolation – or even a response. The Queluz palace chapel was the most important place for both Maria and her husband when he was alive, and they used to attend mass several times a day – so she intensified her devotions, and her fervid imagination started to take over. Her religious passion, especially after the death of Dom Pedro, achieved manic proportions. She no longer seemed to derive comfort from contemplating her supposed saviour and the heavenly inhabitants; she believed demons from the abyss were visiting her. She used inappropriate language to describe what she saw; an acute embarrassment for the rather formal court. Her pitiful condition shocked Beckford, who wrote how she regarded herself being 'damned for all eternity' and lived off barley and oyster stew on Fridays and Saturdays. He related how she was convinced that she saw a black representation of her father standing on a podium of molten iron with evil phantoms dragging it and him down into hell; a mental reconstruction of a medieval doom painting. The country stood transfixed – impotent spectators of this unfolding drama of increasing agony and desperation.

The council of ministers was left with the choice that was no choice, for its leader had to be either the mother who was raving or the dull son who had little idea of what his role was. They hoped for a miracle; that the mother who had tried so hard to be conscientious would recover. They waited. They waited for years; after all, she was the queen, God's minister on earth, and God would have mercy. She thought that God had deserted her. But entirely ineffectual as the son was, João was at least mentally in this world and so controllable. He could sign official documents and had some passing understanding of what was expected of him; so eventually in 1799 Maria was declared incapable of ruling, as her own father had been, and João became prince regent. The council could have made this decision at any time in the previous ten years, but such was the kudos of the monarch that even a discussion about the subject was considered taboo; and even when it was perfectly obvious that the queen's condition was irreversible, the decision was repeatedly postponed. Somehow the day-to-day business of running the country continued.

A more physically unprepossessing pair than João and his wife Carlota Joaquina of Spain can hardly be imagined. They were married by proxy when Carlota was only ten and they didn't see each other until five years later. Their portraits seem flattering. The princess was the eldest daughter of Charles IV of Spain and had only six great-grandparents (Philip V Bourbon of Spain and his wife appear twice) – not that unusual among the royal houses of Iberia and France, where the fruits of endogamy were all too apparent. She was far less than 5ft in height, had a hooked nose, the familiar Habsburg enlarged jaw, bluish lips and uneven teeth, far more body hair than she ought to have had and by all accounts did not take her personal cleanliness very seriously. Her corporeally coarse husband was at least able to father children, and his tiny, ugly, shrewish, ambitious wife was extraordinarily fecund. They had already had four children by the time he became prince regent and there were nine in all; because they were all better-looking than their parents, there were malicious whispers about their parentage. She was the bilious wasp who goaded many in authority in Spain and Portugal with her meddling in the succession of both countries.

Increasing peril for Portugal was the theme of the next eight years, because of threats from abroad. In 1800 Napoleon's France and Spain demanded that the Portuguese give up their political alliance and trading partnerships with Britain. By this time Portugal was dependent on British industry and trade to survive; the countries had been politically allied since 1373. (Portugal is Britain's oldest ally.) Assuming that the British would back them, the Portuguese refused. There followed a Franco-Spanish invasion of the old boundaries of Portugal in 1801, and the invaders secured the town of Olivenca. This was called the War of the Oranges, because the Spanish commander Godoy sent some oranges back to Madrid after their victory, with the observation that he would proceed to Lisbon.

João was forced to sign the Peace of Badajoz, which ceded the province of Olivenca to Spain (it has been claimed back by Portugal ever since), pay France 20 million francs and close all her ports to the British. This was crippling for domestic trade, but there was no choice. For the next four years Spain and France suppressed all forms of Portuguese expression, much as Britain curbed Celtic cultural representations in the nineteenth century. In 1805 teaching in Portuguese and the national currency were banned; local official government documents could only be written in Spanish. Even though the Portuguese ports were free to the British after the Franco-Spanish fleet was destroyed at Trafalgar in October 1805, the Portuguese felt that it was a return to the Spanish dominance that they had experienced in the sixteenth and early seventeenth centuries.

Insult was added to injury in 1807 when the French and Spanish divided Portuguese overseas possessions between them, and proposed to split Portugal itself into three separate areas that could be more easily controlled. Godoy had already concluded a secret agreement that Spain should take over Portugal as part of a greater Iberia. Portuguese nationality and all that the earlier Dukes of Braganza had fought for was in extreme danger. Without a fleet, and with no opposition in the east since the Treaty of Tilsit in 1807, Napoleon needed the Portuguese national marine force to bolster his Continental System and combat the Orders in Council of the British. While the British held dominance of the seas and trade, the French could not possibly beat them into submission so that they could secure Europe. They had tried to starve Britain by blockade in 1800; now the boot was firmly on the other foot. The British advised that war was inevitable, and what Napoleon could not achieve by diplomacy he would get by the mailed fist. João refused to join the Continental System, and in October 1807 the French attacked. The Portuguese were defending their ports; they had had their noses bloodied before, and there was no point in sacrificing lives needlessly – with the inevitable restitutions by force. Lisbon was bloodlessly captured on 1 December. This was the start of what became known as the Peninsular War.

The Portuguese royal family was in great jeopardy. They may not have amounted to much as individuals (all of them were bizarre to look upon and be with; most of them were not very intelligent and one of them was catatonically insane), but they were the Braganzas – the descendants of João IV, the leader of the War of Restoration 160 years before; enduring symbols of the independence of the nation and culture. On 29 November 1807 a strange procession of curtained coaches drove through the straight and elegant streets of Pombal's city to the new port. Everyone who saw the line of coaches knew what it contained, because of the agonised screeches emanating from one of them. This was Maria I and her family fleeing the country at the very last minute into exile overseas. They were only just in time. The French advance guard arrived the next day, and in a gathering storm saw the remnants of a huge fleet disappearing over the horizon. Not only had the Portuguese royal family escaped, but many men-of-war and thirty-one of the merchant marine had also departed – all that could be requisitioned. On them were the civil servants and the court, some 10,000 people, together with 9,000 sailors to man the ships. The fleet was escorted by a squadron of British ships, ensuring that the Braganzas could continue to be monarchs over all their overseas possessions, but not in their homeland.

The royal family arrived in Brazil on 22 January 1808, all of them sea-sick except apparently the mad queen, who was still pleading for her Lord. On 7 March the family entered the Brazilian capital Rio de Janeiro, which became the Portuguese capital until 1821 – even though the Portuguese rose in revolt in their native country within nine months of their occupation. In concert with the British expeditionary force and despite several re-invasions, the valiant Portuguese army slowly pushed the French out of the country, a process complete by 1812 – by which time Napoleon had embarked on a more grandiose campaign in Russia. Maria was still alive at this time, although how much of the outside world was relevant to her it is difficult to say. She screamed with fright when she first saw Brazilian natives performing a dance of welcome about her portable chair: she thought she was finally in hell and that these smiling, hospitable people were devils come to torture her. A Braganza palace was built outside Rio, but Maria didn't live there. She was confined in a Carmelite convent, where on 20 March 1816 her torture finally ceased, and her agonised cries for Jesus to help her ease her pain were silenced forever.

She was brought back to Lisbon and buried in her own enormous neo-classical Basilica de Estrela, built to expiate a vow she had made if she gave birth to a son and heir. Unfortunately for Maria, he had died in his teens in 1788; another of her disappointments.

Even though Portugal was now free from Spanish and French dominance, João continued to live in Rio. Brazil was a vast area – a sizeable empire in its own right – and the prince regent raised the country's status to a separate kingdom in 1815, before his mother's death. Meanwhile, his interfering wife was campaigning for the Spanish Latin American lands to be handed over to her. She also harboured ambitions to reign over northern Argentina. At home, the Portuguese finally lost patience with their absentee king and his support for an increasingly high-handed British presence in internal and military affairs. Inspired by Spain's successful overturning of regal autocracy, they proclaimed the Liberal Revolution in August 1820, with a constitutional monarchy to which João had to swear when he eventually returned in 1821. Poor man, he had hardly been an autocrat; he was too weak for that: he was just content to be king. Carlota significantly refused to sign, and tried to make her numbskull of a husband abdicate in favour of her younger surviving son Miguel. She reckoned without the influence of the British, who exerted far stronger pressure on the constitutionalists; they forced the now ailing king to exile his interfering wife and appoint his daughter Isabel Maria as regent; this post would have been traditionally occupied by Carlota. The constitution ended abruptly on João's death in 1826.

The incompetent king had not nominated which son would succeed him. His son Pedro had become king of Brazil (João had had to recognise Brazilian independence in 1822) and then raised himself to emperor. The rightful king was the new emperor, who favoured the constitutionalist means of rule. However, no-one wanted the two crowns united again, so Pedro abdicated the Portuguese throne in favour of his daughter, Maria da Gloria, then a child of seven, on the condition that when she was of age she should marry João's youngest son Miguel, her uncle; papal dispensation, as in all these cases, would be routinely granted. As a condition they should both accept the constitutional monarchy. Miguel, egged on by his mother Carlota, who as an arch-conservative favoured an autocracy, invaded Portugal and deposed Maria II. For three years afterwards civil war was perpetrated. In Portugal this was called the Liberal War, sometimes known as the War of the Two Brothers, while the aristocrats fought with the constitutionalists. Carlota died with her burning ambitions still frustrated in 1830; it was whispered that in the end she had despaired and had committed suicide. Miguel was eventually forced to abdicate and was exiled, but late in middle age he married a German princess and, because of advantageous marriages secured for their many children, he became known as the grandfather of Europe. He did not live long enough to enjoy this title.

The second Maria was restored to the throne and married advantageously, thereby securing the Portuguese succession for the rest of the century, dying while giving birth to her eleventh child in sixteen years. She was known as the Good Mother, a title that her namesake predecessor might have borne if her destiny had not been so unkind and her genetic ancestry not so damned.

Chapter 13
Ludwig II of Bavaria –
The Swan King Sinks into Oblivion
and Rises Again

Fanatics have their dreams wherewith they weave
A paradise for a sect
'The Fall of Hyperion' – John Keats

The Wittelsbach family is one of the oldest ruling dynasties in the world. It has been part of the European political scene since the twelfth century and in its time has held sway over great tracts of the continent. It has boasted two Holy Roman Emperors, the first king of Greece after their liberation from the Turks and several kings of Bavaria. It has been related to some of the great European royal houses, both past and present. If there are any serious Jacobite Stuarts left, they would regard the present head of the Wittelsbach family, Duke Franz

301

of Bavaria, as being the legitimate Catholic king of the United Kingdom, as Francis II, 'the king over the water', indirectly descended as they are from James II, the last Stuart and Catholic king of England, who escaped into exile in 1688 in what is called the Glorious Revolution. However, this great and autocratic family have not been kings since 1918 and not considered royal since the last-born Crown Prince of Bavaria died on 2 August 1955. As Dukes of Bavaria they have never laid claim to the British throne, although in the 1920s and '30s they suggested a restoration of a German monarchy with them as the ruling family. The escalating eccentricities of the last despotic Wittelsbachs, coupled with the increasing democratisation of the rest of Europe, hastened the end. This kingdom lasted for a little over 110 years; and there were many times during this period when the Bavarians felt that they were not being ruled effectively, because of family members' irresponsible attitude to the business of ruling a small but rich country.

As rulers of areas of Germany including Bavaria, the family had been in charge since 1180 when the then Holy Roman Emperor Frederick I, Barbarossa, whose mother was an early Wittelsbach, deposed Henry the Lion, Duke of Bavaria from the ancient Welf dynasty and gave the fiefdom to Otto I, Duke of Wittelsbach. So their influence grew over the centuries, and they grew in ruling stature from dukes to princes by the end of the sixteenth century, and to self-appointed kings by the beginning of the nineteenth. Ludwig II was the grandson of the first Wittelsbach king of Bavaria, who was extraordinarily popular with his subjects for the way he made himself available to all classes of the population, often going on walkabouts in the streets and chatting to the citizens about what concerned them. When he died, his son Ludwig I initially followed his father's liberal ways, but by 1832 taxes were rising, the king was becoming more dictatorial in personal demands, especially for private, mostly visual arts-based projects, and his private morals were giving cause for public concern. The kings of Bavaria still ruled as autocrats, despite most of the other European crowned heads submitting to some parliamentary or constitutional reform. The Hembach Festival, the democratisation movement where the red, black and gold that would become the national flag of Germany were first seen, was largely ignored by the king, who was more interested in Classical culture, the increasing power of the pope over religious practice, and beautiful women. His extra-marital affairs, especially those with English aristocratic adventuress Lady Jane Digby and the Irish actress Eliza Gilbert, caused the cabinet to turn progressively against him. Miss Gilbert is better known as the dancer Lola Montez. Her influence on the king was perhaps the origin of the phrase 'What Lola wants, Lola gets', memorialised in the famous song from the musical *Damn Yankees*. His long-suffering wife Therese (the celebration of their marriage was the first Oktoberfest in 1810) rose in both popularity and public sympathy, and provided more anti-absolutist ammunition for the pro-democracy movement. Ludwig's dubious talent for composing doggerel about anything made him a laughing-stock. When increasing civil unrest swept over Europe in 1848, even the king saw that the writing was on the wall. To save the kingdom and its inherited privileges, he abruptly abdicated in favour of his eldest son, Maximilian, the second of the name. Miss Montez, now the Countess of Landsfeld, decamped to Switzerland to await her lover in vain.

The new king was somewhat bewildered at his instant rise. He was highly intelligent and academic, and said that he would have liked to have been a professor if he hadn't become king. He reverted to liberal policies and intensified the artistic and intellectual sponsorship of his father. However, he assiduously guarded the independence of Bavaria as had his predecessors, and was increasingly regarded as a reactionary by the democratic movement for a united Germany. The area that would become the German Empire, dominated by Prussia, by far the largest kingdom in area, also comprised a patchwork quilt of states of different jurisdictions ruled by electors, dukes, princes, margraves and others, some of which were impractically tiny; together with three other separate kingdoms, Bavaria, Württemberg and Saxony, all created in the early nineteenth century and each resolved to keep their borders inviolate. The crown heads viewed even confederation with some alarm and suspicion. Maximilian II was as good-natured in his private life as he was recalcitrant in his public defence of archaic forms of government in his public demeanour; however, his health was poor, but it was perhaps still a surprise when he died suddenly after a three day illness, probably typhoid, in March 1864.

His eldest son, Ludwig, was as surprised to be king so quickly as his father must have been on his grandfather's abdication; but he had been strictly brought up to be aware of his responsibilities as head of state from the earliest age – as much because of his father's awareness of his own declining health as the fact that he needed Ludwig to champion continued Bavarian independence from the burgeoning power of Prussia. He knew that any 'unification' would hamstring any remaining power of the smaller states:

Prussia would suffocate any independence, even though borders might remain, and a united Germany would be an economic and political takeover of the south by the north, with all important governmental decisions emanating from Berlin. So Ludwig was brought up remotely from his parents, spoilt by his nurses and strictly controlled by his tutors, who tried to cram eight years of learning into five. He lived a double life almost from the time he knew who he was and what might be expected of him. He began to hear voices while he was playing billiards alone – the schizoid nature of being a prince and also a human being was beginning to have a radical effect on his personality. Ludwig's vivid imagination sometimes took him over: when he first listened to Wagner's *Lohengrin* in his teens he imagined himself to be the Swan Knight. Sometimes it was difficult for him to differentiate one theatrical role from the other as king. He wrote extravagantly of carrying to the throne a heart that beat for his people: 'I will do anything in my power to make my people happy; their welfare, their peace are the conditions of my own happiness.' His sensitive, romantic nature meant that he was deeply affected by the wonderful Bavarian landscape and local nature, especially by the regal beauty of the white swan, an image reinforced in the medieval literature of Wolfram von Eschenbach. He was a poet-knight who lived somewhere in Germany in the twelfth and thirteenth centuries, and about whose life almost everything had been invented.

His grandfather must have encouraged the impressionable young prince in his thoughts about his function as the future king and leader of his people. Ludwig I was still royal, yet not absolute head of state any more and perhaps more importantly with no real responsibilities, so he must have found it extraordinarily difficult not to interfere unofficially in state and private family affairs, including the naming and upbringing of his grandson. Grandfather and grandson shared the same official birthday (there is a story that Ludwig was actually born at 11.30pm on 24 August and his grandfather had the time officially advanced by an hour to 12.28am on the 25th, his birthday and St Louis' day), and despite his parents' wishes insisted on the heir to the throne being named after him. They wanted to call him Otto: his younger brother by almost exactly three years achieved the name. Ludwig often took walks with his grandfather, as his increasingly remote father despaired of his son ever listening to him. So Ludwig's developing eccentricity could be explained as a combination of nature and nurture.

Ludwig's grandfather became a court social irritant. Even when he was king he had often been shabbily dressed and modest in his appearance, but there was always another Ludwig I, self-regarding and extremely unpredictable; he rarely listened to advice while he was king or after his abdication. Ludwig II's younger aunts tended to be rebellious as well. One of them, Alexandra Amalie, was an enthusiast of literature and a minor author and translator. She was unmarried, but entertained various suitors, including Prince Louis Lucien Bonaparte, being refused because of her delicate health – whether mental, physical or both isn't clear. She became the leader of a religious order for noble, unmarried ladies (surely a reinvented pseudo-medieval institution), and demonstrated an obsession for cleanliness throughout her life. Later she became mentally deranged and thought that she had swallowed a glass piano. In 1875 she died in the palace in which Ludwig was born.

Ludwig was anointed king in the room next door to where his father was lying in state; he was pitched into the public gaze at the state funeral a few days later, walking in mourning in the uniform of a cavalry colonel. He had little interest in the army, and because of his isolation during his formative years he suffered from almost paralysing bashfulness and lack of confidence in public. But he was good looking, tall and glamorous, and the Bavarians, romantics that they were, took to him immediately. He seemed to be a fairytale hero-king, which is what they initially called him – *der Märchenkönig*. Ludwig's outward appearance belied his real character. At just eighteen, and although a good linguist with a mathematical brain, the young king was utterly unprepared for his role in a deeply traditional Catholic country when the political scene in the rest of Europe, especially concerning citizens' shifting relationships with their head of state, was changing so rapidly. He had been brought up in some of his father's neo-Gothic homes, which looked back to a fantasised Golden Age of medieval chivalry, and a society in which all classes knew their places and remained in them. He was as much struck by Gothic Revival architecture as many all over Europe – and he had the great composer Richard Wagner's works to inspire him.

Wagner's music had entrammelled Ludwig from early adolescence, especially his 1850 opera *Lohengrin*; the king deeply identified himself with the mystique and symbolism of the eponymous hero. Summoning Wagner to Munich was one of the king's first acts. They made a strange couple: the young, tall, languid, impressionable king, still in his teens, and the capricious, raffish and revolutionary composer, already in his fifties. It is safe to say that if it had not been for

Ludwig's unstinting loyalty and immense financial support the rest of Wagner's operas might not have been written. The composer's reputation, especially his perfidy, was well known when he arrived in 1864, but he was worshipped from the first by Ludwig. Their letters are extraordinarily histrionic, and anyone reading them might be forgiven for thinking that they were written by lovers. Ludwig's adolescence and social inexperience show in his purple prose. He writes from his Alpine retreat in the Midsummer's Day twilight of 1865: 'The evening star sends his gentle light from afar, showing the wanderer his way out of the valley and once again reminding me of my Dear One and his divine works ... the figure of Lohengrin revives anew in my vision; and there I see in my mind Parzival, the hero of the future, searching for salvation, for the single truth.' A month later he effused: 'I long for you; only when I think of my dear one and his work am I truly happy ... Tell me something of "Der Sieger" [a work later abandoned] and "Parzival"! I am yearning to hear. Please quench this burning thirst! Oh, how null is the world! How wretched and vulgar so many men! Their lives revolve in the narrow circle of everyday banality. Oh, if only I had the world behind me!'

There is no evidence that Wagner's written passions were ever homosexual (as far as we know all his many affairs were heterosexual), but he entered into the written fervour with enthusiasm; after all, it was in his interest. It is unlikely that Ludwig was physically attracted to Wagner; he was thirty years older and those years had not been good to him – while the young king cared only to be surrounded by beautiful sycophants. Ludwig paid Wagner's enormous debts out of his own pocket and showered him with honours, his obsessive nature showing in the loyalty he showed in his continued sponsorship of the brilliant but unpredictable, irresponsible and egocentric composer. Wagner visited Ludwig in Hohenschwangau, which in his opinion was 'the Grail castle protected by Parzival's love'. He wrote that he thought that Ludwig was himself 'in a newer, younger, lovelier, rebirth: wholly I, and himself only to be beautiful and powerful'. Ludwig's adoration became quasi-religious, describing Wagner as 'godlike, godlike!' His duty, he wrote to Cosima von Bülow, not realising she was not yet married to Wagner at this point, was 'to live for him, to suffer for him, if that be necessary for his full salvation'.

In a little over a year the cabinet made it plain that they disapproved of Wagner's influence on the impressionable king as much as they had over Lola Montez on his grandfather: he had been involved in some of the political agitation in 1848–9 in Dresden, and Ludwig's closest advisors were concerned that the easily influenced king was too open to Wagner's socially revolutionary ideas. He was already interfering in domestic politics, purporting to speak for the king. The independence of Bavaria had to be preserved at all costs. Baron Karl Ludwig von der Pfordten, the minister-president, wrote to the king, telling him that it was time to make a decision: 'you have to choose between the love and respect of your faithful people and your "friendship" with Richard Wagner'. The inverted commas implied that von der Pfordten thought that there was enough evidence to suspect that the king and Wagner could become intimate, if it hadn't already happened; a mortal sin in the Church's eyes and one which could produce a national crisis. By the end of 1865 Ludwig had been persuaded (he naturally thought he was being forced) to banish Wagner from the country. Apparently the king toyed with the idea of abdication so that he could be constantly with his muse – but by staying king he would have unlimited means to support him. So the price was paid. By remaining king in Bavaria he did not desert Wagner; far from it. He installed him and his mistress Cosima in a comfortable villa on Lake Lucerne in Switzerland, where he could do as he pleased. Ludwig apparently paid for everything. He visited the composer, supposedly incognito, on several occasions.

Operas flowed from Wagner's pen in the next years, and some were premièred in Munich at Ludwig's insistence. But Wagner had more grandiose ideas. He settled on the small town of Bayreuth, in Bavaria, as the site for a purpose-built opera house that would exclusively present his compositions. The foundation stone was laid on Wagner's birthday, 22 May 1872. He adapted the design without the architect's permission, and the opera house opened with the four opera cycle of *Der Ring des Nibelungen*, from 13 to 17 August 1876. Most of the bills were paid by the seemingly bottomless purse of the Bavarian king. Wagner's last opera, *Parsifal*, perhaps composed as a present for his royal supporter, was written specifically to be performed in the opera house's extraordinary acoustics in July 1882 and, apart from some private performances in Munich especially for Ludwig, that was where it was staged until 1913, when the copyright ran out. So anticipated was the staged opera outside Bayreuth that there were performances in several European countries, including Germany, as soon as was possible, on New Year's Day 1914.

Within two years of Ludwig's accession, Bavaria was involved in something she was not able to deal with adequately – war. The country was desperate to preserve its independence, and so was allied with neighbour Austria against the great north German bulwark of Prussia, for the Bavarians and the other small German states feared the expansionist Prussians. The result was unexpected. Austria had the might in men, but the Prussians had the edge in tactics, training and technology. At the battle of Sadowa (or Königgratz), 240,000 Austrians were initially held during the morning of 3 July 1866 by two Prussian armies, who together comprised barely half that number. While they were so gripped, a third Prussian army of 100,000 arrived to deliver the *coup de grâce* in the afternoon. A week later the Bavarians encountered another Prussian force at the spa town of Kissingen. Despite their attractive uniforms and *élan*, the Bavarians were badly equipped and trained; they suffered many casualties and were effectively neutralised as a military force, with their elderly, aristocratic commander killed in action. Ludwig knew that the uniform did not make the soldier; he was nowhere near the battle. After more reverses in Bohemia and Italy, six weeks later the Austrians were forced to the negotiation table. The king must have been advised that political domination by Prussia was bound to become overwhelming sooner or later, and bids for complete independence by any of the small German kingdoms were futile. So perhaps it is not surprising to record that in the Franco-Prussian War of 1870–1, much against his personal will, Bavaria was forced to side with the big, bombastic northern neighbour against the French, whose cultural legacy Ludwig admired so much.

Already he was unpredictable when his judgement as an absolute monarch had to be crucial to the future of his nation. Eduard von Bomhard, Ludwig's attorney-general from 1864 to 1867, made this significant comment just after the king's accession: 'he was mentally gifted in the highest degree but the contents of his mind were stored in a totally disordered fashion'. Not long afterwards he described the king's behaviour, not knowing the accuracy of his prediction: 'I was struck by the way in which, every now and then, just when his expression and whole demeanour seemed to show contentment, he would suddenly straighten up and – looking around him with a serious, even stern expression – would reveal something dark in himself that was in complete contrast to the youthful charm of a moment ago.' This looked like the beginnings of a dual personality. When it came to national judgement, Ludwig's personal agenda always assumed dominance. One can speculate whether the court medical staff had examined his ancestry, which contained Ernst Ludwig IX, Landgrave of Hesse-Darmstadt, who died insane in 1790, and his daughters Karoline, who experienced visions, and Frederica, who became Frederick William II of Prussia's second wife, and included being nocturnal in her portfolio of eccentricities. All the Prussian and therefore German kings descend from her. Perhaps Bavarian Jonahs could speculate that, because of hundreds of years of interbreeding with a succession of daughters of other rulers of small German states, which if they were South German Catholic tended to be related, the Wittelsbach genetic heritage could well be failing; and generations of *rois fainéants* were to ensue, almost as soon as the Bavarian royalty had been established for long enough to assume some sort of parity with other, much more recognised, imperial families of Europe.

The first duty of a king was to ensure a succession, so it was with understandable joy that the Bavarians heard that their young king had become engaged to

Sophie, the sister of the Empress Elisabeth of Austria. Ludwig approached this adventure with romantic over-enthusiasm. The two young people indulged in passionate correspondence as the wedding day approached, but suddenly Ludwig seemed to have doubts. His apparent passion became purely fraternal almost overnight, and Sophie was rejected. The king's diary shows his relief: he wrote that he had 'got rid of' Sophie. 'I longed for, am a-thirst for, freedom. Now I live again after this torturing nightmare.' The over-elaborate prose and the extremes of emotion show a mind in turmoil, not knowing where it was going, and a value system that was coloured by his selfish needs. The king's fervour had no depth of root, and so leapt up and then as quickly shrivelled away. This snub (some would call it betrayal) did little for his diplomatic standing, but Ludwig didn't care about that; he was only interested in his own quality of life. Although he had many close women friends, including the astonishingly beautiful, narcissistic and mercurial Austro-Hungarian Empress Elisabeth herself (they communicated regularly throughout Ludwig's life), he never married.

Ludwig did not marry largely because his sustained passionate enthusiasm was more for men, and an apparently endless troop of fetching male favourites from all classes marched throughout his life. There were the handsome equerry and great horseman Richard Hornig, the cavalry officer Baron von Varicourt, the actor Josef Kainz and a ordinary servant in the royal household called Alfonso Welcker, but the one he was most attached to for longest was Prince Paul von Thurm und Taxis, from the autumn of 1863 to the end of 1866. They corresponded in the most ardent terms. Paul's family derived its wealth from being the Holy Roman Emperor's postmasters, and is one of the richest families in Europe even today. Not all of these attachments were necessarily physical (the Hornig affair was ended by the equerry's marriage), but Ludwig's difficult nature and increasing paranoia meant that all intense relationships were fragile and subject to petty tensions, always instigated by the moody king. In October 1866 the association with Prince Paul, the utterly loyal squire to the so-called perfect knight, ended. He was bewildered as to how he had offended Ludwig, having said or done something that was so inconsequential that he could not even recall it; but the affair was terminated. Once a decision had been made Ludwig was not someone to be swayed, demonstrating the petulance that had been part of his character since the early days. Even though Paul pleaded for an explanation and another chance to justify his action, he achieved neither. Paul never recovered. He is reputed to have had a drunken one night stand with a disreputable actress on the rebound, who weeks later claimed him to be the father of her unborn child. He was forced to enter into a morganatic marriage with her by his noble family, who then disowned him, and he ended his days in 1879, sad and inebriated in Cannes.

Soon the Bavarian cabinet despaired of the king taking a wife and having a family, and looked to his younger brother Otto, who would be a good match in a few years' time. However, as he matured he also showed little inclination to embrace matrimony; the rumour was that his behaviour was becoming even more darkly unpredictable than his brother's. What aristocratic female would take on such a task?

The monarchy and therefore the independence of the country looked to be doomed internally by the failing Wittelsbach genes rather than external political pressure.

Ludwig himself was little concerned with affairs of state; his agenda was to perpetuate the mystique of the German people by leading it down an inspired road that followed the Holy Grail of the perfect life. How much he owed this to Wagner's flattery is difficult to tell, but the composer was quite explicit in his fawning sycophancy, calling the king Parsifal after the perfect knight who found the Grail. Ludwig had already identified himself with Lohengrin, Parsifal's son, the Swan Knight, perhaps because he spent most of his formative years at Hohenschwangau (High Swan) Castle, a neo-gothic edifice that his father had restored and extended near Füssen, the highest town in Bavaria and close to the Austrian border. Not far away the river Lech, which streams in a gorge through Füssen, empties into Swan Lake. The image of the Swan pervaded Ludwig's life, and in his beloved mountains he attempted to create vast neo-medieval dioramas with himself as the chief exhibit, which would justify his self-created image of the Swan Knight resurrected. His father and grandfather had restored castles in neo-Gothic and Romanesque styles – it was popular all over Europe – but Ludwig had to outdo his forebears. The mania for building began early. Inspired by Wagner and his self-engendered image as God's representative on earth, plans for fairy-tale castles were driven forward largely at his expense. Building became Ludwig's obsession. 'I must build or die', he wrote in his diary. Fantastically symbolic structures were begun, the most famous, Neuschwanstein (New Swan Stone) Castle, was begun in 1868, perhaps in part as homage to his grandfather, who had died in the February of that year, but certainly celebrating Richard Wagner and his mystical retelling of German legends. Ludwig had regarded some of the reconstructions and imaginative pseudo-medieval reinventions of the famous French neo-gothic architect Eugene Viollet-le-Duc, and on examination of his palaces it seems that he determined to better him. From riverside rock pinnacles or in broad plains, increasingly fantastical pastiche structures rocketed into the sky or sprawled their way across over -designed landscapes.

Nothing in the architectural style was new; all was rehashed. They were variations on a theme, that of the perfect knight, his possessions and influence, and through that the amplification of the mystique that Ludwig imagined surrounded him. Neuschwanstein was designed by Christian Jank – more a stage designer than an architect – and is situated in a marvellously theatrical setting from all sides; no wonder Disney chose it as one of the inspirations for the fairytale castle that has become the company's famous logo. Jank also had a hand in the design and building of Herrenchiemsee Palace on Herren Island in the Chiemsee lake, with Georg von Dollman (a qualified architect) and interior designer Franz Seitz. Neither of these grandiose schemes was completed at Ludwig's death, but von Dollman was responsible for the two projects that were finished – the Alpine hunting lodge called the King's House on the Schachen (1869–72), with its over-elaborate interior and the Ottoman-inspired opulence of its entire first floor; and Linderhof (1863–86), the homage to Ludwig's other idol, Louis XIV. It was smaller than Versailles but with a longer Hall of Mirrors, which reflected candlelight many hundreds of times for the ever more nocturnal and solitary king – the Moon King as opposed to Le Roi Soleil. However, Ludwig was well aware of his creature comforts: these pseudo-medieval follies were to enjoy the latest in technological innovation. From the first plans, Neuschwanstein possessed hot and cold water on all floors, electric light, steam central heating and hydraulic lifts. Other palaces incorporated the latest inventions: Ludwig, possessing a distinct talent for mathematics, was an enthusiastic patron of technology and founded several technical educational institutions. It is interesting to note that the court architect, Eduard Riedel, although having been active in his father Maximilian's restoration schemes, seemed only peripherally involved in his son's.

These buildings have fascinated later generations, demonstrated by the millions of tourists who visit many of them. Comments have focused on the extraordinary elaboration of the design, which was arguably to the point of bad taste, and the stupendous sums it cost Ludwig to fulfil his architectural dreams. Of course the expense was the least of his worries; it is the nature of obsession that practicalities do not enter into calculations. Ludwig wanted something so grandiose that it would fulfil his personal aspirations. Indeed, another project for which the money simply wasn't there was Falkenstein (Falcon's stone) Castle, the highest medieval structure in Germany. It teetered on the top of a crag like a Cathar stronghold, just on the Bavarian side of the Austrian border, near Pfronten. Over hundreds of years it had degenerated into a picturesque ruin by the time Ludwig bought the site in 1884, with borrowed money that he had no way of repaying. Impressions for another high Gothic fantasy were sought from Jank and then von Dollman, but even their histrionic designs were too conservative for the king and so he turned to Max Schultze, the young inspector of buildings for the von Thurm und Taxis princes. Schultze was aware that money was running out fast, and so he earned his sizeable fee by letting his imagination run riot and creating a stupendously ornate architectural confection based on what contemporary romantic conceit imagined being a 'robber baron' castle – the essence of the picaresque. He was sure it could not be built, firstly because of the fast dwindling sources of finance and secondly because of the king's increasing mental difficulties.

For Ludwig was growing more unpredictable by the day. Always uncomfortable in public, his shyness became such that even the presence of servants sometimes became unbearable. In one of his palaces meals were brought by dumb-waiter to a table that rose out of the floor, which he laid himself. Like his ancestor Queen Frederica of Prussia he stayed up all night in Herrenchiemsee reading alone with the reflected light of a thousand candles, and slept during the day when he was needed to sign documents or meet dignitaries. The court was in despair. Ludwig had no idea of the expense he was engendering, and the final straw came when a power company threatened him with a court summons for unpaid bills. There was no money left. There was no credit to be had. A king could not be expected to soil his hands with mere mercantile utility companies: he was the Moon King, the spirit of the resurgent Germany, the king of a rich country. He simply did not know what to do, and petulantly threatened suicide.

Sometimes hindsight allows us to gain an inkling of the difficulties of vulnerable people who have been pitched into a situation they don't understand. As King Lear's reason cracks, Shakespeare makes the Fool ask him whether he is a 'madman or gentleman or a yeoman'. Lear replies forcefully, 'A King'. For decades he has had things his own way; he thinks he is indestructible, and has never had to fight for what he believes or justify any of his decisions. In emotional terms, therefore, he has never matured; he has never had to. Still psychologically a child, Lear has puerile tantrums when he is thwarted by his ruthless, ungrateful, emasculating elder daughters, whose motives he has misread so grievously. Madness here is a consequence of his actions, but it is also a publicly accepted condition into which he can retreat, and still not take responsibility for his deeds or their costs. Ludwig came from that same absolutist base, which affected who he was to himself, what he represented to his people, what they wanted him to be and the manner in which they regarded him. As a perturbed Prince Hohenlohe commented, admittedly from a somewhat prejudiced north German Protestant point of view, 'So long as the King is encouraged by the sycophancy of the Court and the Government officials, so long will he regard himself as a demi-god who can do what he pleases and for whose pleasure the rest of the world – at any rate Bavaria – was created.' Ludwig progressively regarded himself as an individual apart. His servants, such as he would allow into his presence, were ordered not to look at his face; his valet did so one day, probably inadvertently, and was ordered to wear a black mask thereafter. Ludwig doled out punishments to his servants for misdeeds that none of them knew they had committed – but they were very rarely carried out. He preferred to travel at night no matter the weather, and winters were cruel in the mountains. Seeing his ministers in the middle of the night, Ludwig often did not listen to what they had to say but ordered them to facilitate schemes of his own invention. He was beginning to doubt the validity of the world he lived in, and sent courtiers all over the world to find a place where he could live in peace and undisturbed seclusion.

Perhaps that would have been possible if he could have abdicated, but there was no one of his generation to step into his shoes. His brother Otto was in no condition to rescue the Bavarians: he was in a dreadful state, the king writing to his former governess, Baroness Leonrod in January 1871: '[He] seems to become worse and worse daily. In some respects he is more excitable than Aunt Alexandra, and that is saying a great deal. He often does not go to bed for forty-eight hours. He did not take his boots off for eight weeks … he makes terrible faces, barks like a dog, and at times says the most indecorous things and then is quite normal again for a while.' Otto's last official engagement was the witnessing of the birth of the German Empire later in the year (Ludwig flatly refused to go). His behaviour continued to be embarrassing for both the royal family and the country. In the Corpus Christi celebrations of 1875 he broke through a cordon of soldiers and threw himself on the steps before the high altar of Munich Cathedral, confessing his sins in a loud voice until he was persuaded to be ushered into the nearby vestry. The British *chargé d'affaires* in Munich at the time remarked primly that 'it is certainly as well that this scene did not occur in St George's Chapel, Windsor'. Soon afterwards the royal family had to bow to the inevitable, and after examination by the royal doctors Otto was packed off to Nymphenburg, where he was born, and thence to Furstenried Palace, where he had spent much of his childhood, under the supervision of world pioneer psychiatrist and neurobiologist Dr Johan Bernard von Gudden. He remained there under close watch until his death over thirty years later.

If it hadn't been for Otto's hopeless psychiatric condition, perhaps Ludwig would not have been allowed to remain on the throne for so long. When can a monarch who has abdicated responsibility be forced to abdicate the throne, the source of his power? He was not physically the man he had been when he assumed the throne to so much good will, having become paunchy and unhealthy-looking; photographs show a man looking ever more at unease with himself. During the 1880s, as his thirties progressed, the king became a bloated, egocentric caricature of the handsome, somewhat effete young man who had espoused such ideals as leader of his people twenty years before. The physical evidence of the passage of time and the fruits of his hedonism were all too clear. Contemporary likenesses show his hair thinning at the front, a large goatee beard covering the sagging chin, and his eyes, once clear and gazing into the middle distance, apparently seeking the vision of his destiny, smaller and more suspicious. The photograph of his body lying in state shows a tall but corpulent figure. Ludwig was hardly seen in public, which increased bad feeling. His great friend and mentor Richard Wagner suffered increasingly severe attacks of angina, and finally died in Venice in early 1883. All the advantages Ludwig had had in 1868 had vanished by then; he had frittered them away in high spending and self-regard. The press could not be censored, and foreign correspondents and aristocratic visitors gossiped in their own countries about the crazy king with a mania for building, who in the process was bankrupting himself and his country. After a subsidy from the Prussian government, Ludwig's spending became even more reckless. He seemed to be oblivious to everything but his personal construction agenda. By 1884 he owed 7½ million

German marks, mostly to a consortium of south German banks; eighteen months later his personal debt had nearly doubled. The finance minister told him that the banks simply could not afford to lend him any more. Ludwig's spoiled reaction was typical: 'If a certain sum is not obtained, Linderhof and Herrenchiemsee, my property, will be legally confiscated! If this is not forestalled in good time I will either kill myself promptly or else leave immediately and for ever the accursed land where such an abominable thing could happen.' Ministers and servants scoured lists of financial magnates and vastly wealthy peers from many countries for funds to tide him over. It was rumoured that figures as diverse as the Sultan of Turkey and the Duke of Westminster were approached.

Ludwig's people had been patient, but at last reacted against this now utterly disenchanting ruler; they were eager to be rid of him and his irresponsible, profligate ways. Rumours and myths of his capricious behaviour spread like wildfire. He arranged for the crown prince of Prussia to be kidnapped while he was on holiday in the Italian mountains and kept on a diet of bread and water – vicariously living the idea of the robber baron. Like Caligula, he grew enormously attached to his horse, and on a whim had his grey mare brought to dinner in the royal apartments, where in a panic she smashed everything in sight, including the valuable dinner service. Yet more desperate for immediate funds, Ludwig discussed a scheme where he would mastermind the robbery of the Rothschild bank in Frankfurt. When he consulted Bismarck, the most influential minister in Germany advised him to put his predicament before the Bavarian cabinet and submit to their will. He knew that whatever happened

Ludwig's financial position was so critical that he would inevitably become more of a pawn of the Prussians. Even he could not have predicted what Ludwig would do.

The king was too headstrong, self-deluded and opinionated to follow this advice. He planned to dismiss the cabinet altogether and authorise his personal servants to find alternative individuals to perform the necessary financial miracle. As those servants included his barber it is unlikely that they would have found many suitable replacements; Bismarck was well aware that the king was far too immured financially to emerge from his crisis without severe curtailment of his personal authority. The cabinet itself feared for its own existence, for although they knew that Ludwig's campaign for an alternative administration would not overthrow them, they would be further destabilised and regarded as irresolute in the eyes of the public. The king had gone too far this time and had to be neutralised. But how? He was king: God's representative on earth in one of the most socially and religiously conservative areas of Europe. Assassination, the ultimate sanction, was never contemplated as far as we know.

Temporary deposition because of regal insanity was the obvious reason for relieving Ludwig of his power. The only way that he could be rendered ineffective was by finding a suitable alternative who would bow to the cabinet's resolve more than the present king. The only candidate left who could form a regency in Ludwig's name seemed to be his uncle Luitpold, the third son of King Ludwig I, the passive claimant of the throne of Greece since the death of his deposed brother, Otto. Already well into his sixties, he was unsure how many effective years he had left, and was therefore quite reasonably reluctant to take on a role that was bound to be unpopular initially with the traditionally minded Bavarian people. Political backers for this move had to be sought, and chief among them had to be Bismarck. He made some show of reluctance, but concluded in conversation with the Bavarian envoy to Berlin that 'if the king was unfit to rule because of mental illness, then, in all conscience, I see no reason to keep him on the throne'. Privately he must have rubbed his hands in anticipation of this rich country falling into his lap without him doing anything.

The political deals done, the medical reasoning was researched. Dr von Gudden, the curator of brother Otto, was contacted by a representative of the Bavarian government with a specific request to declare the king incompetent because of mental incapacity. How far von Gudden was influenced in his diagnosis is difficult to say, but his report of 8 June 1886 identified incurable incompetence through advanced paranoia. The king would be unable to govern 'for the entire remainder of his life'. However, the report was compiled without an official face-to-face meeting with the patient. A diagnostic committee of three doctors, including Dr von Gudden, felt that 'The mental powers of His Majesty are disrupted to such an extent that all judgement is lacking, and his thinking is in total contradiction to reality.' They could have concluded this at any time in the previous twenty years. The report continues, 'Gripped by the illusion that he holds absolute power in abundance and made lonely by self-isolation, he stands like a blind man without a guide on the edge of an abyss.'

Ludwig may have had an inkling that something was up. He had tried to persuade Count Durckheim-Montmartin to assemble a bodyguard to protect him for some months before. The day after the report was made public, special commissioners together with Dr von Gudden and his assistant headed for Neuschwanstein where Ludwig was staying, a journey of several hours. He had already ordered the gates to be locked and the local police from Füssen to reinforce the royal guard. The coachman was stopped in the act of hitching the royal coach to a team of horses and told that Prince Luitpold was now the country's ruler. The summer weather was dreadful, cold and damp, and the commissioners hung around outside Neuschwanstein's walls for hours, feeling increasingly bedraggled and useless, before returning in the pouring rain to Hohenschwangau, where they were immediately arrested by the local police on Ludwig's orders and threatened with Byzantine tortures – blinding, flogging and starving while imprisoned in solitary confinement. The situation was becoming farcical. If Ludwig had taken the advice of the unconventional Baroness von Truchess, who happened to be visiting him when the commissioners arrived, he would have fled to the capital where, despite his eccentricities, he was still popular; he might have saved himself. But he remained irresolute, and in that time the government officially announced his deposition and his uncle's regency in his name. Again Ludwig contemplated suicide, but his aide-de-camp refused to visit the local chemist to obtain poison.

The possibility of Ludwig's suicide was uppermost in the mind of the government. Frustrated as he had not been able to poison himself, he was rumoured to have talked of throwing himself from one of Neuschwanstein's many towers, so he was kept under supervision. Quite reasonably, Ludwig asked von Gudden why he had declared him insane when he hadn't examined him. The psychiatrist's reply isn't recorded. Von Gudden advised that Ludwig should be watched from a discreet distance in case he became overwrought, and to make this easier he was moved to his father's castle of Berg on the shores of Lake Starnberg. This was a favourite castle of Ludwig's when he was a boy. They arrived on 12 June at about midday, and strict instructions were given that Ludwig should only be allowed to go for a walk if the psychiatrist accompanied him. His fellow-doctors thought that this might involve danger to both of them, but von Gudden laughed this off. So at 6.45 that evening the king and the tubby little psychiatrist set off on an amble beside the lake shore. They did not intend to go far; the king was tired after the traumatic events of the previous few days and the journey from Neuschwanstein, and he was overweight and unfit. Presently they were out of earshot and soon after that out of sight in the gathering gloom. What they talked about has been the subject of much speculation over the years. Perhaps von Gudden was employing Freud's 'talking cure', which he had been formulating since 1882, to fathom Ludwig's neuroses; perhaps the king subjected the doctor to a stream of vituperation – as he must still have been in shock. At eight o'clock they had not returned, and as the clouds started to pile in the late evening a search party was frantically organised. Darkness fell early as it began to rain again. At nine there was no news, but an hour later, in almost pitch darkness, the king's coat and jacket were discovered in the shallow water of the lake, and his umbrella not far away. Ludwig's body was found almost immediately afterwards, face down in the water. The sixty-two-year-old doctor was floating close by. Both were dead. The king's watch had stopped at 6.45 – behind the times to the last. A simple memorial cross in the shallows now marks the spot where he was found.

Who knows what occurred? The official theory is that the king must have convulsively thrown his coat and jacket off, ridded himself of his umbrella and dashed into the shallow water of the lake in an attempt to end his life. The psychiatrist had tried to stop him, and in the ensuing struggle the water had claimed them both. However, the autopsy showed no water in Ludwig's lungs. Jakob Lidl, the king's fisherman, wrote that the king was shot as he boarded a boat to row out into the middle of the lake, where loyalists were attempting to facilitate an escape, but officially there were no bullet holes in the king's body. Lidl's notes were only discovered after his death, among much more of questionable veracity. There is no explanation of Dr von Gudden's fate or part in this. He cannot have just stood by as a witness, unless he was privy to what was being plotted; did he drown or was he drowned? The king might have had a heart attack from the shock of the cold water and the unaccustomed exercise, even though he was said to be a good swimmer. As was the tradition in the Wittelsbach family, his heart was removed and placed in a silver urn along with his father's and grandfather's in the Chapel of the Mercy in Altotting. After the funeral the two surviving doctors of the commission disagreed with von Gudden's diagnosis of Ludwig's insanity. It was theorised that he might have had schizoid tendencies and addictive traits, demonstrated by his building mania, and guilt because of his homoerotic tendencies – which may have been a factor in his withdrawal from the public gaze. Some have claimed that there is evidence in his behaviour of Asperger's Syndrome. Although there have been requests to subject Ludwig's body to laser and X-ray treatment to ascertain whether there were other injuries and to study frontal lobe brain degeneration, the Wittelsbach family continues to resist what they consider to be an intrusion into their privacy. The controversy will run and run until there is incontrovertible proof, and that will not arrive any time soon.

With Ludwig dead without an heir, and buried in an extravagant, histrionic ceremony (the bouquet on his body was from the Empress Elisabeth of Austria, his cousin and lifelong correspondent), the crown passed to his nearest relative – his brother Otto. What a contrast: he had been securely incarcerated for many years, and although demonstrably insane was still recognised as titular king (Otto I), with his uncle continuing as regent. Otto was so sunk in his own world that he may not even have recognised that he was king; he lingered on for another twenty-seven years until his pathetic life finally ended in 1913. The Bavarians hardly noticed; there were other major military matters to consider. Luitpold, seemingly reluctantly, had become regent for a few days for Ludwig II and then for nearly three decades for Otto I, but the country entered an extended period of stability under his benevolent supervision. Many streets and public buildings in Bavaria are named after him in commemoration of his sensible administration. Under Luitpold, the kingdom of Bavaria and Munich especially experienced a time of great and diverse creative expression. The great writer Thomas Mann said in 1902 that artistically 'Munich shone'. It attracted many other expressive artists; among them a nondescript Austrian drifter and mediocre painter with some talent for architectural drawing, who personally petitioned Otto I's successor, Ludwig III, for entry into the Bavarian army in 1914. His name was Adolf Hitler.

Luitpold's regency lasted until the year before Otto's death, dying still in harness in his ninety-second year. One of his first acts within a week of Ludwig's funeral had been to open the late king's castles to the public, partly to pay off his debts. These fantastical buildings have repaid the country many times over through the millions of tourists who have travelled from near and far to marvel at their astonishing theatricality.

The kingdom of Bavaria ceased to exist under the terms of the treaties that ended the First World War in 1918; and the Wittelsbachs once again became dukes after the last crown prince had died, but the kingdom is remembered, as much as anything else, for the eccentric, egocentric life and architectural legacy of its Swan King, who irresponsibly bankrupted himself and his family and unnecessarily destabilised his kingdom, which he seemed to be convinced was his personal possession. From the rich economic base that the German state of Bavaria now enjoys, especially in Munich, he is still called Unser Kini – our dearest king; the many millions who have been entranced by his romantic legacy have rehabilitated him. Songs, novels, plays and films have been based on his story; the legend is becoming myth. The Germans have profited hugely from this: they can well afford their romanticism, as thousands owe their livelihoods to the *Marcherkonig*. Memories are short and forgiveness divine.

Afterword

*If you would know who controls you, see who you
may not criticise* – Tacitus

We live in uncertain times; we probably
always did. Today the elected chief
executives of some nations have
parliaments and cabinets as modifying
factors and the issue of nationalism is no longer as
strong as it once was, but we seem to be no more in
control of the future than we ever were. Chaos still
seems to prevail. In one universe an anonymous
butterfly shimmers its wings and in another, nations
are inexplicably brought to the brink of catastrophe.
But, despite the vicissitudes brought about by these
individuals, we have struggled through our history with
a modicum of success. There have always been warped
rulers, a lesson and a warning to us all; some self-made,
some whose destiny was pre-ordained.

Even archetypal figures like Louis XIV, the Sun King of France, whose shadow has extended across more than one of these sad stories, was warped in one sense: the cult of personality that surrounded him certainly shaped his view of the world. He is remembered for his long life and reign, his mistresses, his lavish lifestyle, the scandals of his decadent court and the inherent loneliness of his autocracy; but as an absolute ruler he trusted no-one, he emasculated aristocrats who were potential rivals, promoting ministers from the lower classes whose power was dependent on his patronage, and he condemned his son to such brutal treatment that he grew up almost intellectually inert. *Le Roi Soleil* was public property, watched and admired from his rising in the morning to his ritual going to bed. Perhaps the self-reflective world that Louis created and ruled can be summed up by the spectacular Hall of Mirrors – the jewel in the crown of the palace of Versailles. As he perambulated along this magnificent corridor, he could regard himself in every one of seventeen arched mirrors, each made up of twenty-one separate reflections: between his private apartments and his chapel he saw his image over three hundred and fifty times. If this wasn't enough, the ceiling's central roundel featured an allegorical representation of him ruling supreme.

To a greater or lesser extent, monarchs, be they kings or queens, sultans, emperors or tsars, all become insulated, just like Louis, from the vast majority of the populace, their office shrouded in mystery – even when efforts were made to introduce them to the world. We only need to remember Carlos II of Spain visiting the provinces, or Elizabeth I, who travelled from country seat to country seat but rarely saw commoners. The ritual has not changed: when the president of the

United States travels abroad he takes America with him. An aircraft is provided for his exclusive use and his armoured motorcade, brought in a separate aircraft, originates in American car plants. He is surrounded by his familiar, constantly reassuring entourage. Perhaps this insularity, and its inevitable distortion of 'real life', is the modern version of the Hall of Mirrors, reflecting always what the head of state or his ministers would have him see.

There will always be warped rulers as long as we fail to heed previous examples; short-term expediency, self-interest and political pragmatism will continue as national excuses for not acting. *Quis custodiet ipsos custodes?* Juvenal's rhetorical cry echoes down the ages. Who is guarding the guards? No-one has adequately answered this question because it is not in anyone's interest to do so. Thousands will die and millions will be condemned to misery because those who could, did nothing.

The next volume will concentrate on self-made monarchs who were also products of the cult of personality and of their invented bubbles of infallibility and impregnability. When these bubbles failed to burst, still more millions would become innocent victims.